Joe Casad

SAMS
Teach Yourself
TCP/IP
in 24 Hours

SECOND EDITION

SAMS

201 West 103rd St., Indianapolis, Indiana, 46290 USA

Sams Teach Yourself TCP/IP in 24 Hours, Second Edition

Copyright © 2001 by Sams Publishing

International Standard Book Number: 0-672-32085-1

Library of Congress Catalog Card Number: 00-111801

Printed in the United States of America

First Printing: March 2001

04   03   02   01   4   3   2

Trademarks

Warning and Disclaimer

ASSOCIATE PUBLISHER
Jeff Koch

ACQUISITIONS EDITOR
Vicki Harding

DEVELOPMENT EDITOR
Mark Renfrow

MANAGING EDITOR
Matt Purcell

PROJECT EDITOR
Christina Smith

INDEXERS
Diane Brenner
Greg Pearson

PROOFREADER
Candice Hightower

TECHNICAL EDITOR
Terry Ogletree

TEAM COORDINATOR
Vicki Harding

INTERIOR DESIGNER
Gary Adair

COVER DESIGNER
Aren Howell

PAGE LAYOUT
Liz Patterson

Contents at a Glance

Contents

About the Author

JOE CASAD is an engineer who has written widely on computer networking and system administration. He is the lead author of *Sams Teach Yourself TCP/IP in 24 Hours*, First Edition, *MCSE Windows NT Server and Workstation Study Guide*, *MCSE Networking Essentials Training Guide*, *Windows NT Server 4.0 Professional Reference*, and *Windows 98 Professional Reference*. He is currently the senior editor of UnixReview.com.

About the Technical Editor

TERRY OLGETREE is a consultant currently working in New Jersey. He has worked with networked computer systems since 1980, starting out on Digital Equipment PDP computers and Open VMS-based VAX and AlphaServer systems. He has worked with Unix and TCP/IP since 1985 and has been involved with Windows NT since it first appeared. He is the author of *Upgrading and Repairing Networks*, Second Edition, published by Que, and *Windows NT Server 4.0 Networking*, which is volume 4 of *Sams Windows NT Server 4 Resource Library*, published by Sams. In addition, he has contributed chapters to many other books published by Sams and Que, including *Windows NT Server Unleashed* (and the Professional Reference Edition), as well as *Special Edition Using Unix*, Third Edition.

Dedication

To the eternal Maurice, who hastens and chastens.

—Joe Casad

Acknowledgments

Thanks to Jeff Koch for getting this rewrite in the air and to Vicki Harding for keeping it aloft. Thanks to editors Mark Renfrow, T. W. Olgetree, Christina Smith, and Gene Redding for their patience and insight. I would like to acknowledge the following individuals for their contributions to the previous edition of *Sams Teach Yourself TCP/IP in 24 Hours*: Bob Willsey, Sudha Putnam, Walter Glenn, and Art Hammond. And thanks to my wife Barb and my kids, Xander, Mattie, and Bridget, for making my life a joyous excursion into uncharted harmonies, like the fuguing bars of a shape-note song.

Tell Us What You Think!

As the reader of this book, *you* are our most important critic and commentator. We value your opinion and want to know what we're doing right, what we could do better, what areas you'd like to see us publish in, and any other words of wisdom you're willing to pass our way.

As an Associate Publisher for Sams Publishing, I welcome your comments. You can fax, e-mail, or write me directly to let me know what you did or didn't like about this book—as well as what we can do to make our books stronger.

Please note that I cannot help you with technical problems related to the topic of this book, and that due to the high volume of mail I receive, I might not be able to reply to every message.

When you write, please be sure to include this book's title and author as well as your name and phone or fax number. I will carefully review your comments and share them with the author and editors who worked on the book.

Fax: 317-581-4770

E-mail: feedback@samspublishing.com

Mail: Jeff Koch
            Associate Publisher
            Sams Publishing
            201 West 103rd Street
            Indianapolis, IN 46290 USA

Introduction

Welcome to *Sams Teach Yourself TCP/IP in 24 Hours, Second Edition*. This book provides a clear and concise introduction to TCP/IP for newcomers and also for users who have worked with TCP/IP but would like a little more of the inside story. The second edition includes new material on recent developments in TCP/IP and offers a closer look at

- Internet technologies
- Routing and network hardware
- TCP/IP security

You'll find new chapters on topics such as Internet intrusion, security, HTML, and e-mail.

Does Each Chapter Take an Hour?

Each chapter is organized so that you can learn the concepts within one hour. The chapters are designed to be short enough to read all at once. In fact, you should be able to read a chapter in less than one hour and still have time to take notes and reread more complex sections in your one-hour study session.

How to Use This Book

The books in the *Sams Teach Yourself* series are designed to help you learn a topic in a few easy and accessible sessions. *Sams Teach Yourself TCP/IP in 24 Hours, Second Edition* is divided into six parts. Each part brings you a step closer to mastering the goal of proficiency in TCP/IP.

- Part I, "TCP/IP Basics," introduces you to TCP/IP and the TCP/IP protocol stack.
- Part II, "The TCP/IP Protocol System," takes a close look at each of TCP/IP's protocol layers: the Network Access, Internet, Transport, and Application layers. You'll learn about IP addressing and subnetting, as well as physical networks and application services. You'll also learn about the protocols that operate at each of TCP/IP's layers.
- Part III, "Networking with TCP/IP," describes some of the devices, services, and utilities necessary for supporting TCP/IP networks. You'll learn about routing and network hardware, DHCP, and DNS.
- Part IV, "TCP/IP Utilities," introduces some of the common utilities used to configure, manage, and troubleshoot TCP/IP networks. You'll learn about Ping, Netstat, FTP, Telnet, and other network utilities.

- Part V, "TCP/IP and the Internet," describes the world's largest TCP/IP network: the Internet. You'll learn about the structure of the Internet. You'll also learn about HTTP, HTML, and e-mail. Hour 19, "What Hackers Do," describes some common Internet attacks and discusses how to protect your network from intruders.

- Part VI, "Advanced Topics," describes TCP/IP security and discusses the network management protocols RMON and SNMP. You'll also learn about the new IP version 6 standard and some of the new gadgets and services that will populate the Internet of tomorrow. Part VI ends with a case study showing how the components of TCP/IP interact in a real working environment.

The concepts in this book, like TCP/IP itself, are independent of a system and descend from the standards defined in Internet Requests for Comment (RFCs).

How This Book Is Organized

Each hour in *Sams Teach Yourself TCP/IP in 24 Hours, Second Edition* begins with a quick introduction and a list of goals for the hour. You'll also find the following elements.

Main Section

Each hour contains a main section that provides a clear and accessible discussion of the hour's topic. You'll find figures and tables helping to explain the concepts described in the text. Interspersed with the text are special elements called Notes, New Terms, and Tips. These elements come with definitions, descriptions, or warnings that will help you build a better understanding of the material.

These boxes clarify a concept that is being discussed in the text. A Note might add some additional information or provide an example, but Notes typically aren't essential for a basic understanding of the subject. If you're in a hurry, or if you only want to know the bare essentials, you can bypass these sidebars.

NEW TERM   *New Terms* are definitions. You might see a New Term element with an important word or concept that can't be easily described in the main text—or isn't directly related to the main text.

A Tip is a shortcut designed to save you time.

Q&A

Each hour ends with some questions designed to help you explore and test your understanding of the concepts described in the hour. Complete answers to the questions are also provided.

Workshops

Some of the hours that are oriented around real-life configuration topics include Workshops—exercises designed to help you through the details or give you practice with a particular task. Not all hours have Workshops. You'll find them only in hours where a little real-world exploration will help build a better understanding of the material. Even if you don't have the necessary software and hardware to undertake some of the exercises in the Workshop, you might benefit from reading through the exercises to see how to proceed in a real network implementation.

Key Terms

Each hour includes a summary of important key terms that are introduced in the hour. The key terms are compiled into an alphabetized list at the end of each hour.

PART I
TCP/IP Basics

Hour

HOUR 1

What Is TCP/IP?

TCP/IP is a protocol system—a collection of protocols that support network communications. The answer to the question *What is a protocol?* must begin with the question *What is a network?*

This hour describes what a network is and shows why networks need protocols. You'll also learn what TCP/IP is, what it does, and where it began.

At the completion of this hour, you'll be able to

- Define network
- Explain what a network protocol suite is
- Explain what TCP/IP is
- Discuss the history of TCP/IP
- List some important features of TCP/IP
- Identify the organizations that oversee TCP/IP and the Internet
- Explain what RFCs are and where to find them

Networks and Protocols

A network is a collection of computers or computer-like devices that can communicate across a common transmission medium, as shown in Figure 1.1.

FIGURE 1.1

A typical local network.

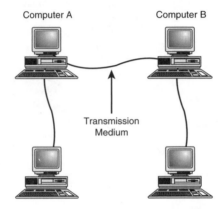

In a network, requests and data from one computer pass across the transmission medium (which might be a network cable or a phone line) to another computer. In Figure 1.1, computer A must be able to send a message or request to computer B. Computer B must be able to understand computer A's message and respond to it by sending a message back to computer A.

A computer interacts with the world through one or more applications that perform specific tasks and manage input and output. If that computer is part of a network, some of those applications must be capable of communicating with applications on other network computers. A *network protocol suite* is a system of common rules that helps to define the complex process of transferring data. The data travels from an application on one computer, through the computer's network hardware, across the transmission medium to the correct destination, and up through the destination computer's network hardware to a receiving application (see Figure 1.2).

The protocols of TCP/IP define the network communication process and, more importantly, define how a unit of data should look and what information it should contain so that a receiving computer can interpret the message correctly. TCP/IP and its related protocols form a complete system defining how data should be processed, transmitted, and received on a TCP/IP network. A system of related protocols, such as the TCP/IP protocols, is called a protocol suite.

The actual act of formatting and processing TCP/IP transmissions is performed by a software component that is known as the vendor's *implementation* of TCP/IP. For instance, Microsoft TCP/IP is a software component that enables Windows NT to process TCP/IP-formatted data and thus to participate in a TCP/IP network. As you read this book, be aware of the following distinction:

- A *TCP/IP standard* is a system of rules defining communication on TCP/IP networks.
- A *TCP/IP implementation* is a software component that performs the functions that enable a computer to participate in a TCP/IP network.

The purpose of the TCP/IP standards is to ensure the compatibility of all TCP/IP implementations regardless of version or vendor.

FIGURE 1.2

The role of a network protocol suite.

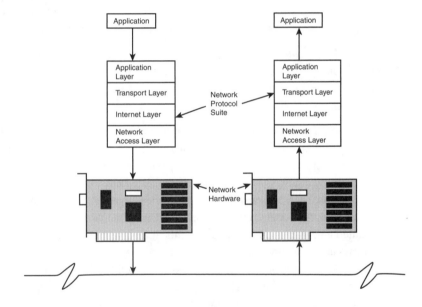

The important distinction between the TCP/IP standards and a TCP/IP implementation is often blurred in popular discussions of TCP/IP, and this is sometimes confusing for readers. For instance, authors often talk about the layers of the TCP/IP model providing services for other layers. In fact, it is not the TCP/IP model that provides services. The TCP/IP model *defines the services that should be provided*. The vendor software implementations of TCP/IP actually provide these services.

The Development of TCP/IP

Present-day TCP/IP networking represents the synthesis of two developments that began in the 1970s and have subsequently revolutionized the world of computing:

- The Internet
- The local area network

The Internet

TCP/IP's design is a result of its historical role as the protocol system for what was to become the Internet. The Internet, like so many other high-tech developments, grew from research originally performed by the United States Department of Defense. In the late 1960s, Defense Department officials began to notice that the military was accumulating a large and diverse collection of computers. Some of those computers weren't networked, and others were grouped in small, closed networks with incompatible proprietary protocols.

NEW TERM *Proprietary*, in this case, means that the technology is controlled by a private entity (such as a corporation). That entity might not have any interest in divulging enough information about the protocol so that users can use it to connect to other (rival) network protocols.

Defense officials began to wonder if it would be possible for these disparate computers to share information. Accustomed as they were to considerations of security, the Defense Department reasoned that, if such a network were possible, it would likely become a target for military attack. One of the primary requirements of this new network, therefore, was that it must be decentralized. Critical services must not be concentrated in a few vulnerable failure points. Because every failure point is vulnerable in the age of the missile, they wanted a network with no failure points at all—where a bomb could land on any part of the infrastructure without bringing down the whole network. These visionary soldiers created a network that became known as ARPAnet, named for the Defense Department's Advanced Research Projects Agency (ARPA). The protocol system that supported this interconnectable, decentralized network was the beginning of what we now know as TCP/IP.

A few years later, when the National Science Foundation wanted to build a network to connect research institutions, it adopted ARPAnet's protocol system and began to build what we know as the Internet. As you'll learn later in this book, the original decentralized vision of ARPAnet survives to this day in the design of the TCP/IP protocol system and is a big part of the success of TCP/IP and the Internet.

Two important features of TCP/IP that provide for this decentralized environment are as follows:

- End node verification: The two computers that are actually communicating—called the end nodes because they are at each end of the chain passing the message—are responsible for acknowledging and verifying the transmission. All computers basically operate as equals, and there is no central scheme for overseeing communications.

- Dynamic routing: Nodes are connected through multiple paths, and the routers choose a path for the data based on present conditions. You'll learn more about routing and router paths in later hours.

The Local Area Network (LAN)

As the Internet began to emerge around universities and research institutions, another network concept, the *local area network (LAN)* was also taking form. LANs developed along with the computer industry and were a response to the need for offices to share computer resources.

Early LAN protocols did not provide Internet access and were designed around proprietary protocol systems. Many did not support routing of any kind. Eventually, some companies began to want a protocol that would connect their incompatible, noncontiguous LANs, and they looked to TCP/IP. As the Internet became more popular, LAN users began to clamor for Internet access, and a variety of solutions began to emerge for getting LAN users connected. Specialized gateways provided the protocol translation necessary for these local networks to reach the Internet. Gradually, LAN software vendors began to provide more complete support for TCP/IP. Recent versions of NetWare, MacOS, and Windows have continued to expand the role of TCP/IP on local networks. TCP/IP grew up around Unix, and all Unix variants are fluent in TCP/IP. The recent popularity of Unix-based systems such as Linux, BSD, Solaris, and Apple OS X has increased the dominance of TCP/IP in the networking world.

> The term *gateway* is used inconsistently in discussions of TCP/IP. A gateway is sometimes just an ordinary router that connects a LAN to a larger network (see the discussion of routers later in this hour), and sometimes the term is used to refer to a routing device that performs some form of protocol translation.

As you'll learn in Hour 3, "The Network Access Layer," the need to accommodate local area networks has caused considerable innovation in the implementation of the hardware-conscious protocols that underlie TCP/IP.

TCP/IP Features

TCP/IP includes many important features that you'll learn about in this book. In particular, pay close attention to the way the TCP/IP protocol suite addresses the following problems:

- Logical Addressing
- Routing
- Name Service
- Error Control and Flow Control
- Application Support

These issues are at the heart of TCP/IP. The following sections introduce these important features. You'll learn more about these features later in this book.

Logical Addressing

A network adapter has a unique and permanent physical address. The physical address is a number that was given to the card at the factory. On a local area network, low-lying hardware-conscious protocols deliver data across the physical network, using the adapter's physical address. There are many network types, and each has a different way of delivering data. On a basic ethernet network, for example, a computer sends messages directly onto the transmission medium. The network adapter of each computer listens to every transmission on the local network to determine if a message is addressed to its own physical address.

 As you'll learn in Hour 9, "Network Hardware," today's ethernet networks are a bit more complicated than the idealized scenario of a computer sending messages directly onto the transmission line. Ethernet networks sometimes contain hardware devices such as switches and hubs to manage the signal.

On large networks, of course, every network adapter can't listen to every message. (Imagine your computer listening to *every* piece of data sent over the Internet.) As the transmission medium becomes more populated with computers, a physical addressing scheme cannot function efficiently. Network administrators often segment networks using devices such as routers in order to reduce network traffic. On routed networks, administrators need a way to subdivide the network into smaller subnetworks (called *subnets*) and impose a hierarchical design so that a message can travel efficiently to its destination. TCP/IP provides this subnetting capability through logical addressing. A *logical address* is an address configured through the network software. In TCP/IP, a computer's logical address is called an *IP address*. As you'll learn in Hour 4,

"The Internet Layer," and Hour 5, "Subnetting," an IP address can include

- A network ID number identifying a network
- A subnet ID number identifying a subnet on the network
- A host ID number identifying the computer on the subnet

The IP addressing system also lets the network administrator impose a sensible numbering scheme on the network so that the progression of addresses reflects the internal organization of the network.

> If your network is isolated from the Internet, you are free to use any IP addresses you want (as long as your network follows the basic rules for IP addressing). If your network will be part of the Internet, however, Internet Corporation for Assigned Names and Numbers (ICANN), which was formed in 1998, will assign a network ID to your network, and that network ID will form the first part of the IP address. (See Hours 4 and 5.)

In TCP/IP, a logical address is resolved to and from the corresponding hardware-specific physical address using the ARP and RARP protocols, which are discussed in Hour 4.

Routing

A *router* is a special device that can read logical addressing information and direct data across the network to its destination. At the simplest level, a router divides a local subnet from the larger network (see Figure 1.3).

FIGURE 1.3

A router connecting a LAN to a large network.

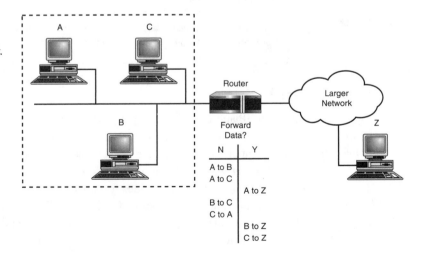

Data addressed to another computer or device on the local subnet does not cross the
router and therefore doesn't clutter up the transmission lines of the greater network. If
data is addressed to a computer outside the subnet, the router forwards the data accordingly. As has already been mentioned this hour, very large networks such as the Internet
include many routers and provide multiple paths from the source to the destination (see
Figure 1.4).

FIGURE **1.4**

A routed network.

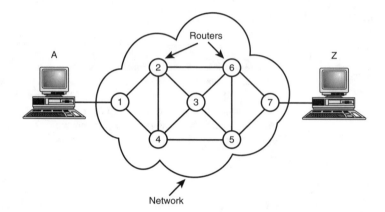

TCP/IP includes protocols that define how the routers will find a path through the network.
You'll learn more about TCP/IP routing and routing protocols in Hour 10, "Routing."

> As you'll also learn in Hour 9, network devices such as bridges, switches, and
> smart hubs also can filter traffic and reduce network traffic. Because these
> devices work with physical addresses rather than logical addresses, they can-
> not perform the complex routing functions shown in Figure 1.4.

Name Resolution

Although the numeric IP address is probably more user friendly than the network
adapter's prefabricated physical address, the IP address is still designed for the
convenience of the computer rather than the convenience of the user. People might
have trouble remembering whether a computer's address is 111.121.131.146 or
111.121.131.156. TCP/IP, therefore, provides for a parallel structure of user-oriented
alphanumeric names, called domain names or DNS names. This mapping of domain
names to an IP address is called *name resolution*. Special computers called *name servers*
store tables showing how to translate these domain names to and from IP addresses.

The computer addresses commonly associated with e-mail or the World Wide Web are expressed as DNS names (for example, `www.microsoft.com`, `falcon.ukans.edu`, and `idir.net`). TCP/IP's name service system provides for a hierarchy of name servers that supply domain name/IP address mappings for DNS-registered computers on the network. This means that the everyday user rarely has to enter or decipher an actual IP address.

DNS is the name resolution system for the Internet and is the most common name resolution method. However, some TCP/IP networks also support other methods for resolving alphanumeric names to IP addresses. Another common name resolution scheme is the Windows Internet Name Services (WINS) for resolving Microsoft Windows NetBIOS names to IP addresses.

You'll learn more about TCP/IP name resolution in Hour 11, "Name Resolution."

Error Control and Flow Control

The TCP/IP protocol suite provides features that ensure the reliable delivery of data across the network. These features include checking data for transmission errors (to ensure that the data that arrives is exactly what was sent) and acknowledging successful receipt of a network message. TCP/IP's Transport layer (see Hour 6, "The Transport Layer") defines many of these error-checking, flow-control, and acknowledgment functions through the TCP protocol. Lower-level protocols at TCP/IP's Network Access layer (see Hour 3) also play a part in the overall system of error control.

Application Support

Several network applications may be running on the same computer. The protocol software must provide some means for determining which incoming packet belongs with each application. In TCP/IP, this interface from the network to the applications is accomplished through a system of logical channels called *ports*. Each port has a number that is used to identify the port. You can think of these ports as logical pipelines within the computer through which data can flow from the application to (and from) the protocol software (see Figure 1.5).

Hour 6 describes TCP and UDP ports at TCP/IP's Transport layer. You'll learn more about application support and TCP/IP's Application layer in Hour 7, "The Application Layer."

The TCP/IP suite also includes a number of ready-made applications designed to assist with various network tasks. Some typical TCP/IP utilities are shown in Table 1.1. You'll learn more about these TCP/IP utilities in Part IV, "TCP/IP Utilities."

FIGURE 1.5
*Applications access the
network through port
addresses.*

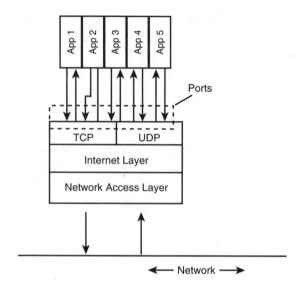

TABLE 1.1   Typical TCP/IP Utilities

Utility	Purpose
ftp	File Transfer
lpr	Printing
ping	Configuration/Troubleshooting
route	Configuration/Troubleshooting
telnet	Remote Terminal Access
traceroute	Configuration/Troubleshooting

Standards Organizations and RFCs

Several organizations have been instrumental in the development of TCP/IP and the
Internet. Another way in which TCP/IP reveals its military roots is in the quantity and
obscurity of its acronyms. Still, a few organizations in the past and present of TCP/IP
deserve mention, as follows:

- Internet Advisory Board (IAB): The governing board that sets policy for the
  Internet and sees to the further development of TCP/IP standards.

- Internet Engineering Task Force (IETF): The branch of the IAB that studies and
  rules on engineering issues. The IETF is divided into workgroups that study particular aspects of TCP/IP and the Internet, such as applications, routing, network
  management, and so forth.

- Internet Research Task Force (IRTF): The branch of the IAB that sponsors long-range research.
- Internet Corporation for Assigned Names and Numbers (ICANN): An organization established in 1998 that coordinates the assignment of Internet domain names, IP addresses, and globally unique protocol parameters such as port numbers (www.icann.com).
- InterNIC: The Internet information service. InterNic keeps a list of ICANN-accredited registration organizations that can assign domain names. Contact InterNIC through the World Wide Web at http://internic.net.

Most of the official documentation on TCP/IP is available through a series of Requests for Comment (RFCs). The library of RFCs includes Internet standards and reports from workgroups. IETF official specifications are published as RFCs. Many RFCs are intended to illuminate some aspect of TCP/IP or the Internet. Anyone can submit an RFC for review. You can either send a proposed RFC to the IETF or you can submit it directly to the RFC editor via e-mail at rfc-editor@rfc-editor.org.

The RFCs provide essential technical background for anyone wanting a deeper understanding of TCP/IP. The list includes several technical papers on protocols, utilities, and services, as well as a few TCP/IP-related poems and Shakespeare takeoffs that, sadly, do not match the clarity and economy of TCP/IP.

You can find the RFCs at several places on the Internet. Try www.rfc-editor.org. A few representative RFCs are shown in Table 1.2.

TABLE 1.2   Representative Examples of the 2,000+ Internet RFCs

Number	Title
791	Internet Protocol
792	Transmission Control Protocol
793	Simple Mail Transfer Protocol
794	File Transfer Protocol
968	Twas the night before start-up
1180	TCP/IP Tutorial
1188	Proposed Standard for transmission of datagrams over FDDI networks
1597	Address Allocation for Private Internets
2000	Internet Official Protocol Standards 2/24/97
2001	The PPP NetBIOS Frames Control Protocol

Summary

This hour describes what networks are and why networks need protocols. You learned that TCP/IP began with the U.S. Defense Department's experimental ARPAnet network and that TCP/IP was designed to provide decentralized networking in a diverse environment.

This hour also covers some important features of TCP/IP, such as logical addressing, name resolution, and application support. It describes some of TCP/IP's oversight organizations and discusses RFCs—the technical papers that serve as the official documentation for TCP/IP and the Internet.

Q&A

Q What is the difference between a protocol standard and a protocol implementation?

A A protocol standard is a system of rules. A protocol implementation is a software component that applies those rules in order to provide networking capability to a computer.

Q Why did the designers of ARPAnet want a decentralized network?

A They envisioned a network that would be used for military purposes, and they didn't want to concentrate critical services in a central location that could become the focus on an attack.

Q Why was end-node verification an important feature of ARPAnet?

A By design, the network was not supposed to be controlled from any central point. The sending and receiving computers, therefore, had to take charge of verifying their own communication.

Q Why do larger networks employ name resolution?

A IP addresses are difficult to remember and easy to get wrong. DNS-style domain names are easier to remember because they let you associate a word or name with the IP address.

Key Terms

Review the following list of key terms:

ARPAnet—An experimental network that was the birthplace of TCP/IP.

Domain name—An alphanumeric name associated with an IP address through TCP/IP's DNS system.

1

Gateway—A router that connects a LAN to a larger network. The term gateway sometimes applies specifically to a router that performs some kind of protocol conversion.

IP address—A logical address used to locate a computer or other networked device (such as a printer) on a TCP/IP network.

Logical address—A network address configured through the protocol software.

Name service—A service that associates human-friendly alphanumeric names with network addresses.

Physical address—A permanent address burned into a network adapter in the factory.

Port—An internal address that provides an interface between an application and TCP/IP's Transport layer.

Protocol system—A system of standards and procedures that enables computers to communicate over a network.

RFC (Request for Comment)—An official technical paper providing relevant information on TCP/IP or the Internet. You can find the RFCs at several places on the Internet. Try www.rfc-editor.org.

Router—A network device that forwards data by logical address and can also be used to segment large networks into smaller subnetworks.

TCP/IP—A network protocol suite used on the Internet and also on many other networks around the world.

Hour 2

How TCP/IP Works

TCP/IP is a system (or suite) of protocols, and a protocol is a system of rules and procedures. For the most part, the hardware and software of the communicating computers carry out the rules of TCP/IP communications—the user does not have to get involved with the details. Still, a working knowledge of TCP/IP is essential if you want to navigate through the configuration and troubleshooting problems you'll face with TCP/IP networks.

This hour describes the TCP/IP protocol system and shows how the components of TCP/IP work together to send and receive data across the network.

At the completion of this hour, you will be able to

- Describe the layers of the TCP/IP protocol system and the purpose of each layer
- Describe the layers of the OSI protocol model and explain how the OSI layers relate to TCP/IP
- Explain TCP/IP protocol headers and how data is enclosed with header information at each layer of the protocol stack
- Name the data package at each layer of the TCP/IP stack
- Discuss the TCP, UDP, and IP protocols and how they work together to provide TCP/IP functionality

The TCP/IP Protocol System

Before looking at the elements of TCP/IP, it is best to begin with a brief review of the responsibilities of a protocol system.

A protocol system such as TCP/IP must be capable of the following tasks:

- Dividing messages into manageable chunks of data that will pass efficiently through the transmission medium.
- Interfacing with the network adapter hardware.
- Addressing—The sending computer must be capable of targeting data to a receiving computer. The receiving computer must be capable of recognizing a message that it is supposed to receive.
- Routing data to the subnet of the destination computer, even if the source subnet and the destination subnet are dissimilar physical networks.
- Performing error control, flow control, and acknowledgment: For reliable communication, the sending and receiving computers must be able to identify and correct faulty transmissions and control the flow of data.
- Accepting data from an application and passing it to the network.
- Receiving data from the network and passing it to an application.

To accomplish the preceding tasks, the creators of TCP/IP settled on a modular design. The TCP/IP protocol system is divided into separate components that theoretically function independently from one another. Each component is responsible for a piece of the communication process.

The advantage of this modular design is that it lets vendors easily adapt the protocol software to specific hardware and operating systems. For instance, the Network Access layer (as you'll learn in Hour 3, "The Network Access Layer") includes functions relating to a specific LAN architecture, such as token ring or ethernet. Because of TCP/IP's modular design, a vendor such as Microsoft does not have to build a completely different software package for token ring TCP/IP (as opposed to ethernet TCP/IP) networks. The upper layers are not affected; only the Network Access layer must change.

The TCP/IP protocol system is subdivided into layered components that each perform specific duties (see Figure 2.1). This model, or *stack*, comes from the early days of TCP/IP, and it is sometimes called the TCP/IP model. The official TCP/IP protocol layers and their functions are as follows. Compare the functions in the list with the responsibilities listed earlier in this section, and you'll see how the responsibilities of the protocol system are distributed among the layers.

The four-layer model shown in Figure 2.1 is a common model for describing TCP/IP networking, but it isn't the only model. The ARPAnet model, for instance, as described in RFC 871, describes three layers: the Network Interface layer, the Host-to-Host layer, and the Process-Level/Applications layer. Other descriptions of TCP/IP call for a five-layer model, with Physical and Data Link layers in place of the Network Access layer (to match OSI). Still other models may exclude either the Network Access or the Application layer, which are less uniform and harder to define than the intermediate layers.

The names of the layers also vary. The ARPAnet layer names still appear in some discussions of TCP/IP, and the Internet layer is sometimes called the Internetwork layer or the Network layer.

This book uses the four-layer model, with names shown in Figure 2.1.

FIGURE 2.1
The TCP/IP model's protocol layers.

| Application Layer |
| Transport Layer |
| Internet Layer |
| Network Access Layer |

- Network Access layer—Provides an interface with the physical network. Formats the data for the transmission medium and addresses data for the subnet based on physical hardware addresses. Provides error control for data delivered on the physical network.

- Internet layer—Provides logical, hardware-independent addressing so that data can pass among subnets with differing physical architectures. Provides routing to reduce traffic and support delivery across the internetwork. (The term *internetwork* refers to an interconnected, greater network of LANs, such as what you find in a large company or on the Internet.) Relates physical addresses (used at the Network Access layer) to logical addresses.

- Transport layer—Provides flow control, error control, and acknowledgment services for the internetwork. Serves as an interface for network applications.

- Application layer—Provides applications for network troubleshooting, file transfer, remote control, and Internet activities. Also supports the network Application Programming Interfaces (APIs) that enable programs written for a particular operating environment to access the network.

Part II, "The TCP/IP Protocol System," provides more detailed descriptions of the activities at each of these TCP/IP protocol layers.

When the TCP/IP protocol system prepares a piece of data for transmission across the network, each layer on the sending machine adds a layer of information to the data that will be relevant to the corresponding layer on the receiving machine. For instance, the Internet layer of the computer sending the data adds a header with some information that is significant to the Internet layer of the computer receiving the message. This process is sometimes referred to as encapsulation. At the receiving end these headers are removed as the data is passed up the protocol stack.

> The term *layer* is used throughout the computer industry for protocol component levels such as the ones shown in Figure 2.1. Header information is applied in layers to the data as it passes through the components of the protocol stack. (You'll learn more about this later in this hour.) When it comes to the components themselves, however, the term layer is somewhat metaphorical.
>
> Diagrams such as Figure 2.1 are meant to show that the data passes across a series of interfaces. As long as the interfaces are maintained, the processes within one component are not affected by the processes in other components. If you turned Figure 2.1 sideways, it would look more like an assembly line, and this is also a useful analogy for the relationship of the protocol components. The data stops at each point in the line and, as long as it arrives at each point as specified, the components can operate independently.

TCP/IP and the OSI Model

The networking industry has a standard seven-layer model for network protocol architecture called the Open Systems Interconnection (OSI) model. The OSI model represents an effort by ISO, an international standards organization, to standardize the design of network protocol systems in order to promote interconnectivity and open access to protocol standards for software developers.

TCP/IP was already on the path of development when the OSI standard architecture appeared and, strictly speaking, TCP/IP does not conform to the OSI model. However, the two models did have similar goals, and there was enough interaction among the designers of these standards that they emerged with a certain compatibility. The OSI model has been very influential in the growth and development of protocol implementations, and it is quite common to see the OSI terminology applied to TCP/IP. Figure 2.2 shows the relationship between the four-layer TCP/IP standard and the seven-layer OSI model. Note that the OSI model divides the duties of the Application layer into three layers: Application, Presentation, and Session. OSI splits the activities of the Network Interface layer into a Data Link layer and a Physical layer. This increased subdivision adds some complexity, but it also adds flexibility for developers by targeting the protocol layers to more specific services.

FIGURE 2.2
The seven-layer OSI model.

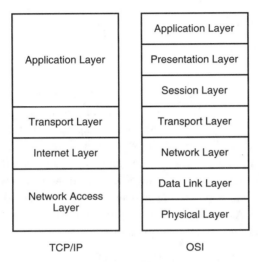

The seven layers of the OSI model are as follows:

- Physical layer—Converts the data into the stream of electric or analog pulses that will actually cross the transmission medium and oversees the transmission of the data.
- Data Link layer—Provides an interface with the network adapter; maintains logical links for the subnet.
- Network layer—Supports logical addressing and routing.
- Transport layer—Provides error control and flow control for the internetwork.
- Session layer—Establishes sessions between communicating applications on the communicating computers.
- Presentation layer—Translates data to standard format; manages encryption and data compression.
- Application layer—Provides a network interface for applications; supports network applications for file transfer, communications, and so forth.

It is important to remember that the TCP/IP model and the OSI model are standards, not implementations. Real-world implementations do not always map cleanly to the models shown in Figures 2.1 and 2.2, and the perfect correspondence depicted in Figure 2.2 is also a matter of some discussion within the industry.

Notice that the OSI and TCP/IP models are most similar at the important Transport and Internet (called Network in OSI) layers. These layers include the most identifiable and distinguishing components of the protocol system, and it is no coincidence that protocol systems are sometimes named for their Transport and Network layer protocols. As you'll learn later in this book, the TCP/IP protocol suite is named for TCP, a Transport layer protocol, and IP, an Internet/Network layer protocol.

Data Packages

The important thing to remember about the TCP/IP protocol stack is that each layer plays a role in the overall communication process. Each layer invokes services that are necessary for that layer to perform its role. As an outgoing transmission passes down through the stack, each layer includes a bundle of relevant information called a *header* along with the actual data. The little data package containing the header and the data then becomes the data that is repackaged at the next lower level with the next lower layer's header. This process is shown in Figure 2.3. The reverse process occurs when data is received on the destination computer. As the data moves up through the stack, each layer unpacks the corresponding header and uses the information.

As the data moves down through the stack, the effect is a little like the nested Russian wooden dolls you may have seen; the innermost doll is enclosed in another doll, which is then enclosed in another doll, and so on. At the receiving end, the data packages will be unpacked, one by one, as the data climbs back up the protocol stack. The Internet layer on the receiving machine will use the information in the Internet layer header. The Transport layer will use the information in the Transport layer header. At each layer, the package of data takes a form that will provide the necessary information to the corresponding layer on the receiving machine. Because each layer is responsible for different functions, the form of the basic data package is very different at each layer.

> The networking industry has as many analogies as it has acronyms, and the Russian doll analogy, like any of the others, illustrates a point but must not be taken too far. It is worth noting that on a physical network such as ethernet, the data is typically broken into smaller units at the Network Access layer. A more accurate analogy would call for this lowest layer to break the concentric doll system into smaller pieces, encapsulate those pieces into tinier dolls, then grind those tiny dolls into a pattern of ones and zeros. The ones and zeroes will be received, reconstituted into tiny dolls, and rebuilt into the concentric doll system. The complexity of this scenario causes many to eschew the otherwise-promising analogy of the dolls.

FIGURE 2.3
At each layer, the data is repackaged with that layer's header.

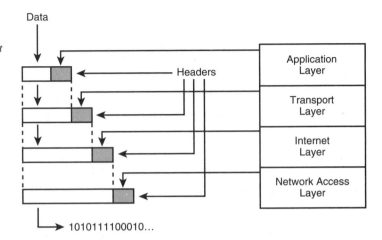

The data packet looks different at each layer, and at each layer it goes by a different name. The names for the data packages created at each layer are as follows:

- The data package created at the Application layer is called a *message.*
- The data package created at the Transport layer, which encapsulates the Application layer message, is called a *segment* if it comes from the Transport layer's TCP protocol. If the data package comes from the Transport layer's UDP protocol, it is called a *datagram.*
- The data package at the Internet layer, which encapsulates the Transport layer segment, is called a *datagram.*
- The data package at the Network Access layer, which encapsulates and may subdivide the datagram, is called a *frame*. This frame is then turned into a bitstream at the lowest sublayer of the Network Access layer.

You'll learn more about the data packages for each layer in Part II.

A Quick Look at TCP/IP Networking

The practice of describing protocol systems in terms of their layers is widespread and nearly universal. The layering system does provide insights into the protocol system, and it's impossible to describe TCP/IP without first introducing its layered architecture. However, focusing solely on protocol layers also creates some limitations.

First, talking about protocol layers rather than protocols introduces additional abstraction to a subject that is already excruciatingly abstract. Second, itemizing the various protocols as subheads within the greater topic of a protocol layer can give the false impression that all protocols are of equal importance. In fact, though every protocol has a role to play, most of the functionality of the TCP/IP suite can be described in terms of only a few of its most important protocols. It is sometimes useful to view these important protocols in the foreground, against the backdrop of the layering system described earlier in this hour.

Figure 2.4 describes the basic TCP/IP protocol networking system. Of course, there are additional protocols and services in the complete package, but Figure 2.4 shows most of what is going on.

FIGURE 2.4

A quick look at the basic TCP/IP networking system.

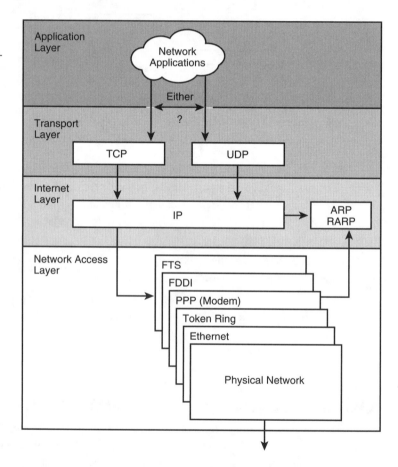

The basic scenario is as follows:

1. Data passes from a TCP/IP application, or from a network application program interface, through a TCP or UDP port to either of the two Transport layer protocols (TCP or UDP). Programs can access the network through either TCP or UDP, depending on the program's requirements.

- TCP is a connection-oriented protocol. As you'll learn in Hour 6, "The Transport Layer," connection-oriented protocols provide more sophisticated flow control and error checking than connectionless protocols. TCP goes to great effort to guarantee the delivery of the data. TCP is more reliable than UDP, but the additional error checking and flow control mean that TCP is slower than UDP.

  - UDP is a connectionless protocol. It is faster than TCP, but it is not as reliable. UDP offloads more of the error-checking responsibilities to the application.

2. The data segment passes to the Internet level, where the IP protocol provides logical-addressing information and encloses the data into a datagram.

3. The IP datagram enters the Network Access layer, where it passes to software components designed to interface with the physical network. The Network Access layer creates one or more data frames designed for entry onto the physical network. In the case of a LAN system such as ethernet, the frame may contain physical address information obtained from lookup tables maintained using the Internet layer ARP and RARP protocols. (ARP, Address Resolution Protocol, translates IP addresses to physical addresses. RARP, Reverse Address Resolution Protocol, translates physical addresses to IP addresses.)

4. The data frame is converted to a stream of bits that is transmitted over the network medium.

Of course, there are endless details describing how each protocol goes about fulfilling its assigned tasks. For instance, how does TCP provide flow control, how do ARP and RARP map physical addresses to IP addresses, and how does IP know where to send a datagram addressed to a different subnet? These questions are explored later in this book. You'll also learn more about the TCP/IP protocols and about the processes described in this section in later hours.

Summary

In this hour, you learned about the layers of the TCP/IP protocol stack and how those layers interrelate. You also learned how the classic TCP/IP model relates to the seven-layer OSI networking model. At each layer in the protocol stack, data is packaged into the form that is most useful to the corresponding layer on the receiving end. This hour discusses the process of encapsulating header information at each protocol layer and outlines the different terms used at each layer to describe the data package. Lastly, you got a quick look at how the TCP/IP protocol system operates from the viewpoint of some of its most important protocols: TCP, UDP, IP, ARP, and RARP.

Q&A

Q **What is the principle advantage of TCP/IP's modular design?**

A Because of TCP/IP's modular design, the TCP/IP protocol stack can adapt easily to specific hardware and operating environments.

Q **What functions are provided at the Network Access layer?**

A The Network Access layer provides services related to the specific physical network.

Q **Which OSI layer corresponds to the TCP/IP Internet layer?**

A TCP/IP's Internet layer corresponds to the OSI Network layer.

Q **Why is header information enclosed at each layer of the TCP/IP protocol stack?**

A Because each protocol layer on the receiving machine needs different information to process the incoming data, each layer on the sending machine encloses header information.

Key Terms

Review the following list of key terms:

Application layer—The layer of the TCP/IP stack that supports network applications and provides an interface to the local operating environment.

Datagram—The data package passed from the Internet layer to the Network Access layer, or a data package passed from UDP at the Transport layer to the Internet layer.

Frame—The data package created at the Network Access layer according to the specification of the physical network.

Header—A bundle of protocol information attached to the data at each layer of the protocol stack.

Internet layer—The layer of the TCP/IP stack that provides logical addressing and routing.

IP (Internet Protocol)—The Internet layer protocol that provides logical addressing and routing capabilities.**Modular design**—A design that calls for the complete system to be built from individual components that pass information across well-defined interfaces.

Message—In TCP/IP networking, a message is the data package passed from the Application layer to the Transport layer. The term is also used generically to describe a message from one entity to another on the network. The term doesn't always refer to an Application layer data package.

Modular Design—A design that calls for the complete system to be built from individual components that pass information across well-defined interfaces.

Network Access layer—The layer of the TCP/IP stack that provides an interface with the physical network.

Segment—The data package passed from TCP at the Transport layer to the Internet layer.

TCP (Transmission Control Protocol)—A Transport layer, reliable, connection-oriented protocol.

Transport layer—The layer of the TCP/IP stack that provides error control and acknowledgment and serves as an interface for network applications.

UDP (User Datagram Protocol)—A Transport layer, non-reliable, connectionless protocol.

2

PART II
The TCP/IP Protocol System

Hour

HOUR 3

The Network Access Layer

At the base of the TCP/IP protocol stack is the Network Access layer, the collection of services and specifications that provide and manage access to the network hardware. In this hour you'll learn about the duties of the Network Access layer and how the Network Access layer relates to the OSI model. This hour also looks at some common physical network technologies you'll find in the Network Access layer.

At the completion of this hour, you'll be able to

- Explain what the Network Access layer is
- Discuss how TCP/IP's Network Access layer relates to the OSI networking model
- Explain what a network architecture is
- List the contents of an ethernet frame
- Identify the methods that ethernet, token ring, and FDDI use for controlling access to the transmission medium

Protocols and Hardware

The Network Access layer is the most mysterious and least uniform of TCP/IP's layers. Basically, the Network Access layer manages all the services and functions necessary to prepare the data for the physical network. These responsibilities include

- Interfacing with the computer's network adapter.
- Coordinating the data transmission with the conventions of the appropriate access method. You'll learn more about access methods later in this hour.
- Formatting the data into a unit called a *frame* and converting that frame into the stream of electric or analog pulses that passes across the transmission medium.
- Checking for errors in incoming frames.
- Adding error-checking information to outgoing frames so that the receiving computer can check the frame for errors.
- Acknowledging receipt of data frames and resending frames if acknowledgment is not received.

Of course, any formatting tasks performed on an outgoing frame must occur in reverse when the frame reaches its destination and is received by the computer to which it is addressed.

The Network Access layer defines the procedures for interfacing with the network hardware and accessing the transmission medium. Below the surface of TCP/IP's Network Access layer, you'll find an intricate interplay of hardware, software, and transmission-medium specifications. Unfortunately, at least for the purposes of a concise description, there are many different types of physical networks that all have their own conventions, and any one of these physical networks can form the basis for the Network Access layer. You'll learn about these physical network types later in this hour. A few examples include

- Ethernet
- Token ring
- FDDI
- PPP (Point-to-Point Protocol, through a phone modem)

Not every networked computer is on a LAN. The network-access software may provide support for something other than a standard network adapter and a LAN cable. One of the most common alternatives is a modem connection to a remote network, such as the connection you establish when you dial in to an Internet service provider (ISP). Modem protocol standards such

> as Serial Line Internet Protocol (SLIP) and Point-to-Point Protocol (PPP) pro-
> vide network access for the TCP/IP protocol stack through a modem connec-
> tion. You'll learn more about these protocols in Hour 8, "Dial-Up TCP/IP."

The good news is that the Network Access layer is almost totally invisible to the everyday user. The network adapter driver, coupled with key low-level components of the
operating system and protocol software, manages most of the tasks relegated to the
Network Access layer, and a few short configuration steps are usually all that is required
of a user. These steps are becoming simpler with the improved plug-and-play features of
desktop operating systems.

As you read through this hour, remember that the logical, IP-style addressing discussed in
Hours 1, 2, 4, and 5 exist entirely in the software. The protocol system requires additional
services to deliver the data across a specific LAN system and up through the network adapter
of a destination computer. These services are the purview of the Network Access layer.

3

It is worth mentioning that the diversity, complexity, and invisibility of the
Network Access layer has caused some authors to exclude it from discussions
of TCP/IP completely, asserting instead that the stack rests on LAN drivers
below the Internet Access layer. This viewpoint has some merit, but the
Network Access layer really is part of TCP/IP, and no discussion of the network-
communication process is complete without it.

The Network Access Layer and the OSI Model

As Hour 2, "How TCP/IP Works," mentioned, TCP/IP is officially independent of the
seven-layer OSI networking model, but the OSI model is often used as a general framework for understanding protocol systems. OSI terminology and concepts are particularly
common in discussions of the Network Access layer because the OSI model provides
additional subdivisions to the broad category of network access. These subdivisions reveal
a bit more about the inner workings of this layer. The OSI model has been influential with
computer networking vendors, and the recent trend toward multiprotocol standards such
as NDIS and ODI (discussed later in this section) has accentuated the need for a common
terminology that the OSI model provides.

As Figure 3.1 shows, the TCP/IP Network Access layer roughly corresponds to the OSI
Physical and Data Link layers. The OSI Physical layer is responsible for turning the data
frame into a stream of bits suitable for the transmission medium. In other words, the OSI

Physical layer manages and synchronizes the electrical or analog pulses that form the actual transmission. On the receiving end, the Physical layer reassembles these pulses into a data frame.

FIGURE 3.1

OSI and the Network Access layer.

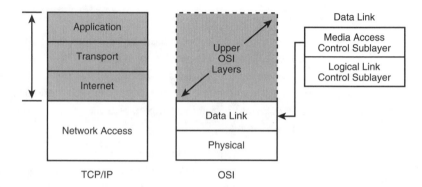

The OSI Data Link layer performs two separate functions and is accordingly subdivided into the following two sublayers:

- Media Access Control (MAC)—This sublayer provides an interface with the network adapter. The network adapter driver, in fact, is often called the MAC driver, and the hardware address burned into the card at the factory is often referred to as the MAC address.

- Logical Link Control (LLC)—This sublayer performs error-checking functions for frames delivered over the subnet and manages links between devices communicating on the subnet.

In real network protocol implementations, the distinction between the layers of TCP/IP and OSI systems has become further complicated by the development of the Network Driver Interface Specification (NDIS) and Open Data-Link Interface (ODI) specification. NDIS (developed by Microsoft and 3Com Corp.) and ODI (developed by Apple and Novell) are designed to let a single protocol stack (such as TCP/IP) use multiple network adapters and to let a single network adapter use multiple upper-layer protocols. This effectively enables the upper-layer protocols to float independently of the network access system, which adds great functionality to the network but also adds complexity and makes it even more difficult to provide a systematic discussion of how the software components interrelate at the lower layers.

Network Architecture

In practice, local area networks are not really thought of in terms of protocol layers but by what is called *LAN architecture* or *network architecture*. (Sometimes a network architecture is referred to as a LAN type or a LAN technology.) A network architecture, such as ethernet, provides a bundle of specifications governing media access, physical addressing, and the interaction of the computers with the transmission medium. When you decide on a network architecture, you are in effect deciding on a design for the Network Access layer.

A network architecture is a design for the physical network and a collection of specifications defining communications on that physical network. The communication details are dependent on the physical details, so the specifications usually come together as a complete package. These specifications include considerations such as the following:

- Access method—An access method is a set of rules defining how the computers will share the transmission medium. To avoid data collisions, computers must follow these rules when they transmit data.
- Data frame format—The IP-level datagram from the Internet layer is encapsulated in a data frame with a predefined format. The data enclosed in the header must supply the information necessary to deliver data on the physical network. You'll learn more about data frames later in this hour.
- Cabling type—The type of cable used for a network has an effect on certain other design parameters, such as the electrical properties of the bitstream transmitted by the adapter.
- Cabling rules—The protocols, cable type, and electrical properties of the transmission have an effect on the maximum and minimum lengths for the cable and for the cable connector specifications.

Details such as cable type and connector type are not the direct responsibility of the Network Access layer, but in order to design the software components of the Network Access layer, developers must assume a specific set of characteristics for the physical network. Thus, the network access software must come with a specific hardware design.

Physical Addressing

As you learned in Part I, "TCP/IP Basics," the Network Access layer is necessary in order to relate the logical IP address, which is configured through the protocol software with the actual permanent physical address of the network adapter. The physical address is burned into the card at the factory. Data frames sent across the LAN must use this physical address to identify the source and destination adapters, but the lengthy physical address (48 bits in the case of ethernet) is so unfriendly that it is impractical for people to use. Also, encoding the physical address at higher protocol levels compromises the flexible modular architecture of TCP/IP, which requires that the upper layers remain independent of physical details. TCP/IP uses the Address Resolution Protocol (ARP) and Reverse Address Resolution Protocol (RARP) to relate IP addresses to the physical addresses of the network adapters on the local network. ARP and RARP provide a link between the logical IP addresses seen by the user and the (effectively invisible) hardware addresses used on the LAN.

You'll learn about ARP and RARP in Hour 4, "The Internet Layer."

Anatomy of a Frame

The Network Access layer software accepts a datagram from the Internet layer and converts that data to a form that is consistent with the specifications of the physical network (see Figure 3.2). Because many forms of physical networks exist, there are many formats for data at the Network Access layer, and it would not be easy or useful to describe all these formats in detail.

FIGURE 3.2

The Network Access layer formats data for the physical network.

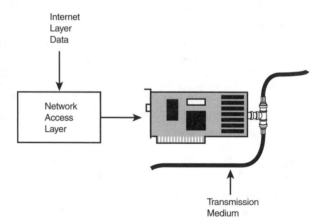

As an example of what happens to the data at the Network Access layer, consider the case of ethernet, the most common of the LAN architectures. When the ethernet software receives a datagram from the Internet layer, it performs the following steps:

1. Breaks IP layer data into smaller chunks, if necessary, which will be sent in the data field of the ethernet frames. The total size of the ethernet frame must be between 64 bytes and 1,518 bytes (not including the preamble).

2. Packages the chunks of data into frames. Each frame includes data as well as other information that the network adapters on the ethernet need in order to process the frame. An IEEE 802.3 ethernet frame includes the following:

Preamble: A sequence of bits used to mark the beginning of the frame (8 bytes, the last of which is the 1-byte Start Frame Delimiter).

Recipient address: The 6-byte (48-bit) physical address of the network adapter that is to receive the frame.

Source address: The 6-byte (48-bit) physical address of the network adapter that is sending the frame.

Length: A 2-byte (16-bit) field indicating the size of the data field.

Data: The data that is transmitted with the frame.

Frame Check Sequence (FCS): A 4-byte (32-bit) checksum value for the frame. The FCS is a common means of verifying data transmissions. The sending computer calculates a Cyclical Redundancy Check (CRC) value for the frame and encodes the CRC value in the frame. The receiving computer then recalculates the CRC and checks the FCS field to see if the values match. If the values don't match, some data was lost or changed during transmission.

3. Passes the data frame to lower-level components corresponding to OSI's physical layer, which will convert the frame into a bitstream and send it over the transmission medium.

The other network adapters on the ethernet receive the frame and check the destination address. If the destination address matches the address of the network adapter, the adapter software processes the incoming frame and passes the data to higher layers of the protocol stack.

IEEE 802.3 is not the only ethernet standard. The Ethernet II standard, used by some vendors, has a slightly different frame format.

LAN Technologies

The most common network architectures are the following:

- Ethernet, including variants such as the following:

    10BASE-2 (an ethernet standard using thin coaxial cable)

    10BASE-5 (an ethernet standard using thick coaxial cable)

10BASE-T (an ethernet standard using twisted-pair cable in a star configuration)

100BASE-TX (a standard similar to 10BASE-T with faster transmissions speed (100Mbps)

- Token ring

> The Institute of Electrical and Electronic Engineers (IEEE) has produced a set of standards for LAN architectures. Although token ring and ethernet were both created before the IEEE standards, the IEEE specifications for IEEE 802.3 (ethernet) and IEEE 802.5 (token ring) now provide vendor-neutral standards for these important LAN technologies.

The following sections will examine ethernet and token ring in greater detail, along with another LAN technology: FDDI.

Ethernet

Ethernet and its newer sibling Fast Ethernet, are the LAN technologies most commonly used today. Ethernet has become popular because of its modest price; Ethernet cable is inexpensive and easily installed. Ethernet network adapters and Ethernet hardware components are also relatively inexpensive.

On ethernet networks, all computers share a common transmission medium. Ethernet uses an access method called Carrier Sense Multiple Access with Collision Detect (CSMA/CD) for determining when a computer is free to transmit data on to the access medium. Using CSMA/CD, all computers monitor the transmission medium and wait until the line is available before transmitting. If two computers try to transmit at the same time, a collision occurs. The computers then stop, wait for a random time interval, and attempt to transmit again.

CSMA/CD can be compared to the protocol followed by a room full of polite people. Someone who wants to speak first listens to determine if anybody else is currently speaking (this is the Carrier Sense). If two people start speaking at the same moment, then both people will detect this, stop speaking, and wait before speaking again (this is Collision Detect).

Traditional ethernet works well under light-to-moderate use but suffers from high collision rates under heavy use. Some of the newer ethernet variants, which may include intelligent hubs or switches, support higher traffic levels. You'll learn more about hubs and switches in Hour 9, "Network Hardware."

Ethernet is capable of using a variety of media. Ethernet networks typically operate at baseband speeds of either 10Mbps or 100Mbps. 1000Mbps (Gigabit) Ethernet systems are now available and may soon be common. Table 3.1 lists terms used to identify cabling media, speeds, and maximum distances. Wireless ethernet is also becoming popular. 10BASE-2 and 10BASE-5 coaxial ethernet networks were once very common. Figure 3.3 shows a coaxial 10BASE-2 network. Note that the computers are attached to a single cable that acts as the shared transmission medium. In recent years, hub-based ethernet variants such as 10BASE-T (see Figure 3.4) have become vastly more popular. On a 10BASE-T network, the computers are attached to a central hub. 10BASE-2 and 10BASE-T may appear to be dissimilar, but internally they are both still ethernet.

TABLE 3.1 Ethernet Media Technology

Technology Name	Media Type	Operating Speed	Maximum Distance
10BASE-2	Thin coax	10 megabits	185 meters
10BASE-5	Thick coax	10 megabits	500 meters
10BASE-T	CAT3 or CAT5 UTP	10 megabits	100 meters
10BASE-F	Fiber optic	10 megabits	2,000 meters
100BASE-TX	CAT 5 UTP or STP	100 megabits	100 meters
100BASE-FX	Fiber optic	100 megabits	2,000 meters

3

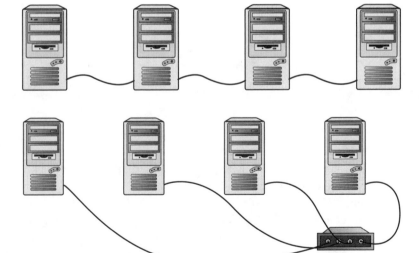

FIGURE 3.3
A 10BASE-2 coaxial ethernet network.

FIGURE 3.4
A 10BASE-T hub-based ethernet network.

Token Ring

Token ring technology uses a completely different concept for allowing network adapters to transmit data on the media. This access method is known as *token passing*.

Under the token passing access method, the computers on the LAN are connected so that data is passed around the network in a logical ring (see Figure 3.5). The token ring configuration calls for the computers to be wired to a central hub called a MAU or MSAU. Figure 3.5 may not look like a ring, but the MSAU is wired so that the data passes from one computer to the next in a circular motion. The computers pass a packet of data called a *token* around the network. Only the computer that holds the token can transmit a message on to the ring.

FIGURE 3.5

A token ring.

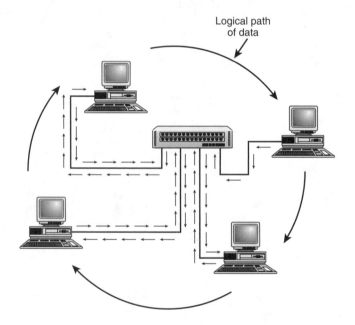

Token ring is technically more sophisticated than ethernet, and it includes a number of built-in diagnosis and correction mechanisms that can help troubleshoot network problems. Also, because data is transmitted in a more orderly fashion, token ring does not suffer as badly under heavy data traffic. Almost everything about token ring is more expensive than ethernet by comparison—the cable, the network adapter cards, and the other components as well.

Token ring typically operates at either 4Mbps or 16Mbps. It is also available at 100Mbps.

FDDI

Fiber Distributed Data Interface (FDDI) is an expensive LAN technology that employs a pair of fiber-optic rings. One ring is considered primary and the second ring is principally there to repair the primary ring in the event of a breakdown. FDDI uses a token passing access method similar to token ring.

Like token ring, FDDI also has error-detection and correction capabilities. In a normally operating FDDI ring, the token passes by each machine every so often. If the token is not seen within the maximum amount of time that it takes to circulate the largest ring, it indicates a problem has occurred such as a broken cable.

Fiber-optic cable such as the cable used with FDDI can support very large volumes of data over large distances.

Other Network-Access Technologies

LAN technologies such as ethernet are common throughout the mechanized world, but there are many other ways to connect computers. Any networking technology must have some means of preparing data for the physical network and, therefore, any TCP/IP technology must have a Network Access layer. As was already mentioned, a modem is another means of supporting a network connection. You'll learn more about modems in Hour 8. Wide area network (WAN) technologies support connections that operate over greater distances but often at slower transmission rates. WAN connections require specialized hardware that, as you might guess, requires specialized software at the Network Access layer.

Summary

In this hour you learned about the Network Access layer, the most diverse and arguably the most complex layer in the TCP/IP protocol stack. The Network Access layer defines the procedures for interfacing with the network hardware and accessing the transmission medium. There are many types of LAN architectures and therefore many different forms that the Network Access layer can take. This hour also described the contents of an ethernet frame and briefly discussed ethernet, token ring, and FDDI.

Q&A

Q What types of services are defined at the Network Access layer?

A The Network Access layer includes services and specifications that manage the process of accessing the physical network.

Q Which OSI layers correspond to the TCP/IP network Access layer?

A The Network Access layer roughly corresponds with the OSI Data Link layer and Physical layer.

Q What are the two most common LAN architectures?

A The most common LAN architectures are ethernet, with its several cabling variants, and token ring.

Q What is CSMA/CD?

A CSMA/CD is Carrier Sense Multiple Access with Collision Detect, a network-access method used by ethernet. Under CSMA/CD, the computers on a network wait for a moment to transmit and, if two computers attempt to transmit at once, they both stop, wait for a random interval, and transmit again.

Q What is token passing?

A Token passing is a network-access method used by token ring and FDDI. A packet of data called a token circulates around the network. Only the computer with the token can transmit data.

Key Terms

Review the following list of key terms:

Access method—A procedure for regulating access to the transmission medium.

CRC (Cyclical Redundancy Check)—A checksum calculation used to verify the contents of a data frame.

CSMA/CD—The network access method used by ethernet.

Data frame—A package of data transmitted over an ethernet network.

Data Link layer—The second layer of the OSI model.

Ethernet—A very popular LAN architecture, using the CSMA/CD network-access method.

FDDI—A token passing network architecture using fiber-optic cable.

Logical Link Control sublayer—A sublayer of OSI's Data Link layer that is responsible for error checking and managing links between devices on the subnet.

Media Access Control sublayer—A sublayer of OSI's Data Link layer that is responsible for the interface with the network adapter.

Network architecture—A complete specification for a physical network, including specifications for access method, data frame, and network cabling.

Physical address—A permanent network address, burned into the adapter card by the manufacturer, that is used to deliver data across the physical network.

Physical layer—The first OSI layer, responsible for translating the data frame into a bit-stream suitable for the transmission medium.

Preamble—A series of bits marking the beginning of a data frame transmission.

Token passing—The network access method used by token ring.

Token ring—A LAN architecture featuring a ring topology and a token-passing network access method.

3

HOUR 4

The Internet Layer

As you learned in the preceding hour, the computers on a single network segment such as an ethernet LAN can communicate with each other using the physical addresses available at the Network Access layer. How, then, does an e-mail message get from Carolina to California and arrive precisely at its destination? As you'll learn in this hour, the protocols at the Internet layer provide for delivery beyond the subnet. This hour discusses the important Internet layer protocols IP, ARP, and ICMP.

At the completion of this hour, you will be able to

- Explain the purpose of IP, ARP, and ICMP
- Explain what a network ID and host ID are
- Explain what an octet is
- Convert a dotted decimal address to its binary equivalent
- Convert a 32-bit binary IP address into dotted decimal notation
- Describe the contents of an IP header
- Explain the purpose of the IP address
- Identify the network ID and host ID fields for Class A, B, and C addresses

Addressing and Delivering

As you learned in Hour 3, "The Network Access Layer," a computer communicates with
the network through a network interface device such as a network adapter card. The network interface device has a unique physical address and is designed to receive data sent
to that physical address. This physical address is burned into the card when it is manu-
factured. A device such as an ethernet card does not know any of the details of the upper
protocol layers. It does not know its IP address or whether an incoming frame is being
sent to Telnet or FTP. It just listens to incoming frames, waits for a frame addressed to its
own physical address, passes that frame up the stack.

This physical addressing scheme works very well on an individual LAN segment. A network that consists of only a few computers on an uninterrupted medium can function with
nothing more than physical addresses. Data can pass directly from network adapter to network adapter using the low-level protocols associated with the Network Access layer.
(The non-routable NetBEUI protocol is a holdover from this simpler era in networking.)

Unfortunately, on a routed network, it is not possible to deliver data by physical address.
The discovery procedures required for delivering by physical address do not work across
a router interface. Even if they did work, delivery by physical address would be cumbersome because the permanent physical address built into a network card does not allow
you to impose a logical structure on the address space.

TCP/IP therefore makes the physical address invisible and instead organizes the network
around a logical, hierarchical addressing scheme. This logical addressing scheme is maintained by the IP protocol at the Internet layer. The logical address is called the *IP address*.
Another Internet layer protocol called Address Resolution Protocol (ARP) assembles a
table that maps IP addresses to physical addresses. This ARP table is the link between the
IP address and the physical address burned into the network adapter card.

On a routed network (see Figure 4.1), the TCP/IP software uses the following strategy
for sending data on the network:

1. If the destination address is on the same network segment as the source computer,
   the source computer sends the packet directly to the destination. The IP address is
   resolved to a physical address using ARP, and the data is directed to the destination
   network adapter.

2. If the destination address is on a different segment from the source computer, the
   following process begins:

   a. The datagram is directed to a gateway. A *gateway* is a device on the local
      network segment that is capable of forwarding a datagram to other network
      segments. (As you'll learn in Hour 9, "Network Hardware," and Hour 10,

"Routing," a gateway is basically a router.) The gateway address is resolved to a physical address using ARP, and the data is sent to the gateway's network adapter.

b. The datagram is routed through the gateway to a higher-level network segment (refer to Figure 4.1) where the process is repeated. If the destination address is on the new segment, the data is delivered to its destination. If not, the datagram is sent to another router.

c. The datagram passes through the chain of routers to the destination segment, where the destination IP address is mapped to a physical address using ARP and the data is directed to the destination network adapter.

FIGURE 4.1

The gateway receives datagrams addressed to other networks.

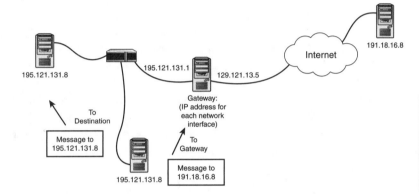

To deliver data on a complex routed network, the Internet layer protocols must therefore be able to

- Identify any computer on the network.
- Provide a means for determining when a message must be sent through the gateway.
- Provide a hardware-independent means of identifying the destination network segment so that the datagram will pass efficiently through the routers to the correct segment.
- Provide a means for converting the logical IP address of the destination computer to a physical address so that the data can be delivered to the network adapter of the destination computer.

In this hour you'll learn about the important IP addressing system, and you'll learn how TCP/IP delivers datagrams on a complex network using the Internet layer's IP and ARP. You'll also learn about the Internet layer's ICMP protocol, which provides error detection and troubleshooting.

Internet Protocol (IP)

The IP protocol provides a hierarchical, hardware-independent addressing system and offers the services necessary for delivering data on a complex, routed network. Each network adapter on a TCP/IP network has a unique IP address.

> Descriptions of TCP/IP often talk about a *computer* having an IP address. A computer is sometimes said to have an IP address because most computers have only one network adapter. However, computers with multiple network adapters are also common. A computer that is acting as a router or a proxy server, for instance, must have more than one network adapter and therefore has more than one IP address. The term *host* is often used for a network device associated with an IP address.
>
> Under many operating systems, it is also possible to assign more than one IP address to a single network adapter.

IP addresses on the network are organized so that you can tell the location of the host—the network or subnet where the host resides—by looking at the address (see Figure 4.2). In other words, part of the address is a little like a ZIP Code (describing a general location), and part of the address is a little like the street address (describing an exact location within that general area).

It is easy for a person to look at Figure 4.2 and say, "Every address that starts with 192.132.134 must be in Building C." A computer, though, requires a bit more hand-holding. The IP address is therefore divided into two parts:

- The network ID
- The host ID

The owners of a network can also impose an additional hierarchical level by assigning a subnet ID. You'll learn more about subnets and subnet IDs in Hour 5, "Subnetting."

> Study this hour and Hour 5 together. Until you learn about subnet IDs, you haven't really mastered the art of IP addressing.

As you'll learn later in this hour, the IP module of the protocol software can determine from the address itselfwhat part of the address is the network ID and what part is the host ID.

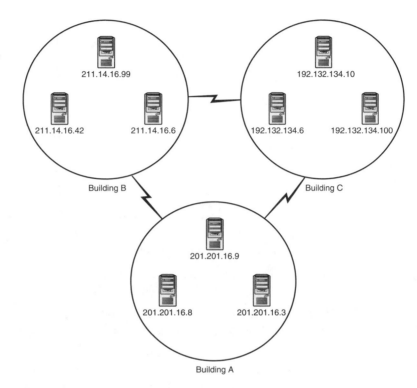

<figure>
FIGURE 4.2

You can tell the network by looking at the address.
</figure>

IP Header Fields

Every IP datagram begins with an IP header. The TCP/IP software on the source computer constructs the IP header. The TCP/IP software at the destination uses the information enclosed in the IP header to process the datagram. The IP header contains a great deal of information, including the IP addresses of the source and destination computers, the length of the datagram, the IP version number, and special instructions to routers.

For additional information about IP headers see RFC 791.

The minimum size for an IP header is 20 bytes. Figure 4.3 shows the contents on the IP header.

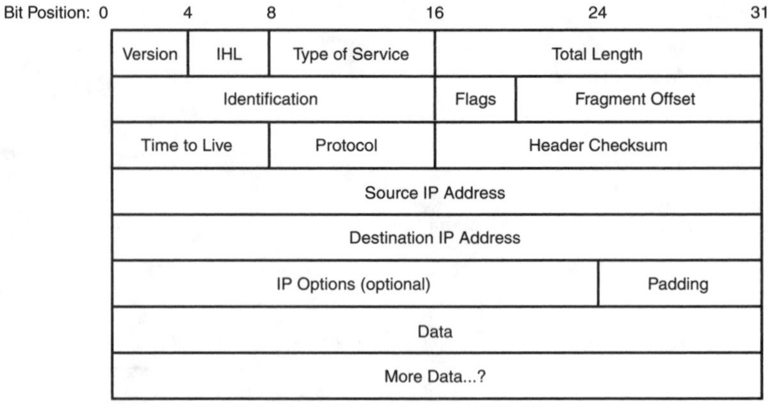

FIGURE 4.3
IP header fields.

The header fields in Figure 4.3 are as follows:

- **Version** This 4-bit field indicates which version of IP is being used. The current version of IP is 4. The binary pattern for 4 is 0100.

- **IHL (Internet Header Length)** This 4-bit field gives length of the IP header in 32-bit words. The minimum header length is five 32-bit words. The binary pattern for 5 is 0101.

- **Type of Service** The source IP can designate special routing information. Some routers ignore the Type of Service field, although this field recently has received more attention with the emergence of Quality of Service (QoS) technologies. The primary purpose of this 8-bit field is to provide a means of prioritizing datagrams that are waiting to pass through a router. Most implementations of IP today simply put all zeros in this field.

- **Total Length** This 16-bit field identifies the length, in octets, of the IP datagram. This length includes the IP header and the data payload.

- **Identification** This 16-bit field is an incrementing sequence number assigned to messages sent by the source IP. When a message is sent to the IP layer and it is too large to fit in one datagram, IP fragments the message into multiple datagrams, giving all datagrams the same identification number. This number is used on the receiving end to reassemble the original message.

- **Flags** The indicates fragmentation possibilities. The first bit is unused and should always have a value of zero. The next bit is called the DF (Don't Fragment) flag. The DF flag signifies whether fragmentation is allowed (value = 0) or not (value =1), The next bit is the MF (More Fragments) flag, which tells the receiver that more fragments are on the way. When MF is set to 0, no more fragments need to be sent or the datagram never was fragmented.

- **Fragment Offset**   This 13-bit field is a numeric value assigned to each successive fragment. IP at the destination uses the fragment offset to reassemble the fragments into the proper order. The offset value found here expresses the offset as a number of 8-byte units.

- **Time to Live**   This 8-bit field indicates the amount of time in seconds or *router hops* that the datagram can survive before being discarded. Every router examines and decrements this field by at least 1, or by the number of seconds the datagram is delayed inside the router. The datagram is discarded when this field reaches zero.

NEW TERM   A *hop* or a *router hop* correlates to a router that a datagram travels through on its way to its destination. If a datagram passes through five routers before arriving at its destination, the destination is said to be five hops, or five router hops, away.

- **Protocol**   This 8-bit for the protocol that will receive the data payload. A datagram with the protocol identifier 6 (binary 00000110) is passed up the stack to the TCP module, for example. The following are some common protocol values:

Protocol Name	Protocol Identifier
ICMP	1
TCP	6
UDP	17

- **Header Checksum**   This field holds a 16-bit calculated value to verify the validity of the header only. This field is recomputed in every router as the TTL field decrements.

- **Source IP Address**   This 32-bit field holds the address of the source of the datagram.

- **Destination IP Address**   This 32-bit field holds the destination address of the datagram and is used by the destination IP to verify correct delivery.

- **IP Options**   This field supports a number of optional header settings primarily used for testing, debugging, and security. Options include Strict Source Route (a specific path router path that the datagram should follow), Internet Timestamp (a record of timestamps at each router), and security restrictions.

- **Padding**   The IP Options field may vary in length. The Padding field provides additional zero bits so that the total header length is an exact multiple of 32 bits. (The header must end after a 32-bit word because the IHL field measures the header length in 32-bit words.)

- **IP Data Payload**   This field typically contains data destined for delivery to TCP or UDP (in the Transport layer), ICMP, or IGMP. The amount of data is variable but could include thousands of bytes.

4

IP Addressing

An IP address is a 32-bit binary address. This 32-bit address is subdivided into four 8-bit segments called *octets*. Humans do not work well with 32-bit binary addresses or even 8-bit binary octets, so the IP address is almost always expressed in what is called *dotted decimal* format. In dotted decimal format, each octet is given as an equivalent decimal number. The four decimal values ($4 \times 8 = 32$ bits) are then separated with periods. Eight binary bits can represent any whole number from 0 to 255, so the segments of a dotted decimal address are decimal numbers from 0 to 255. You have probably seen examples of dotted decimal IP addresses on your computer, in this book, or in other TCP/IP documents. A dotted decimal IP address looks like this: 209.121.131.14.

Part of the IP address is used for the network ID, and part of the address is used for the host ID. One complication is that the portion of the address allotted to the network ID varies, depending on the address. Most IP addresses fall into the following address classes:

- **Class A addresses** The first 8 bits of the IP address are used for the network ID. The final 24 bits are used for the host ID.
- **Class B addresses** The first 16 bits of the IP address are used for the network ID. The final 16 bits are used for the host ID.
- **Class C addresses** The first 24 bits of the IP address are used for the network ID. The final 8 bits are used for the host ID.

More bits lead to more bit combinations. As you might guess, the Class A format provides a small number of possible network IDs and a huge number of possible host IDs for each network. A Class A network can support approximately 2^{24}, or 16,777,216 hosts. A Class C network, on the other hand, can provide host IDs for only a small number of hosts (approximately 2^8, or 256), but many more combinations of network IDs are available in the Class C format.

You might be wondering how a computer or router knows whether to interpret an IP address as a Class A, Class B, or Class C address. The designers of TCP/IP wrote the address rules such that the class of an address is obvious from the address itself. The first few bits of the binary address specify whether the address should be interpreted as a Class A, Class B, or Class C address (see Table 4.1). The rules for interpreting addresses are as follows:

- If the 32-bit binary address starts with a 0 bit, the address is a Class A address.
- If the 32-bit binary address starts with the bits 10, the address is a Class B address.
- If the 32-bit binary address starts with the bits 110, the address is a Class C address.

This scheme (thankfully) is easy to convert to dotted decimal notation because these rules have the effect of limiting the range of values for the first term in the dotted decimal address. For instance, since a Class A address must have a 0 bit in the leftmost place of the first octet, the first term in a Class A dotted decimal address cannot be higher than 127. You'll learn more about converting binary numbers to decimal later in this hour. For purposes of this discussion, Table 4.1 shows the address ranges for Class A, B, and C networks. Note that some address ranges are listed as excluded addresses. Certain IP address ranges are not assigned to networks because they are reserved for special uses. You'll learn more about special IP addresses later in this hour.

TABLE 4.1 Address Ranges for Class A, B, and C Networks

Address Class	Binary Address Must Begin with	First Term of Dotted Decimal Address Must Be	Excluded Addresses
A	0	0 to 127	`10.0.0.0` to `10.255.255.255` `127.0.0.0` to `127.255.255.255`
B	10	128 to 191	`172.16.0.0` to `172.31.255.255`
C	110	192 to 223	`192.168.0.0` to `192.168.255.255`

4

The Internet specifications also define special-purpose Class D and Class E addresses. You'll learn more about Class D and Class E addresses later in this hour.

The owner of a network can divide the network into smaller sub-networks called *subnets*. Subnetting essentially borrows some of the bits of the host ID to create additional networks within the network. As you can probably guess, Class A and B networks, with their large host ID address spaces, make extensive use of subnetting. Subnetting is also used on Class C networks. You'll learn more about subnetting in Hour 5.

Theoretically, every computer on the Internet must have a unique IP address. In practice, the use of proxy server software and Network Address Translation (NAT) devices makes it possible for unregistered and non-unique addresses to operate on the Internet. You'll learn more about NAT devices in Hour 9.

Converting a 32-Bit Binary Address to Dotted Decimal Format

Binary (base 2) numbers are similar to decimal (base 10) numbers except that the place values are multiples of 2 instead of multiples of 10. As Figure 4.4 shows, a decimal whole number begins with the ones place on the right, and each successive value to the left is a higher multiple of 10. A value of a decimal number is just the sum of the values for each decimal place. For instance, (as shown) the value of the decimal number 126,325 is determined as follows: $(1 \times 100{,}000) + (2 \times 10{,}000) + (6 \times 1000) + (3 \times 100) + (2 \times 10) + (5 \times 1) = 126{,}325$.

FIGURE 4.4

The base 10 number system.

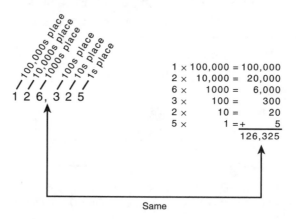

A binary whole number also starts with the ones place on the right. Each successive value to the left is a higher multiple of 2 (see Figure 4.5).

FIGURE 4.5

The binary (base 2) number system.

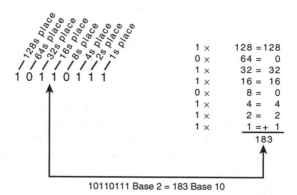

Computers work in binary because a bit pattern of zeroes and ones corresponds easily to the discrete on and off states used within digital circuitry.

To determine the decimal equivalent of a binary value, add the place values of any bit that holds a one. Remember that the IP address is comprised of four octets that must each be converted separately to decimal format. Following is an example showing how to convert a 32-bit binary IP address to dotted decimal format.

Convert the binary address 01011001000111011100110000011000.

1. First break the address into 8-bit octets:

   Octet 1: 01011001

   Octet 2: 00011101

   Octet 3: 11001100

   Octet 4: 00011000

2. Convert each octet to a decimal number. This process is illustrated in Table 4.2.

TABLE 4.2 Converting a Binary Address to Dotted Decimal Format

Octet	Binary Value	Calculation	Decimal Value
1	01011001	1+8+16+64	89
2	00011101	1+4+8+16	29
3	11001100	4+8+64+128	204
4	00011000	8+16	24

3. Write out the decimal equivalent values in order from left to right. Separate the values with periods:

   The address is: `89.29.204.24`

If you need more practice converting a binary address to dotted decimal format, check the Workshop section at the end of this hour.

You can use the Windows Calculator accessory to convert binary numbers to and from decimal. Select the View menu and choose Scientific. The Bin radio button places the calculator in binary mode. The Dec radio button puts the number back in decimal.

Converting a Decimal Number to a Binary Octet

The process of converting a decimal number to binary is a matter of going backward through the process shown in Figure 4.5. If you need to convert a dotted decimal address to a 32-bit binary address, convert each period-separated number in the address to a binary octet and then concatenate the octets. The following procedure shows how to convert the decimal number 207 to a binary octet.

 This procedure assumes you started with a decimal number representing an IP address octet. If the number you are converting is higher than 255, you'll need to extend the binary place value diagram shown in Figure 4.5 and adapt the procedure accordingly.

To convert the decimal number 207 to a binary octet, follow these steps:

1. Compare the decimal number you want to convert (in this case 207) to the number 128. If the decimal number is greater than or equal to 128, subtract 128 and write down a 1. If the decimal number is less than 128, subtract 0 and write down a 0.

    $207 > 128$

    $207 - 128 = 79$

    Write down 1 for the 128s place

    Answer so far: 1

2. Take the result from step 1 (79 in this case) and compare it to the number 64. If the decimal number is greater than or equal to 64, subtract 64 and write down a 1. If the decimal number is less than 64, subtract 0 and write down a 0.

    $79 > 64$

    $79 - 64 = 15$

    Write down a 1 for the 64s place

    Answer so far: 11

3. Take the result from step 2 (15 in this case) and compare it to the number 32. If the decimal number is greater than or equal to 32, subtract 32 and write down a 1. If the decimal number is less than 32, subtract 0 and write down a 0.

    $15 < 32$

    $15 - 0 = 15$

    Write down a 0 in the 32s place

    Answer so far: 110

4. Compare the result from step 3 to the number 16. If the number is greater than 16, subtract 16 and write down a 1. If the number is less than 16, subtract 0 and write down a 0.

    $15 < 32$

    $15 - 0 = 15$

    Write down a 0 in the 16s place

    Answer so far: 1100

5. Compare the result of step 4 to the number 8. If the decimal number is greater than 8, subtract 8 and write down a 1. If the decimal number is less than 8, subtract 0 and write down a 0.

    $15 > 8$

    $15 - 8 = 7$

    Write down a 1 in the 8s place

    Answer so far: 11001

6. Compare the result of step 5 to the number 4. If the decimal number is greater than 4, subtract 4 and write down a 1. If the decimal number is less than 4, subtract 0 and write down a 0.

    $7 > 4$

    $7 - 4 = 3$

    Write down a 1 in the 4s place

    Answer so far: 110011

7. Compare the result of step 6 to the number 2. If the decimal number is greater than 2, subtract 2 and write down a 1. If the decimal number is less than 2, subtract 0 and write down a 0.

    $3 > 2$

    $3 - 2 = 1$

    Write down a 1 in the 2s place

    Answer so far: 1100111

8. If the result of step 8 is a 1, write down a 1. If the result of step 8 is a 0, write down a 0.

    $1 = 1$

    Write down a 1 in the ones place

    Final answer: 11001111

You have now converted the decimal number 207 to its binary equivalent 11001111.

Classes D and E

As you learned earlier in this hour, the IP specifications also provide for Class D and Class E addresses.

Most TCP/IP communication is either host-to-host (sent from one source computer to one destination computer) or broadcast (sent to all computers on the segment or network). Class D addresses, on the other hand, are used for multicasting. A *multicast* is a single message sent to a subset of the network. The four leftmost bits of a Class D network address always start with the binary pattern 1110, which corresponds to decimal numbers 224 through 239.

> The Internet Group Management Protocol (IGMP) is an Internet layer protocol used in conjunction with multicasting and Class D addresses.

The Internet RFCs specify a number of permanent multicast addresses. Multicasting is an advanced topic and is not covered in any greater depth in this ook.

Class E networks are considered experimental. They are not normally used in any production environment.

The five leftmost bits of a Class E network always start with the binary pattern 11110, which corresponds to decimal numbers 240 through 247.

Special IP Addresses

A few IP addresses have special meanings and are not assigned to specific hosts. An all-zero host ID refer to the network itself. For instance, the IP address 129.152.0.0 refers to the Class B network with the network ID 129.152.

An all-ones host ID signifies a broadcast. A broadcast is a message sent to all hosts on the network. The IP address 129.152.255.255 is the broadcast address for the Class B network with the network ID 129.152. (Note that the dotted decimal term 255 corresponds to the all-ones binary octet 11111111.)

The address 255.255.255.255 can also be used for broadcast on the network.

Addresses beginning with the term 127 are loopback addresses. A message addressed to a loopback address is sent by the local TCP/IP software to itself. The loopback address is used to verify that the TCP/IP software is functioning. See the discussion of the ping utility in Hour 13, "Connectivity Utilities." The loopback address 127.0.0.1 is commonly used.

RFC 1597 also reserves some IP address ranges for private networks. The assumption is that these private address ranges are not connected to the Internet, so the addresses don't have to be unique. In today's world, these private address ranges are often used for the protected network behind network translation devices:

- 10.0.0.0 to 10.255.255.255
- 172.16.0.0 to 172.31.255.255
- 192.168.0.0 to 192.168.255.255

See Hour 9 for more on network translation devices.

Address Resolution Protocol (ARP)

As you learned earlier in this hour, the computers on a local network use an Internet layer protocol called Address Resolution Protocol (ARP) to map IP addresses to physical addresses. A host must know the physical address of the destination network adapter in order to send any data to it. For this reason, ARP is a very important protocol. However, TCP/IP is implemented in such a way that ARP and all the details of physical address translation are almost totally invisible to the user. As far as the user is concerned, a network adapter is identified by its IP address. Behind the scenes, though, the IP address must be converted to a physical address in order for a message to reach its destination. (See Hour 3.)

Each host on a network segment maintains a table in memory called the *ARP table* or *ARP cache*. The ARP cache associates the IP addresses of other hosts on the network segment with physical addresses (see Figure 4.6). When a host needs to send data to another host on the segment, the host checks the ARP cache to determine the physical address of the recipient. The ARP cache is assembled dynamically. If the address that is to receive the data is not currently listed in the ARP cache, the host sends a broadcast called an *ARP request frame* (see Figure 4.6).

The ARP request frame contains the unresolved IP address. The ARP request frame also contains the IP address and physical address of the host that sent the request. The other hosts on the network segment receive the ARP request, and the host that owns the unresolved IP address responds by sending its physical address to the host that sent the request. The newly resolved IP-address-to-physical-address mapping is then added to the ARP cache of the requesting host.

Typically, the entries in the ARP cache expire after a pre-determined period. When the lifetime of an ARP entry expires, the entry is removed from the table. The resolution process begins again the next time the host needs to send data to the IP address of the expired entry.

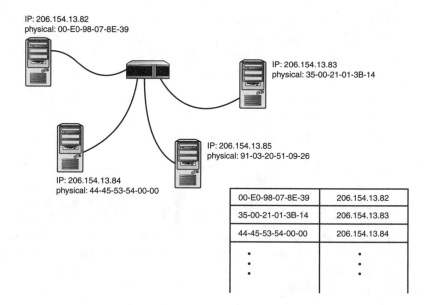

FIGURE 4.6
ARP maps IP addresses to physical addresses.

RARP

RARP stands for Reverse ARP. RARP is the opposite of ARP. ARP is used when the IP address is known but the physical address is not known. RARP is used when the physical address is known but the IP address is not known. RARP is often used in conjunction with the BOOTP protocol to boot diskless workstations.

NEW TERM *BOOTP (boot PROM).* Many network adapters contain an empty socket for insertion of an integrated circuit known as a boot PROM. The boot PROM has a protocol (BOOTP) that starts as soon as the computer is powered on. It loads an operating system into the computer by reading it from a network server instead of a local disk drive. The operating system located on the server is pre-built for a specific IP address. The MAC address selects which copy of the operating system to download into the remote boot computer.

Internet Control Message Protocol (ICMP)

Data sent to a remote computer often travels through one or more routers; these routers can encounter a number of problems in sending the message to its ultimate destination. Routers use Internet Control Message Protocol (ICMP) messages to notify the source IP of these problems. ICMP is also used for other diagnosis and troubleshooting functions.

The most common ICMP messages are listed here. Quite a few other conditions generate ICMP messages but their frequency of occurrence is quite low.

- Echo Request and Echo Reply ICMP is often used during testing. When a technician uses the ping command to check connectivity with another host, he is using ICMP. ping sends a datagram to an IP address and requests the destination computer to return the data sent in a response datagram. The commands actually being used are the ICMP Echo Request and Echo Reply.
- Source Quench If a fast computer is sending large amounts of data to a remote computer, the volume can overwhelm the router. The router might use ICMP to send a Source Quench message to the source IP to ask it to slow down the rate at which it is shipping data. If necessary, additional source quenches can be sent to the source IP.
- Destination Unreachable If a router receives a datagram that cannot be delivered, ICMP returns a Destination Unreachable message to the source IP. One reason that a router cannot deliver a message is a network that is down due to equipment failure or maintenance.
- Time Exceeded ICMP sends this message to the source IP if a datagram is discarded because TTL reaches zero. This indicates that the destination is too many router hops away to reach with the current TTL value, or it indicates router table problems that cause the datagram to loop through the same routers continuously.

NEW TERM A *routing loop* occurs when a datagram circulates through the same routers continuously and never reaches its destination. Suppose three routers are located in Los Angeles, San Francisco, and Denver. The Los Angeles router sends datagrams to San Francisco, which sends them to Denver, which sends them back to Los Angeles again. The datagram becomes trapped and will circulate continuously through these three routers until the TTL reaches zero. A routing loop should not occur, but occasionally it does. A routing loop sometimes occurs when a network administrator places static routing entries in a routing table.

- Fragmentation Needed ICMP sends this message if it receives a datagram with the Don't Fragment bit set and if the router needs to fragment the datagram in order to forward it to the next router or the destination.

Summary

In this hour you learned about the Internet layer protocols IP, ARP, RARP, and ICMP. IP provides a hardware-independent addressing system for delivering data over the network. You learned about binary and dotted decimal IP address formats and about the IP address classes A, B, C, D, and E. You also learned about ARP, a protocol that resolves IP addresses to physical addresses. RARP is the opposite of ARP, a protocol that lets a disk-less computer query a server for its own IP address. ICMP is a protocol used for diagnosis and testing.

Q&A

Q **A 32-bit binary number is more easily identified after converting it into what format?**

A Dotted decimal notation

Q **ARP returns what type of information when given an IP address?**

A The corresponding physical address

Q **If a router is unable to keep up with the volume of traffic, what type of ICMP message is sent to the source IP?**

A A Source Quench message

Q **What class does an IP address belong to that starts with the binary pattern 110 as the three leftmost bits?**

A A Class C network

Workshop

Convert the following binary octets to their decimal number equivalents.

00101011	Answer = 43
01010010	Answer = 82
11010110	Answer = 214
10110111	Answer = 183
01001010	Answer = 74
01011101	Answer = 93
10001101	Answer = 141
11011110	Answer = 222

Convert the following decimal numbers to their binary-octet equivalents.

13	Answer = 00001101
184	Answer = 10111000
238	Answer = 11101110
37	Answer = 00100101
98	Answer = 01100010
161	Answer = 10100001
243	Answer = 11110011
189	Answer = 10111101

Convert the following 32-bit IP addresses into dotted decimal notation.

11001111 00001110 00100001 01011100	Answer = 207.14.33.92
00001010 00001101 01011001 01001101	Answer = 10.13.89.77
10111101 10010011 01010101 01100001	Answer = 189.147.85.97

4

Key Terms

Review the following list of key terms:

Address Resolution Protocol (ARP)—A key Internet layer protocol used to obtain the physical address associated with an IP address. ARP maintains a cache of recently resolved physical-address-to-IP-address pairs.

Class A, B, C, D, and E—A classification system for IP addresses. The network class determines how the address is subdivided into a network ID and host ID.

Host ID—A portion of the IP address that refers to a node on the network. Each node within a network should have an IP address that contains a unique host ID.

Internet Control Message Protocol (ICMP)—A key Internet layer protocol used by routers to send messages that inform the source IP of routing problems. Also used by the ping command to determine the status of other hosts on the network.

Internet Protocol (IP)—A key Internet layer protocol used for addressing, delivering, and routing datagrams.

Multicast—Allows datagrams to be delivered to a group of hosts simultaneously.

Network ID—A portion of the IP address that identifies the network. All computers on a network should contain an IP address with the same network ID. Note that in this case a network is a physical subdivision of some larger internetwork (refer to Figure 4.2).

Reverse Address Resolution Protocol—A TCP/IP protocol that returns an IP address if given a physical address. This protocol is typically used by a diskless workstation that has a remote boot PROM installed in its network adapter.

HOUR 5

Subnetting

Subnetting is the process of dividing a block of IP addresses assigned as a Class A, B, or C network into multiple smaller blocks of addresses. This hour addresses the needs and benefits of subnetting, as well as the steps and procedures you should follow to generate a subnet mask.

At the completion of this hour, you will be able to

- Explain how subnets and supernets are used
- Explain the benefits of subnetting
- Develop a subnet mask that meets business needs
- Describe supernetting and CIDR notation

Subnets in TCP/IP

The address class system described in Hour 4, "The Internet Layer," enables all hosts to identify the network ID in an IP address and send a datagram to the correct network. However, identifying a network segment by its Class A, B, or C network ID presents some limitations. The principal limitation of the address class system is that it doesn't provide any logical subdivision of the address space beneath the network level.

Figure 5.1 shows a Class A network. As described in Hour 4, datagrams arrive efficiently at the gateway and pass into the `99.0.0.0` address space. However, the picture gets more complicated when you consider how to deliver the datagram once it passes into the `99.0.0.0` address space. A Class A network has room for over 16 million host IDs. This network could include millions of hosts, way more than would be possible on a single subnet.

FIGURE 5.1

Delivering data to a Class A network.

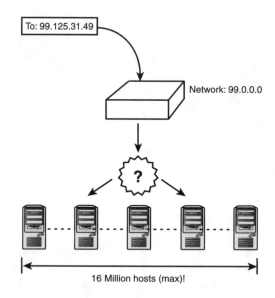

To: 99.125.31.49

Network: 99.0.0.0

?

16 Million hosts (max)!

To provide for more efficient delivery on a large network, the address space can be subdivided into smaller network segments (see Figure 5.2). Segmenting into separate physical networks increases the overall capacity of the network and therefore enables the network to use a greater portion of the address space. In this common scenario, the routers that separate the segments within the address space need some indication of where to deliver the data. They can't use the network ID because every datagram sent to the network has the same network ID (`99.0.0.0`). Though it might be possible to organize the address space by host ID, such a solution would be very cumbersome, inflexible, and totally impractical on a network with 16 million hosts. The only practical solution is to create some subdivision of the address space beneath the network ID so that the hosts and routers can tell from the IP address which network segment should receive the delivery.

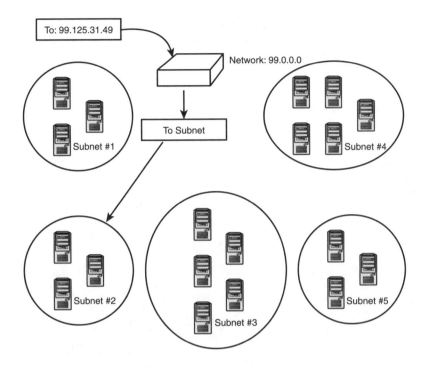

FIGURE 5.2
Organizing the network for efficient delivery.

To: 99.125.31.49

Network: 99.0.0.0

To Subnet

Subnet #1

Subnet #2

Subnet #3

Subnet #4

Subnet #5

TCP/IP provides a second tier of logical organization beneath the network ID through what is called a subnet. A *subnet* is a logical division of the network address space. The routers can deliver a datagram to a subnet address within the network (generally corresponding to a network segment), and once the datagram reaches the subnet, it can be resolved to a physical address using ARP (see Hour 4).

You are probably wondering where this subnet address comes from, since all 32 bits of the IP address are used for the network ID and the host ID. The answer is that the designers of TCP/IP provided a means to borrow some of the bits from the host ID to designate a subnet address. A parameter called the *subnet mask* tells how much of the address should be used for the subnet ID and how much is left for the actual host ID.

Like an IP address, a subnet mask is a 32-bit binary number. The bits of the subnet mask are arranged in a pattern that reveals the subnet ID of the IP address to which the mask is associated. Figure 5.3 shows an IP address/subnet mask pair. Each bit position in the subnet mask represents a bit position in the IP address. The subnet mask uses a 1 for every bit in the IP address that is part of the network ID or subnet ID. The subnet mask

5

uses a 0 to designate any bit in the IP address that is part of the host ID. You can think of the subnet mask as a map used for reading the IP address. Figure 5.4 shows the allocation of address bits in a subnetted network versus a non-subnetted network.

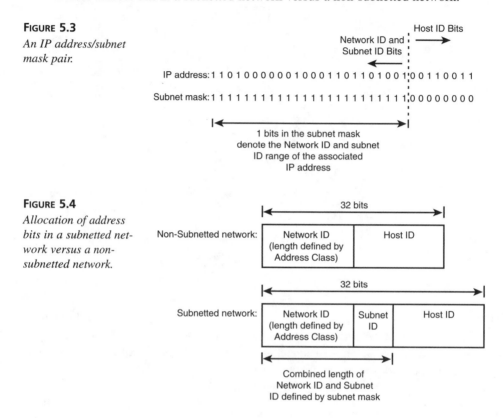

FIGURE 5.3

An IP address/subnet mask pair.

FIGURE 5.4

Allocation of address bits in a subnetted network versus a non-subnetted network.

The routing tables used by routers and hosts on a subnetted network include information on the subnet mask associated with each IP address. (You'll learn more about routing in Hour 10, "Routing.") As Figure 5.5 shows, an incoming datagram is routed to the network using the network ID field, which is determined by the address class (see Hour 4). Once the datagram reaches the network, it is routed to the proper segment using the subnet ID. After it reaches the segment, the host ID is used to deliver the datagram to the correct computer.

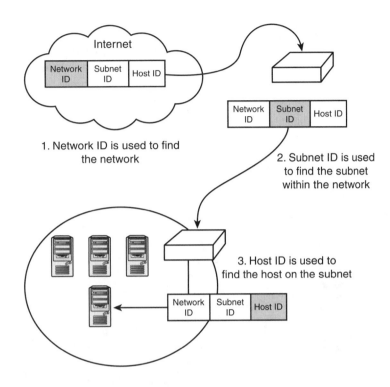

FIGURE 5.5
Incoming datagrams on a subnetted network.

1. Network ID is used to find the network

2. Subnet ID is used to find the subnet within the network

3. Host ID is used to find the host on the subnet

Converting a Subnet Mask to Dotted Decimal Notation

5

The network administrator typically assigns a subnet mask to each host as part of the TCP/IP configuration. If the host receives an IP address through DHCP (see Hour 12, "Dynamic Host Configuration Protocol (DHCP)"), the DHCP server can assign a subnet mask along with the IP address.

Subnet masks must be carefully calculated and must reflect the internal organization of the network. All the hosts within a subnet should have the same subnet ID and subnet mask. For the benefit of people, the subnet mask is usually expressed in dotted decimal notation similar to the notation used for an IP address.

As you'll recall from the preceding section, the subnet mask is a 32-bit binary number. You can convert the binary subnet mask to a dotted decimal address using the address conversion techniques described in Hour 4. A subnet mask is usually much easier to convert to dotted decimal format than an IP address. As you'll recall, the subnet mask bits

representing the IP address's network ID and the subnet ID are 1 bits. The bits representing the IP address's host ID are 0 bits. This means that (with a few rare and bewildering
exceptions) the 1 bits are all on the left and the 0 bits are all on the right. Any full octet
of ones in the subnet mask will appear as 255 (binary 11111111) in the dotted decimal
subnet mask. Any full octet of zeros will appear as 0 (binary 00000000) in the subnet
mask. Hence, the common subnet mask

11111111111111111111111100000000

is expressed in dotted decimal notation as 255.255.255.0. Likewise, the subnet mask:

11111111111111110000000000000000

is expressed in dotted decimal notation as 255.255.0.0.

As you can see, it is very easy to determine the dotted decimal equivalent of a subnet
mask that divides the address at an octet boundary. However, some subnet masks do not
divide the address at an octet boundary. In that case, you must simply determine the decimal equivalent of the mixed octet (the octet containing both ones and zeros).

To convert a binary subnet mask to dotted decimal notation, follow these steps:

1. Divide the subnet mask into octets by writing the 32-bit binary subnet mask with
   periods inserted at the octet boundaries:

   11111111.11111111.11110000.00000000

2. For every all-ones octet, write down 255. For every all-zeros octet, write down 0.

3. Convert the mixed octet to decimal using the binary conversion techniques discussed in Hour 4. To summarize, add up the bit position values for all one bits
   (refer to Figure 4.5).

4. Write down the final dotted decimal address:

   255.255.240.0

   In most cases, this dotted decimal subnet mask is the value you will enter as part of
   a computer's TCP/IP configuration.

Working with Subnets

The subnet mask defines how many bits after the network ID will be used for the subnet
ID. The subnet ID can vary in length, depending on the value you select for the subnet
mask. As the subnet ID grows larger, fewer bits are left for the host ID. In other words, if
your network has many subnets, you will be limited to fewer hosts on each subnet. If you
have only a few subnets and require only a few bits for the subnet ID, you can place
more hosts on a subnet.

> Note that the address class also defines how many bits will be available for the subnet ID. The mask
>
> 11111111111111111110000000000000
>
> specifies 19 bits for the network ID and subnet ID together. If this mask is used with a Class B address (which has a 16-bit network ID), only three bits are available for subnetting. If the same mask is used with a Class A address (which has an 8-bit network ID), 11 bits are available for subnetting.

The assignment of subnet IDs (and hence the assignment of a subnet mask) depends on your network configuration. The best solution is to plan your network first and determine the number and location of all network segments, then assign each segment a subnet ID. You'll need enough subnet bits to assign a unique subnet ID to each subnet. Save room, if possible, for additional subnet IDs in case your network expands.

A simple example of subnetting is a Class B network in which the third octet (the third term in the dotted decimal IP address) is reserved for the subnet number. In Figure 5.6, the network 129.100.0.0 is divided into four subnets. The IP addresses on the network are given the subnet mask 255.255.255.0, signifying that the network ID and subnet mask span three octets of the IP address. Because the address is a Class B address (see Hour 4), the first two octets in the address form the network ID. Subnet A in Figure 5.6 therefore has the following parameters:

Network ID: 129.100.0.0

Subnet ID: 0.0.128.0

Host IDs of either all ones or all zeros cannot be assigned. The configuration shown in Figure 5.6 therefore supports a possible 254 subnets and 254 addresses per subnet. This is a very sensible solution as long as you don't have more than 254 addresses on a subnet and as long as you have access to a Class B network address (which are getting harder to find).

It often isn't possible to assign a full octet to the subnet ID. On a Class C network, for instance, if you assigned a full octet to the subnet ID, you wouldn't have any bits left for the host ID. Even on a Class B network, you may not be able to use a full octet for the subnet ID, because you may need to make room for more than 254 hosts on a subnet. The subnetting rules do not require you to place the subnet ID at an octet boundary. The concept of a subnet ID that doesn't fall on an octet boundary is easy to visualize in binary form but becomes a bit more confusing when you return to dotted decimal format.

5

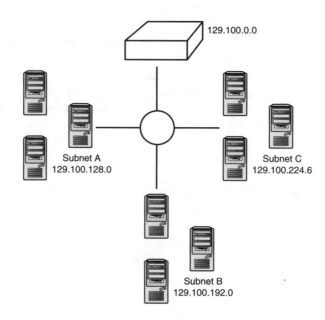

FIGURE **5.6**

A subnetted Class B network.

Consider a Class C network that must be divided into five small subnets. The class addressing rules provide 8 bits after the network ID to use for the subnet ID and the host ID in a Class C network. You could designate 3 of those bits for the subnet ID using this subnet mask:

11111111111111111111111111100000

The remaining five bits are then available for the host ID. The three bits of the subnet ID provide eight possible bit patterns. As mentioned earlier, the official subnetting rules exclude the all-ones pattern and the all-zeros pattern from the pool of subnet IDs (although many routers actually support the assignment of the all-ones or all-zeros sub-net ID). In any case, this configuration is sufficient for five small subnets. The five bit places of the host ID offer 32 possible bit combinations. Excluding the all-zeros pattern and the all-ones pattern, the subnets could each hold 30 hosts.

To express this subnet mask in dotted decimal notation, follow the procedure described in the preceding section:

1. Add periods to mark the octet boundaries:

   11111111.11111111.11111111.11100000

2. Write down 255 for each all-ones octet. Convert the mixed octet to decimal:

   128+64+32=224

3. The dotted decimal version of this subnet mask is `255.255.255.224`

Suppose you start placing hosts on this subnetted network (see Figure 5.7). Because this network is a Class C network, the first three octets will be the same for all hosts. To obtain the fourth octet of the IP address, simply write down the binary subnet ID and host ID in their respective bit positions. In Figure 5.7, for instance, the subnet ID field for Subnet C has the bit pattern 011. Because this pattern is on the left end of the octet, the bit positions of the subnet ID actually represent the pattern 01100000, which means that the subnet number is 96. If the host ID is 17 (binary 10001), the fourth octet is `01110001`, which converts to 113. The IP address of this host is therefore `212.114.32.113`.

FIGURE 5.7
A subnetted Class C network.

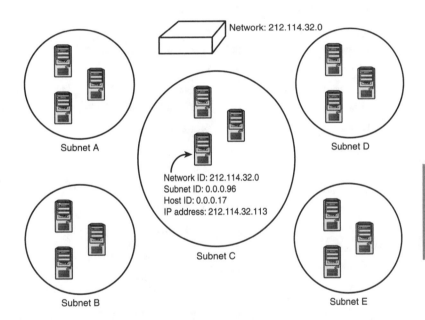

Table 5.1 shows the binary pattern equivalents of the dotted notation subnet masks. This table shows all valid subnet mask patterns. Note that some of these patterns are not very practical and are included here for illustration purposes only. The Description column in Table 5.1 tells how many additional ones bits are present beyond the ones bits present in the default mask provided by the class designation. These mask bits are available for the subnet ID. For example, the default Class A mask has eight one bits; the row that displays 2 mask bits means there are eight plus two or a total of 10 ones bits present in the subnet mask.

TABLE 5.1   Subnet Mask Dotted Notation to Binary Pattern

Description	Dotted Notation	Binary Pattern
Class A		
Default Mask	255.0.0.0	11111111 00000000 00000000 00000000
1 subnet bit	255.128.0.0	11111111 10000000 00000000 00000000
2 subnet bits	255.192.0.0	11111111 11000000 00000000 00000000
3 subnet bits	255.224.0.0	11111111 11100000 00000000 00000000
4 subnet bits	255.240.0.0	11111111 11110000 00000000 00000000
5 subnet bits	255.248.0.0	11111111 11111000 00000000 00000000
6 subnet bits	255.252.0.0	11111111 11111100 00000000 00000000
7 subnet bits	255.254.0.0	11111111 11111110 00000000 00000000
8 subnet bits	255.255.0.0	11111111 11111111 00000000 00000000
9 subnet bits	255.255.128.0	11111111 11111111 10000000 00000000
10 subnet bits	255.255.192.0	11111111 11111111 11000000 00000000
11 subnet bits	255.255.224.0	11111111 11111111 11100000 00000000
12 subnet bits	255.255.240.0	11111111 11111111 11110000 00000000
13 subnet bits	255.255.248 0	11111111 11111111 11111000 00000000
14 subnet bits	255.255.252.0	11111111 11111111 11111100 00000000
15 subnet bits	255.255.254.0	11111111 11111111 11111110 00000000
16 subnet bits	255.255.255.0	11111111 11111111 11111111 00000000
17 subnet bits	255.255.255.128	11111111 11111111 11111111 10000000
18 subnet bits	255.255.255.192	11111111 11111111 11111111 11000000
19 subnet bits	255.255.255.224	11111111 11111111 11111111 11100000
20 subnet bits	255.255.255.240	11111111 11111111 11111111 11110000
21 subnet bits	255.255.255.248	11111111 11111111 11111111 11111000
22 subnet bits	255.255.255.252	11111111 11111111 11111111 11111100
Class B		
Default Mask	255.255.0.0	11111111 11111111 00000000 00000000
1 subnet bit	255.255.128.0	11111111 11111111 10000000 00000000
2 subnet bits	255.255.192.0	11111111 11111111 11000000 00000000
3 subnet bits	255.255.224.0	11111111 11111111 11100000 00000000
4 subnet bits	255.255.240.0	11111111 11111111 11110000 00000000
5 subnet bits	255.255.248.0	11111111 11111111 11111000 00000000

TABLE 5.1   continued

Description	Dotted Notation	Binary Pattern
	Class B	
6 subnet bits	255.255.252.0	11111111 11111111 11111100 00000000
7 subnet bits	255.255.254.0	11111111 11111111 11111110 00000000
8 subnet bits	255.255.255.0	11111111 11111111 11111111 00000000
9 subnet bits	255.255.255.128	11111111 11111111 11111111 10000000
10 subnet bits	255.255.255.192	11111111 11111111 11111111 11000000
11 subnet bits	255.255.255.224	11111111 11111111 11111111 11100000
12 subnet bits	255.255.255.240	11111111 11111111 11111111 11110000
13 subnet bits	255.255.255.248	11111111 11111111 11111111 11111000
14 subnet bits	255.255.255.252	11111111 11111111 11111111 11111100
	Class C	
Default subnet mask	255.255.255.0	11111111 11111111 11111111 00000000
1 subnet bit	255.255.255.128	11111111 11111111 11111111 10000000
2 subnet bits	255.255.255.192	11111111 11111111 11111111 11000000
3 subnet bits	255.255.255.224	11111111 11111111 11111111 11100000
4 subnet bits	255.255.255.240	11111111 11111111 11111111 11110000
5 subnet bits	255.255.255.248	11111111 11111111 11111111 11111000
6 subnet bits	255.255.255.252	11111111 11111111 11111111 11111100

5

Classless Internet Domain Routing

Class A addresses are long gone, and the world is quickly running out of Class B addresses. Many Class C addresses are still available, but the small address space of a Class C network (254 hosts maximum) is a severe limitation in the high-volume game of Internet service providers (ISPs). It is possible to assign a range of Class C networks to a network owner who needs more than 254 addresses. However, treating multiple Class C networks as separate entities when they are all going to the same place only clutters up routing tables unnecessarily.

Classless Internet Domain Routing (CIDR) is a technique that allows a block of network IDs to be treated as a single entity in routing tables. CIDR groups a range of network IDs into a single address entry using what is called a *supernet mask*. You can think of a supernet mask as something like the opposite of a subnet mask. Instead of designating additional bits for identifying the network, the supernet mask in effect takes bits away from the network ID. The addresses in the range are therefore identified by the network address bits that the networks in the range hold in common. For example, an ISP might be assigned all Class C addresses in the range 204.21.128.0 11001100000101011000000000000000 to 204.21.255.255 11001100000101011111111111111111.

In this case, the network addresses are identical up to the seventeenth bit counting from the left. The supernet mask would therefore be 11111111111111110000000000000000, which is equivalent to the dotted decimal mask 255.255.128.0.

The address block is specified using the lowest address in the range followed by the supernet mask. A common notation for a CIDR address/mask pair is to show the number of mask bits after the address with a slash (/) separator. Hence, the CIDR range in the preceding example would be specified as 204.21.128.0/17.

Of course, CIDR addressing can be used only if the routers on the network support it.

Summary

Subnetting is a commonly used technique to better utilize the IP addresses. Subnetting adds an intermediate tier to the IP addressing structure, providing a means for grouping IP addresses in the address space below the network ID. Subnetting is a common feature on networks that include multiple physical segments separated by routers.

Q&A

Q How large is the subnet ID field on a Class B network with the mask 255.255.0.0?

A Zero bits (no subnet ID field). The mask 255.255.0.0 is the default condition for a Class B network. All 16 mask bits are used for the network ID, and no bits are available for subnetting.

Q A network admin calculates that he'll need 21 mask bits for his network. What subnet mask should he use?

A 21 mask bits: 11111111111111111111100000000000 is equivalent to two full octets plus an additional 5 bits. Each full octet is expressed in the mask as 255. The five bits in the third octet are equivalent to 128+64+32+16+8= 248. The mask is 255.255.248.0.

Q **You have a Class C network address. You also have employees at 10 locations, and each location has no more than 12 people. What subnet mask or masks would enable you to install a workstation for each user?**

A `255.255.255.240`

Q **Billy wants to use 3 subnet bits for subnetting on a Class A network. What should he use for a subnet mask?**

A A Class A network means that the first octet will be devoted to the network ID. The first octet of the mask is equivalent to 255. The three subnet bits in the second octet are equivalent to: 128+64+32= 224. The subnet mask is 255.224.0.0.

Q **What IP addresses are assigned in the CIDR range `212.100.192.0/20`?**

A The `/20` supernet parameter specifies that 20 of the IP address will be constant and the rest will vary. The binary version of the initial address is

`11010100.01100100.11000000.00000000`

The first 20 bits of the highest address must be the same as the initial address, and the rest of the address bits can vary. Show the varying bits as the opposite end of the range (all ones instead of all zeros):

`11010100.01100100.11001111.11111111`

The address range is `212.100.192.0` to `212.100.207.255`.

Key Terms

Review the following list of key terms:

CIDR—Classless Internet Domain Routing. A technique that allows a block of network IDs to be treated as a single entity.

subnet—A logical subdivision of the address space defined by a TCP/IP network ID.

subnet mask—Used to assign some of the bits of an IP address to a subnet ID.

supernet—Enables you to combine several networks into a larger network.

5

HOUR 6

The Transport Layer

The Transport layer provides an interface for network applications and offers optional error checking, flow control, and verification for network transmissions. This hour describes some important Transport layer concepts and introduces the TCP and UDP protocols.

At the completion of this hour, you will be able to

- Describe the basic duties of the Transport layer
- Explain the difference between a connection-oriented protocol and a connectionless protocol
- Explain how Transport layer protocols provide an interface to network applications through ports and sockets
- Describe the differences between TCP and UDP
- Identify the fields that make up the TCP header
- Describe how TCP opens and closes a connection
- Describe how TCP sequences and acknowledges data transmissions
- Identify the four fields that comprise the UDP header

Introducing the Transport Layer

The TCP/IP Internet layer, as you learned in Hour 4, "The Internet Layer," and Hour 5, "Subnetting," is full of useful protocols that are effective at providing the necessary addressing information so that data can make its journey across the network. Addressing and routing, however, are only part of the picture. The developers of TCP/IP knew they needed another layer above the Internet layer that would cooperate with IP by providing additional necessary features. Specifically, they wanted the Transport layer protocols to provide the following:

- An interface for network applications—a way for applications to access the network. The designers wanted to be able to target data not just to a destination computer, but to a particular application running on the destination computer.

- A mechanism for multiplexing/demultiplexing. *Multiplexing,* in this case, means accepting data from different applications and computers and directing that data to the intended recipient application on the receiving computer. In other words, the Transport layer must be capable of simultaneously supporting several network applications and managing the flow of data to the Internet layer. On the receiving end, the Transport layer must accept the data from the Internet layer and direct it to multiple applications. This is known as *demultiplexing.* Another aspect of multiplexing/demultiplexing is that a single application can simultaneously maintain connections with more than one computer.

- Error checking, flow control, and verification. The protocol system needs an overall scheme that ensures delivery of data between the sending and receiving machines.

The last item (error checking, flow control, and verification) is the most open ended. Questions of quality assurance always balance on questions of benefit and cost. An elaborate quality assurance system can increase your certainty that a delivery was successful, but you pay for it with increased network traffic and slower processing time. For many applications, this additional assurance simply isn't worth it. The Transport layer, therefore, provides two pathways to the network, each with the interfacing and multiplexing/demultiplexing features necessary for supporting applications, but each with a very different approach to quality assurance, as follows:

- Transport Control Protocol (TCP)—TCP provides extensive error control and flow control to ensure the successful delivery of data. TCP is a connection-oriented protocol.

- User Datagram Protocol (UDP)—UDP provides extremely rudimentary error checking and is designed for situations when TCP's extensive control features are not necessary. UDP is a connectionless protocol.

You'll learn more about connection-oriented and connectionless protocols and about the TCP and UDP protocols later in this hour.

Transport Layer Concepts

Before moving to a more detailed discussion of TCP and UDP, it is worth pausing for a moment to focus on a few of the important concepts:

- Connection-oriented and connectionless protocols
- Ports and sockets
- Multiplexing

These important concepts are essential to understanding the design of the Transport layer. You'll learn about these concepts in the following sections.

Connection-Oriented and Connectionless Protocols

In order to provide the appropriate level of quality assurance for any given situation, developers have come up with two alternative network protocol archetypes:

- A connection-oriented protocol establishes and maintains a connection between communicating computers and monitors the state of that connection over the course of the transmission. In other words, each package of data sent across the network receives an acknowledgment, and the sending machine records status information to ensure that each package is received without errors, retransmitting the data if necessary. At the end of the transmission, the sending and receiving computers gracefully close the connection.
- A connectionless protocol sends a one-way datagram to the destination and doesn't worry about officially notifying the destination machine that data is on the way. The destination machine receives the data and doesn't worry about returning status information to the source computer.

Figure 6.1 shows two people demonstrating connection-oriented communication. Of course, they are not intended to show the true complexity of digital communications but simply to illustrate the concept of a connection-oriented protocol.

6

FIGURE **6.1**

*A connection-oriented
protocol.*

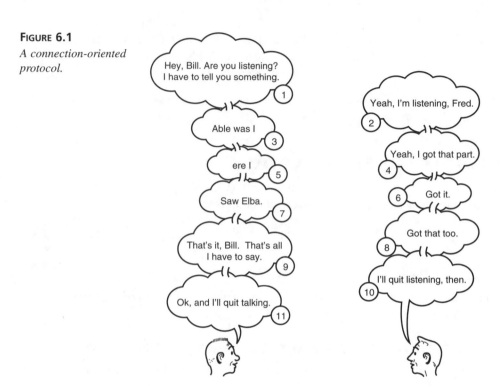

FIGURE **6.1**

*A connection-oriented
protocol.*

Figure 6.2 shows how the same data would be sent using a connectionless protocol.

FIGURE **6.2**

*A connectionless
protocol.*

Ports and Sockets

The Transport layer serves as an interface between network applications and the network
and provides a method for addressing network data to particular applications. In the TCP/IP
system, applications can address data through either the TCP or UDP protocol module
using port numbers. A *port* is a predefined internal address that serves as a pathway from
the application to the Transport layer or from the Transport layer to the application (see
Figure 6.3). For instance, a client computer typically contacts a server's FTP application
through TCP port 21.

FIGURE 6.3

A port address targets data to a particular application.

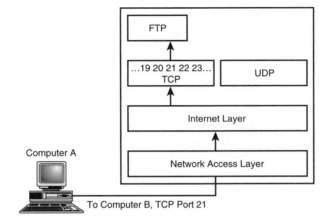

A closer look at the Transport layer's application-specific addressing scheme reveals that TCP and UDP data is actually addressed to what is called a socket. A *socket* is an address formed by concatenating the IP address and the port number. For instance, the socket number 111.121.131.141.21 refers to port 21 on the computer with the IP address 111.121.131.141.

Figure 6.4 shows how computers using TCP exchange socket information when they form a connection.

FIGURE 6.4

Exchanging the source and destination socket numbers.

The following is an example of how a computer accesses an application on a destination machine through a socket:

1. Computer A initiates a connection to an application on Computer B through a well-known port. A *well-known port* is a port number that is assigned to a specific application by ICANN. See Tables 6.1 and 6.2 for lists of some well-known TCP and UDP ports. Combined with the IP address, the well-known port becomes the destination socket address for Computer A. The request includes a data field telling Computer B which socket number to use when sending back information to Computer A. This is Computer A's source socket address.

6

2. Computer B receives the request from Computer A through the well-known port and directs a response to the socket listed as Computer A's source address. This socket becomes the destination address for messages sent from the application on Computer B to the application on Computer A.

You'll learn more about how to initiate a TCP connection later in this hour.

TABLE 6.1   Well-Known TCP Ports

Service	TCP Port Number	Brief Description
tcpmux	1	TCP port service multiplexor
compressnet	2	Management utility
compressnet	3	Compression utility
echo	7	Echo
discard	9	Discard or null
systat	11	Users
daytime	13	Daytime
netstat	15	Network status
qotd	17	Quote of the Day
chargen	19	Character generator
ftp-data	20	File Transfer Protocol data
ftp	21	File Transfer Protocol control
telnet	23	Terminal network connection
smtp	25	Simple Mail Transport Protocol
nsw-fe	27	NSW user system
time	37	Time server
name	42	Host name server
domain	53	Domain name server (DNS)
nameserver	53	Domain name server (DNS)
gopher	70	Gopher service
rje	77	Remote job entry
finger	79	Finger
http	80	WWW service
link	87	TTY link
supdup	95	SUPDUP protocol
hostnames	101	sri-nic host name server

TABLE 6.1 continued

Service	TCP Port Number	Brief Description
iso-tsap	102	ISO-TSAP
x400	103	X.400 mail service
x400-snd	104	X.400 mail send
pop	109	Post Office Protocol
pop2	109	Post Office Protocol 2
pop3	110	Post Office Protocol 3
portmap	111	
sunrpc	111	SUN RPC service
auth	113	Authentication service
sftp	115	Secure FTP
path	117	UUCP path service
uucp-path	117	UUCP path service
nntp	119	Usenet Network News Transfer Protocol
nbsession	139	NetBIOS session service
NeWS	144	News
tcprepo	158	TCP repository

TABLE 6.2 Well-Known UDP Ports

Service	UDP Port Number	Description
echo	7	Echo
discard	9	Discard or null
systat	11	Users
daytime	13	Daytime
netstat	15	Network status
qotd	17	Quote of the Day
chargen	19	Character generator
time	37	Time server
name	42	Host Name server
domain	53	Domain name server (DNS)
nameserver	53	Domain name server (DNS)
bootps	67	Bootstrap protocol service/DHCP

6

TABLE 6.2 continued

Service	UDP Port Number	Description
bootpc	68	Bootstrap protocol client/DHCP
tftp	69	Trivial File Transfer Protocol
portmap	111	
sunrpc	111	SUN RPC service
ntp	123	Network Time Protocol
nbname	137	NetBIOS name
nbdatagram	148	NetBIOS datagram
sgmp	153	
snmp	161	Simple Network Management Protocol
snmp-trap	162	Simple Network Management Protocol trap

Multiplexing/Demultiplexing

The socket addressing system enables TCP and UDP to perform another important Transport layer task: multiplexing and demultiplexing. As described earlier, multiplexing is the act of braiding input from several sources into a single output, and demultiplexing is the act of receiving input from a single source and delivering it to multiple outputs (see Figure 6.5).

FIGURE 6.5
Multiplexing and demultiplexing.

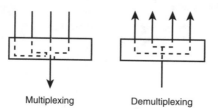

Multiplexing   Demultiplexing

Multiplexing/demultiplexing enables the lower levels of the TCP/IP stack to process data without regard to which application initiated that data. All associations with the originating application are settled at the Transport layer, and data passes to and from the Internet layer in a single, application-independent pipeline.

The key to multiplexing and demultiplexing is the socket address. Because the socket address combines the IP number with the port number, it provides a unique identifier for a specific application on a specific machine. See the Telnet server depicted in Figure 6.6. All client machines use the well-known port address TCP 23 to contact the Telnet server, but the destination socket for each of the connecting PCs is unique. Likewise, all network applications running on the Telnet server use the server's IP address, but only the Telnet service uses the socket address, consisting of the server's IP address plus TCP port 23.

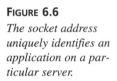

FIGURE 6.6
The socket address uniquely identifies an application on a particular server.

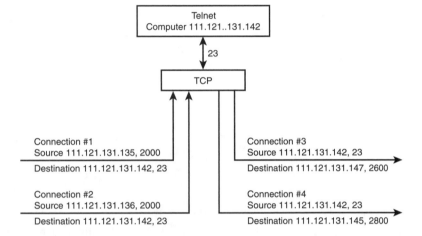

Understanding TCP and UDP

As this hour has already mentioned, TCP is a connection-oriented protocol that provides extensive error control and flow control. UDP is a connectionless protocol with much less sophisticated error control. You might say that TCP is built for reliability, and UDP is built for speed. Applications that must support interactive sessions, such as Telnet and FTP, tend to use TCP. Applications that do their own error checking or that don't need much error checking tend to use UDP.

A software developer designing a network application can choose whether to use TCP or UDP as a transport protocol. UDP's simpler control mechanisms should not necessarily be considered limiting. First of all, less quality assurance does not necessarily mean lower quality. The extra checks and controls provided by TCP are entirely unnecessary for many applications. In cases where error control and flow control are necessary, some developers prefer to provide those control features within the application itself, where they can be customized for the specific need, and to use the leaner UDP transport for network access. UDP-based services such as TCP/IP's Remote Procedure Call (RPC) can support advanced and sophisticated applications, but those applications must take responsibility for more error control and flow control tasks than if they reached the stack through TCP.

6

TCP: The Connection-Oriented Transport Protocol

This hour has already described TCP's connection-oriented approach to communication. TCP has a few other important features that warrant mentioning:

- Stream-oriented processing—TCP processes data in a stream. In other words, TCP can accept data a byte at a time rather than as a preformatted block. TCP formats the data into variable-length segments, which it will pass to the Internet layer.

- Resequencing—If data arrives at the destination out of order, the TCP module is capable of resequencing the data to restore the original order.

- Flow control—TCP's flow control feature ensures that the data transmission won't outrun or overrun the destination machine's capability to receive the data. This is especially critical in a diverse environment in which there may be considerable variation of processor speeds and buffer sizes.

- Precedence and security—The Department of Defense specifications for TCP call for optional security and priority levels that can be set for TCP connections. Many TCP implementations, however, do not provide these security and priority features.

- Graceful close—TCP is as careful about closing a connection as it is about opening a connection. The graceful close feature ensures that all segments have been sent and received before a connection is closed.

A close look at TCP reveals a complex system of announcements and acknowledgments supporting TCP's connection-oriented structure. The following sections take a closer look at TCP data format, TCP data transmission, and TCP connections. The technical nature of this discussion should reveal how complex TCP really is. This discussion of TCP also underscores the fact that a protocol is more than just a data format: It is a whole system of interacting processes and procedures designed to accomplish a set of well-defined objectives.

As you learned in Hour 2, "How TCP/IP Works," layered protocol systems such as TCP/IP operate through an information exchange between a given layer on the sending machine and the corresponding layer on the receiving machine. In other words, the Network Access layer on the sending machine communicates with the Network Access layer on the receiving machine, the Internet layer on the sending machine communicates with the Internet layer on the receiving machine, and so forth.

The TCP software communicates with the TCP software on the machine to which it has established (or wants to establish) a connection. In any discussion of TCP, if you hear the phrase "Computer A establishes a connection with Computer B," then what that really means is that the TCP software of Computer A has established a connection with the

TCP software of Computer B, both of which are acting on behalf of a local application. The subtle distinction yields an interesting observation concerning the concept of end-node verification that was introduced in Hour 1, "What Is TCP/IP?"

Recall that end nodes are responsible for verifying communications on a TCP/IP network. (The end nodes are the nodes that are actually attempting to communicate—as opposed to the intermediate nodes, which forward the message.) In a typical internet-working situation (see Figure 6.7), the data is passed from the source subnet to the desti-nation subnet by routers. These routers typically operate at the Internet layer—the layer below the Transport layer. (You'll learn more about routers in Hour 10, "Routing.") The important point is that the routers are not concerned with the information at the Transport level. They simply pass on the Transport layer data as cargo for the IP datagram, which attaches its own header information and sends the datagram on its way. The control and verification information encoded in a TCP segment is intended solely for the TCP soft-ware of the destination machine. This speeds up routing over TCP/IP internetworks (because routers do not have to participate actively in TCP's elaborate quality assurance ritual) and at the same time enables TCP to fulfill the Department of Defense's objective of providing a network with end-node verification.

FIGURE 6.7
Routers forward but do not process Transport layer data.

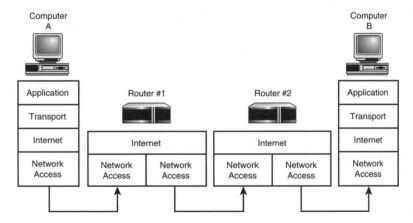

TCP Data Format

The TCP header format is shown in Figure 6.8. The complexity of this structure reveals the complexity of TCP and the many facets of its functionality.

FIGURE **6.8**

TCP segment data format.

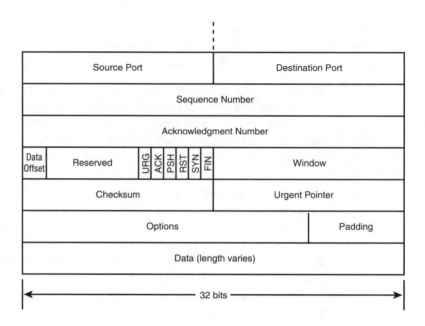

The fields are as follows. You'll have a better idea of how these data fields are used after reading the next section, which discusses TCP connections:

- Source Port (16-bit)—The port number assigned to the application on the source machine.

- Destination Port (16-bit)—The port number assigned to the application on the destination machine.

- Sequence Number (32-bit)—The sequence number of the first byte in this particular segment, unless the SYN flag is set to 1. If the SYN flag is set to 1, the Sequence Number field provides the initial sequence number (ISN), which is used to synchronize sequence numbers. If the SYN flag is set to 1, the sequence number of the first octet is one greater than the number that appears in this field (in other words, ISN +1).

- Acknowledgment Number (32-bit)—The acknowledgment number acknowledges a received segment. The value is the *next* sequence number the receiving computer is expecting to receive, in other words, the sequence number of the last byte received +1.

- Data offset (4 bits)—A field that tells the receiving TCP software how long the header is and, therefore, where the data begins. The data offset is expressed as an integer number of 32-bit words.

- Reserved (6 bits)—Reserved for future use. The Reserved field provides room to accommodate future developments of TCP and must be all zeros.
- Control flags (1 bit each)—The control flags communicate special information about the segment.
  - URG—A value of 1 announces that the segment is urgent and the Urgent Pointer field is significant.
  - ACK—A value of 1 announces that the Acknowledgment Number field is significant.
  - PSH—A value of 1 tells the TCP software to push all the data sent so far through the pipeline to the receiving application.
  - RST—A value of 1 resets the connection.
  - SYN—A value of 1 announces that sequence numbers will be synchronized, marking the beginning of a connection. See the discussion of the three-way handshake, later in this hour.
  - FIN—A value of 1 signifies that the sending computer has no more data to transmit. This flag is used to close a connection.
- Window (16-bit)—A parameter used for flow control. The window defines the range of sequence numbers beyond the last acknowledged sequence number that the sending machine is free to transmit without further acknowledgment.
- Checksum (16-bit)—A field used to check the integrity of the segment. A receiving computer performs a checksum calculation based on the segment and compares the value to the value stored in this field. TCP and UDP include a pseudo-header with IP addressing information in the checksum calculation. See the discussion of the UDP pseudo-header later in this hour.
- Urgent Pointer (16-bit)—An offset pointer pointing to the sequence number that marks the beginning of any urgent information.
- Options—Specifies one of a small set of optional settings.
- Padding—Extra zero bits (as needed) to ensure that the data begins on a 32-bit boundary.
- Data—The data being transmitted with the segment.

TCP needs all these data fields to successfully manage, acknowledge, and verify network transmissions. The next section shows how the TCP software uses some of these fields to manage the tasks of sending and receiving data.

6

TCP Connections

Everything in TCP happens in the context of a connection. TCP sends and receives data through a connection, which must be requested, opened, and closed according to the rules of TCP.

As you learned earlier in this hour, one of the reasons for TCP is to provide an interface so that applications can have access to the network. That interface is provided through the TCP ports and, in order to provide a connection through the ports, the TCP interface to the application must be open. TCP supports two open states:

- Passive open—A given application process notifies TCP that it is prepared to receive incoming connections through a TCP port. Thus, the pathway from TCP to the application is opened in anticipation of an incoming connection request.

- Active open—An application requests that TCP initiate a connection with another computer that is in the passive open state. (Actually, TCP can also initiate a connection to a computer that is in the active open state, in case both computers are attempting to open a connection at once.)

In a typical situation, an application wanting to receive connections, such as an FTP server, places itself and its TCP port status in a passive open state. On the client computer, the FTP client's TCP state is most likely closed until a user initiates a connection from the FTP client to the FTP server, at which time the state for the client becomes active open. The TCP software of the computer that switches to active open (that is, the *client*) then initiates the exchange of messages that leads to a connection. That exchange of information, the so-called three-way handshake, will be discussed later in this hour.

New Term   A *client* is a computer requesting or receiving services from another computer on the network.

New Term   A *server* is a computer offering services to other computers on the network.

TCP sends segments of variable length; within a segment, each byte of data is assigned a sequence number. The receiving machine must send an acknowledgment for every byte it receives. TCP communication is thus a system of transmissions and acknowledgments. The Sequence Number and Acknowledgment Number fields of the TCP header (described in the preceding section) provide the communicating TCP software with regular updates on the status of the transmission.

A separate sequence number is not encoded with each individual byte. Instead, the Sequence Number field in the header gives the sequence number of the first byte of data in a segment.

There is one exception to this rule. If the segment occurs at the beginning of a connection (see the description of the three-way handshake later in this section), the Sequence Number field contains the ISN, which is actually one less than the sequence number of the first byte in the segment. (The first byte is ISN +1.)

If the segment is received successfully, the receiving computer uses the Acknowledgment Number field to tell the sending computer which bytes it has received. The Acknowledgment Number field in the acknowledgment message will be set to the last received sequence number +1. In other words, the Acknowledgment Number field defines which sequence number the computer is prepared to receive next.

If an acknowledgment is not received within the specified time period, the sending machine retransmits the data beginning with the byte after the last acknowledged byte.

Establishing a Connection

In order for the sequence/acknowledgment system to work, the computers must synchronize their sequence numbers. In other words, Computer B must know what initial sequence number (ISN) Computer A used to start the sequence. Computer A must know what ISN Computer B will use to start the sequence for any data Computer B will transmit.

This synchronization of sequence numbers is called a *three-way handshake*. The three-way handshake always occurs at the beginning of a TCP connection. The three steps of a three-way handshake are as follows:

1. Computer A sends a segment with

   SYN = 1

   ACK = 0

   Sequence Number = X (where X is Computer A's ISN)

   The active open computer (Computer A) sends a segment with the SYN flag set to 1 and the ACK flag set to 0. SYN is short for *synchronize*. This flag, as described earlier, announces an attempt to open a connection. This first segment header also contains the initial sequence number (ISN), which marks the beginning of the sequence numbers for data that Computer A will transmit. The first byte transmitted to Computer B will have the sequence number ISN +1.

2. Computer B receives Computer A's segment and returns a segment with

   SYN = 1 (still in synchronization phase)

   ACK = 1 (the Acknowledgment Number field will contain a value)

   Sequence number = Y, where Y is Computer B's ISN

   Acknowledgment number = M + 1, where M is the last sequence number received from Computer A

6

3. Computer A sends a segment to Computer B that acknowledges receipt of Computer B's ISN:

   `SYN = 0`

   `ACK = 1`

   Sequence number = next sequence number in series (M+1)

   Acknowledgment number = N + 1 (where N is the last sequence number received from Computer B)

After the three-way handshake, the connection is open, and the TCP modules transmit and receive data using the sequence and acknowledgment scheme described earlier in this section.

TCP Flow Control

The Window field in the TCP header provides a flow control mechanism for the connection. The purpose of the Window field is to ensure that the sending computer doesn't send too much data too quickly, which could lead to a situation in which data is lost because the receiving computer can't process incoming segments as quickly as the sending computer can transmit them. The flow control method used by TCP is called the *sliding window* method. The receiving computer uses the Window field to define a window of sequence numbers beyond the last acknowledged sequence number that the sending computer is authorized to transmit. The sending computer cannot transmit beyond that window until it receives the next acknowledgment.

Closing a Connection

When it is time to close the connection, the computer initiating the close, Computer A, places a segment in the queue with the FIN flag set to one. The application then enters what is called the *fin-wait state*. In the fin-wait state, Computer A's TCP software continues to receive segments and processes the segments already in the queue, but no additional data is accepted from the application. When Computer B receives the FIN segment, it returns an acknowledgment to the FIN, sends any remaining segments, and notifies the local application that a FIN was received. Computer B sends a FIN segment to Computer A, which Computer A acknowledges, and the connection is closed.

UDP: The Connectionless Transport Protocol

UDP is much simpler than TCP, and it doesn't perform any of the functions listed in the preceding section. However, there are a few observations about UDP that this hour should mention.

First, although UDP is sometimes described as having no error-checking capabilities, in fact, it is capable of performing rudimentary error checking. It is best to characterize UDP as having the capability for limited error checking. The UDP datagram includes a checksum value that the receiving machine can use to test the integrity of the data. (Often, this checksum test is optional and can be disabled on the receiving machine to speed up processing of incoming data.) The UDP datagram includes a pseudo-header that encompasses the destination address for the datagram, thus providing a means of checking for misdirected datagrams. Also, if the receiving UDP module receives a datagram directed to an inactive or undefined UDP port, it returns an ICMP message notifying the source machine that the port is unreachable.

Second, UDP does not offer the *resequencing* of data provided by TCP. Resequencing is most significant on a large network, such as the Internet, where the segments of data might take different paths and experience significant delays in router buffers. On local networks, the lack of a resequencing feature in UDP typically does not lead to unreliable reception.

UDP's lean, connectionless design makes it the protocol of choice for network broadcast situations. A *broadcast* is a single message that will be received and processed by all computers on the subnet. Understandably, if the source computer had to simultaneously open a TCP-style connection with every computer on the subnet in order to send a single broadcast, the result could be a significant erosion of network performance.

The primary purpose of the UDP protocol is to expose datagrams to the Application layer. The UDP protocol itself does very little and therefore employs a simple header structure. The RFC that describes this protocol, RFC 768, is only three pages in length. As mentioned earlier, UDP does not retransmit missing or corrupted datagrams, sequence datagrams received out of order, eliminate duplicated datagrams, acknowledge the receipt of datagrams, or establish or terminate connections. UDP is primarily a mechanism for application programs to send and receive datagrams without the overhead of a TCP connection. The application can provide for any or all of these functions, if they are necessary for the application's purpose.

The UDP header consists of four 16-bit fields. See Figure 6.9 for the layout of the UDP datagram header.

6

FIGURE 6.9

The UDP datagram header and data payload.

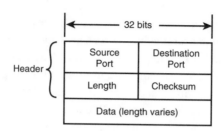

The following list describes these fields:

- Source Port—This field occupies the first 16 bits of the UDP header. This field typically holds the UDP port number of the application sending this datagram. The value entered in the Source Port field is used by the receiving application as a return address when it is ready to send a response. This field is considered optional, and it is not required that the sending application include its port number. If the sending application does not include its port number, the application is expected to place 16 zero bits into the field. Obviously if there is no valid source port address, the receiving application will be unable to send a response. However, this might be the desired functionality, as in the case of an SNMP-trap message, which is a unidirectional message where no response is expected.

- Destination Port—This 16-bit field holds the port address to which the UDP software on the receiving machine will deliver this datagram.

- Length—This 16-bit field identifies the length in octets of the UDP datagram. The length includes the UDP header as well as the UDP data payload. Because the UDP header is eight octets in length, the value will always be at least 8.

- Checksum—This 16-bit field is used to determine whether the datagram was corrupted during transmission. The checksum is the result of a special calculation performed on a string of binary data. In the case of UDP, the checksum is calculated based on a pseudo-header, the UDP header, the UDP data, and possibly the filler zero octets to build an even octet length checksum input. The checksums generated at the source and verified at the destination allow the client application to determine if the datagram has been corrupted.

Because the actual UDP header does not include the source or destination IP address, it is possible for the datagram to be delivered to the wrong computer or service. Part of the data used for the checksum calculation is a string of values extracted from the IP header known as the *pseudo-header*. The pseudo-header provides destination IP addressing information so that the receiving computer can determine whether a UDP datagram has been misdelivered.

A Note About Firewalls

A *firewall* is a system that protects a local network from attack by unauthorized users attempting to access the LAN from the Internet. The word firewall has entered the lexicon of Internet jargon, and it is one of many computer terms that can fall within a wide range of definitions. Firewalls perform a number of functions. However, one of the most basic features of a firewall is something that is pertinent to this hour.

That important feature is the capability of a firewall to block off access to specific TCP and UDP ports. The word firewall, in fact, is sometimes used as a verb, meaning to close off access to a port.

For example, to initiate a Telnet session with the server, a client machine must send a request to Telnet's well-known port address, TCP port 23. (*Telnet* is a utility that lets the client computer serve as a terminal for the server. You'll learn more about Telnet in Hour 15, "Remote Access Utilities.") Unauthorized use of Telnet can sometimes pose a security threat. To increase security, the server can be configured to stop using port 23 to access Telnet; for that matter, the server can simply stop using the Telnet application, but that extreme solution would prohibit authorized users on the LAN from using Telnet for authorized activities. (Why have it if you're not going to use it?) An alternative would be to install a firewall as shown in Figure 6.10 and configure that firewall to block access to TCP port 23. The result is that users on the LAN, from inside the firewall, have free access to TCP port 23 on the server. Users from the Internet, outside the LAN, do not have access to the server's TCP port 23 and therefore cannot access the server through Telnet. In fact, users from the Internet cannot use Telnet at all to access any computer on the LAN.

FIGURE **6.10**
A typical firewall scenario.

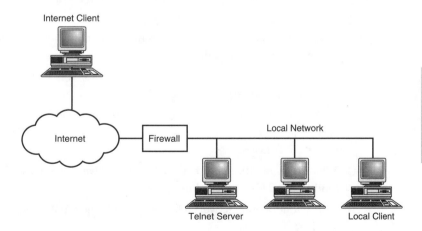

6

This scenario uses Telnet and TCP port 23 as an example. Firewalls typically block access to any or all ports that may pose a security threat. Network administrators often block access to all ports except those that are absolutely necessary, such as a port that handles incoming e-mail. You often find devices that provide the company's Internet presence, such as a Web server, placed outside the firewall, so that access to the Internet device will not result in unauthorized access to the LAN.

> Just as a firewall can keep outside users from accessing services within the network, it can keep inside users from accessing services outside the network.

Summary

This hour covered some key features of TCP/IP's Transport layer. You learned about connection-oriented and connectionless protocols, multiplexing and demultiplexing, and ports and sockets. This hour also introduced TCP/IP's Transport layer protocols, TCP and UDP, and described some important TCP and UDP features. You learned how TCP fulfills the TCP/IP objective of providing end-node verification. You also learned about TCP data format, flow control, and error recovery, and the three-way handshake TCP uses to open a connection. This hour also described the format of a UDP header.

Q&A

Q Why are multiplexing and demultiplexing necessary?

A If TCP/IP did not provide multiplexing and demultiplexing, only one application could use the network software at a time, and only one computer could connect to a given application at a time.

Q Why would a software developer use UDP for a transport protocol when TCP offers better quality assurance?

A TCP's quality assurance comes at the price of slower performance. If the extra error control and flow control of TCP are not necessary, UDP is a better choice because it is faster.

Q Why do applications that support interactive sessions, such as Telnet and FTP, tend to use TCP rather than UDP?

A TCP's control and recovery features provide the reliable connection necessary for an interactive session.

Q **Why would a network administrator want to use a firewall to intentionally close off Internet access to a TCP or UDP port?**

A Internet firewalls close off access to specific ports in order to deny Internet users access to the applications that use those ports. Firewalls can also close off access to the Internet so that users on the internal LAN cannot make use of certain services available on the Internet.

Q **Why don't routers send TCP connection acknowledgments to the computer initiating a connection?**

A Routers operate at the Internet layer (below the Transport layer) and therefore do not process TCP information.

Q **Would a functioning FTP server most likely be in a passive open, active open, or closed state?**

A A working FTP server would most likely be in a passive open state, ready to accept an incoming connection.

Q **Why is the third step in the three-way handshake necessary?**

A After the first two steps, the two computers have exchanged ISN numbers, so theoretically they have enough information to synchronize the connection. However, the computer that sent its ISN in step 2 of the handshake still hasn't received an acknowledgment. The third step acknowledges the ISN received in the second step.

Q **Which field is optional in the UDP header and why?**

A The Source Port field. Because UDP is a connectionless protocol, the UDP software on the receiving machine does not have to know the source port. The source port is provided as an option in case the application receiving the data needs the source port for error checking or verification.

Q **What happens if the source port is equal to 16 zero bits?**

A The application on the destination machine will be unable to send a response.

Key Terms

Review the following list of key terms:

ACK—A control flag specifying that the Acknowledgment Number field in the TCP header is significant.

Acknowledgment Number field—A field in the TCP header specifying the next sequence number the computer is expecting to receive. The acknowledgment number, in effect, acknowledges the receipt of all sequenced bytes prior to the byte specified in the acknowledgment number.

Active open—A state in which TCP is attempting to initiate a connection.

Checksum—A 16-bit calculated field used to ensure detection of corrupted datagrams.

Connection-oriented protocol—A protocol that manages communication by establishing a connection between the communicating computers.

Connectionless protocol—A protocol that transmits data without establishing a connection with the remote computer.

Control flag—A 1-bit flag with special information about a TCP segment.

Demultiplexing—Directing a single input to several outputs.

Destination Port—The TCP or UDP port number of the application on the destination machine that will be the recipient of the data in a TCP segment or UDP datagram.

FIN—A control flag used in the process of closing a TCP connection.

Firewall—A device that protects a network from unauthorized Internet access.

Initial sequence number (ISN)—A number that marks the beginning of the range of numbers a computer will use for sequencing bytes transmitted through TCP.

Multiplexing—Combining several inputs into a single output.

Passive open—A state in which the TCP port (usually a server application) is ready to receive incoming connections.

Port—An internal address that provides an interface from an application to a Transport layer protocol.

Pseudo-header—A structure derived from fields from the IP header that is used to calculate the TCP or UDP checksum and to verify that the datagram has not been delivered to the wrong destination due to alteration of information in the IP header.

Resequencing—Assembling incoming TCP segments so that they are in the order in which they were actually sent.

Segment—A package of TCP data and header information.

Sequence Number—A unique number associated with a byte transmitted through TCP.

Sliding window—A window of sequence numbers that the receiving computer has authorized the sending computer to send. The sliding window flow control method is the method used by TCP.

Socket—The network address for a particular application on a particular computer, consisting of the computer's IP address followed by the port number of the application.

Source Port—The TCP or UDP port number of the application sending a TCP segment or UDP datagram.

Stream-oriented input—Continuous (byte by byte) input, rather than input in predefined blocks of data.

SYN—A control flag signifying that sequence number synchronization is taking place. The SYN flag is used at the beginning of a TCP connection as part of the three-way handshake.

TCP—A reliable connection-oriented Transport protocol in the TCP/IP suite.

Three-way handshake—A three-step procedure that synchronizes sequence numbers and begins a TCP connection.

UDP—A non-reliable connectionless transport protocol in the TCP/IP suite.

Well-known port—Predefined standard port numbers for common applications. Well-known ports are specified by the ICANN.

6

HOUR 7

The Application Layer

At the top of TCP/IP's stack is the Application layer, a loose collection of networking components perched above the Transport layer. This hour describes some of the kinds of Application layer components and shows how those components help bring the user to the network. Specifically, this hour examines application layer services, operating environments, and network applications.

At the completion of this hour, you'll be able to

- Describe what the Application layer is
- Describe some of the Application layer's network services
- Show how NetBIOS over TCP/IP brings TCP/IP networking to NetBIOS environments
- Define IPX tunneling
- List some of TCP/IP's important utilities

What Is the Application Layer?

The Application layer is the top layer in TCP/IP's protocol suite. In the Application layer, you'll find network applications and services that communicate with lower layers through the TCP and UDP ports discussed in Hour 6, "The Transport Layer." You might ask why the Application layer is considered part of the stack at all, because the TCP and UDP ports form such a well-defined interface to the network. But it is important to remember that, in a layered architecture such as TCP/IP, *every* layer is an interface to the network. The Application layer must be as aware of TCP and UDP ports as the Transport layer is and must channel data accordingly.

TCP/IP's Application layer is really an assortment of network-aware software components sending information to and receiving information from the TCP and UDP ports. These Application layer components are not really parallel in the sense of being logically similar or equivalent. Some of the components at the Application layer are simple utilities that collect information about the network configuration. Other Application layer components might be a user interface system (such as the X Window interface) or an Application Program Interface (API), such as NetBIOS, that supports a desktop operating environment. Some Application layer components provide services for the network, such as file and print services or name resolution services. (You'll learn more about name resolution in Hour 11, "Name Resolution.") This hour shows you some of the kinds of services and applications that are usually found in the Application layer. The actual implementation of these components hinges on details of programming and software design.

But first this hour begins with a quick comparison of TCP/IP's Application layer with the corresponding layers defined through TCP/IP's counterpart, the OSI model.

The TCP/IP Application Layer and OSI

As was mentioned in Hour 2, "How TCP/IP Works," TCP/IP does not officially conform with the seven-layer OSI networking model. The OSI model, however, has been very influential in the development of networking systems, and the recent trend toward multi-protocol networking has increased reliance on OSI terminology and concepts. The Application layer can draw from a vast range of operating and networking environments, and in many of those environments the OSI model is an important tool for defining and describing network systems. A look at the OSI model will help you understand the processes that take place at the TCP/IP Application layer.

The TCP/IP Application layer corresponds with the OSI Application, Presentation, and Session layers (see Figure 7.1). The extra subdivisions of the OSI model (three layers instead of one) provide some additional organization of features that TCP/IP theorists have traditionally grouped into the heading of *Application-level* (sometimes called *Process/Application-level*) services.

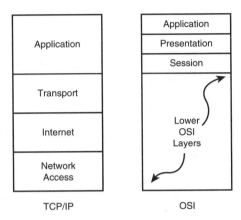

FIGURE 7.1

A comparison of TCP/IP's and OSI's Application layers.

Descriptions of the OSI layers corresponding to TCP/IP's Application layer are as follows:

- Application layer—OSI's Application layer (not to be confused with TCP/IP's Application layer) has components that provide services for user applications and support network access.

- Presentation layer—The Presentation layer translates data into a platform-neutral format and handles encryption and data compression.

- Session layer—The Session layer manages communication between applications on networked computers. This layer provides some functions related to the connections that aren't available through the Transport layer, such as name recognition and security.

All of these services are not necessary for all applications and implementations. In the TCP/IP model, implementations are not required to follow the layering of these OSI subdivisions, but overall the duties defined for OSI's Application, Presentation, and Session layers fall within the range of the TCP/IP Application layer's responsibility.

Network Services

Many Application layer components are network services. In earlier hours you might have read that a layer of the protocol system provides services for other layers of the system. In many cases, these services are a well-defined, integral part of the protocol system. In the case of the Application layer, the services are not all required for the operation of the protocol software and are more likely provided for the direct benefit of a user or to link the network with the local operating system.

7

The features available at the Application layer include the following:

- File and print services
- Name resolution services
- Redirector services

Other important network services, such as mail services and network management services, are discussed in other hours.

File and Print Services

A server is a computer that provides services for other computers. Two common types of servers are file servers and print servers.

A print server operates a printer and fulfills requests to print documents on that printer. A file server operates a data storage device, such as a hard drive, and fulfills requests to read or write data to that device.

Because file service and print service are such common networking activities, they are often thought of together. Often the same computer (or sometimes even the same service) provides both file and print service capabilities. Whether or not they're together, the theory is the same. Figure 7.2 shows a typical file service scenario. A request for a file comes across the network and up through the protocol layers to the Transport layer, where it is routed through the appropriate port to the file server service.

FIGURE 7.2

File service.

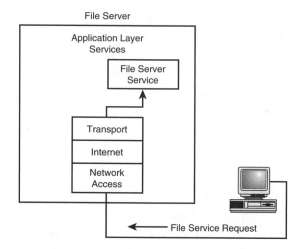

> Figure 7.2 is a schematic drawing showing only the basic components as
> they relate to TCP/IP. In a real protocol and operating system implementa-
> tion, additional layers or components might assist with forwarding the data
> to the file server service. For instance (as you'll learn later in this hour), in a
> Windows environment, WinSock provides an interface for the TCP/IP
> Transport layer with Windows applications.

Name Resolution Services

As you learned in Hour 1, "What Is TCP/IP?," *name resolution* is the process of mapping
IP addresses to predefined, user-friendly alphanumeric names. The domain name service
(DNS) provides name resolution for the Internet and can also provide name resolution
for isolated TCP/IP networks. DNS uses *name servers* to resolve DNS name queries. A
name server service runs at the Application layer of the name server computer and communicates with other name servers to exchange name resolution information. Other name
resolution systems exist, most notably Microsoft's NetBIOS name resolution through
Windows Internet Naming Service (WINS).

Name resolution is an example of an Application layer service that functions integrally
with lower protocol layers and actively participates in the interactions of the protocol
stack. DNS or WINS queries are initiated by the protocol software of the client machine,
rather than by a user or user application. A user references a domain name, and the
underlying protocol software resolves that name to an IP address using name resolution.

Redirectors

In order to integrate the local environment with the network, some network operating
systems use a service called a *redirector*. A redirector is sometimes called a requester.

A redirector intercepts service requests in the local computer and checks to see whether
the request should be fulfilled locally or forwarded to another computer on the network.
If the request is addressed to a service on another machine, the redirector redirects the
request to the network (see Figure 7.3).

A redirector enables the user to access network resources as if they were part of the local
environment. For instance, a remote disk drive could appear as a local disk drive on the
client machine.

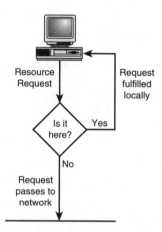

FIGURE 7.3
A redirector.

APIs and the Application Layer

An Application Programming Interface (API) is a predefined collection of functions that a program can use to access other parts of the operating environment. Programs use API functions to communicate with the operating system. A network protocol stack is a classic application of the API concept. As is shown in Figure 7.4, a network API provides an interface from the application to the protocol stack. The application program uses functions from the API to open and close connections and write or read data to the network.

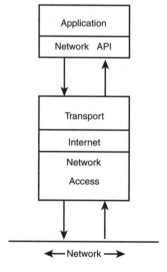

FIGURE 7.4
A network API enables an application to access the network through TCP/IP.

The Sockets API was originally developed for BSD Unix as an interface for applications to access the TCP/IP protocol stack. Sockets is now used widely on other systems as a program interface for TCP/IP. The Windows version of the Sockets interface is known as WinSock. In Windows 3.1 and earlier, the user had to install and configure an implementation of WinSock to set up TCP/IP networking. Starting with Windows 95, Microsoft built WinSock directly into the Windows operating system.

Network APIs such as the Sockets API receive data through a socket (see Hour 6) and pass that data to the application. These APIs therefore are operating at the Application layer.

Operating Environments and the Application Layer

The local operating system (or the network operating system) might have its own layered components that assist with providing users with access to the network. These components typically function above the TCP and UDP ports and are thus within the province of the Application layer. In some cases, however, the interaction of these components with the protocol stack is so unique that, in effect, the result is best understood as an entirely different stack.

You'll learn about some of the upper-layer user-environment components in the following sections, which cover TCP/IP with NetBIOS and TCP/IP with NetWare. Other network systems provide similar solutions for access to TCP/IP.

> It is worth noting that the Application layer isn't the only layer where vendors have contributed additional components in order to adapt TCP/IP to their environments. For instance, lower-level structures related to specifications such as NDIS and ODI (see Hour 2) are common in protocol implementations.

TCP/IP with NetBIOS

Windows, OS/2, and certain other operating systems use an interface called NetBIOS to access network resources. NetBIOS, which was originally developed by IBM, is a collection of network services and an API designed to give applications access to those services. NetBIOS was originally developed to provide a vendor-neutral program interface for LAN-based proprietary protocols. As TCP/IP became more popular on computer-based

7

LANs, vendors and developers began to see the advantage of providing TCP/IP connectivity to the many NetBIOS-based applications and operating systems. RFCs 1001 and 1002 provide a protocol standard for linking NetBIOS with TCP/IP.

NetBIOS locates computers by computer name (often called NetBIOS name). Computer names appear in the Windows Network Neighborhood utility. To resolve NetBIOS computer names to IP addresses, the network needs an entire name resolution system that is separate from DNS. This NetBIOS-based name resolution is provided in a layer called *NetBIOS over TCP/IP* (NBT), which is located between the Transport layer and the NetBIOS interface. You'll learn more about NetBIOS name resolution in Hour 11.

As you may have noticed, the NetBIOS computer naming system is entirely separate from the DNS naming system. The need for two names to reference one computer is downright confusing in the context of TCP/IP. However, it is important to remember that NetBIOS was developed for non-TCP/IP network systems and only later was integrated with TCP/IP.

In recent years, it has become increasingly clear that NetBIOS may have outlived its usefulness. Microsoft's Windows 2000 Active Directory environment emphasizes DNS and de-emphasizes NetBIOS as a means of locating network resources. However, the huge user base of NetBIOS-based systems means that Microsoft will undoubtedly continue to support NetBIOS.

TCP/IP with NetWare

A few years ago, Novell NetWare was the most popular LAN networking system in the world. Novell had already developed its own protocol suite (called IPX/SPX) before TCP/IP began its rise to prominence. IPX/SPX is a full-featured protocol system with its own error control and logical addressing. With the recent upsurge of interest in TCP/IP, developers and systems engineers started to wonder if it would be possible to integrate IPX/SPX networks with TCP/IP without disturbing the NetWare-related upper layers of the IPX/SPX stack.

An interesting solution emerged, known as *IPX tunneling*. IPX tunneling is defined in RFC 1234, "Tunneling IPX Traffic Through IP Networks."

In IPX tunneling, the IPX/SPX stack is grafted onto the UDP protocol of the TCP/IP stack (see Figure 7.5). The IPX protocol layer performs logical addressing functions similar to IP for the Novell network. Data passes down from IPX to UDP (see Hour 6), where it enters the TCP/IP stack and is encoded in an IP datagram, and delivered to the physical network.

FIGURE 7.5

An IP stack supporting IPX.

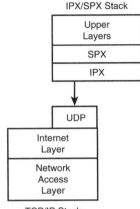

IPX tunneling and solutions similar to it produce a sort of hybrid protocol stack that is not easily described with the four-layer TCP/IP model. It is perhaps a matter of opinion whether the IPX superstructure riding above the Transport layer qualifies as an Application layer component, and most experts would describe this situation as upper-layer IPX/SPX protocols resting on the IPX/SPX Network layer, resting on TCP/IP's Transport layer. However, this IPX component supports applications at the top and links to the UDP ports beneath, so if it is included anywhere in this discussion of TCP/IP layering, the Application layer is an appropriate place to mention it. The fact that IPX tunneling is even possible is a tribute to TCP/IP's flexibility and versatility.

> Like the rest of the computer industry, Novell is well aware of the emergence of TCP/IP as the dominant routable protocol. Recent versions of NetWare have increased NetWare's support for TCP/IP, which is now the primary NetWare networking protocol (beginning with NetWare 5). Hybrid solutions such as IPX tunneling therefore are less important but will continue to exist as long as IPX/SPX networks remain in the world.

TCP/IP Utilities

Other residents of the Application layer are TCP/IP's utilities. The TCP/IP utilities originally were developed around the Internet and early Unix networks. These utilities are now used to configure, manage, and troubleshoot TCP/IP networks throughout the world, and versions of these utilities are now available with Windows NT Server and other network operating systems.

7

This book classifies the TCP/IP utilities into four categories: connectivity utilities, file transfer and access utilities, remote access utilities, and Internet utilities. Some of the Internet applications shown in Table 7.1 are newer and less Unix-like than the other applications in the table, but they are similar in that they provide the user with access to information and resources across a TCP/IP network.

TABLE 7.1 TCP/IP Utilities

Utility	Description
Connectivity Utilities	
IPConfig	A Windows utility that displays TCP/IP configuration settings. (The Unix utility ifconfig is similar.)
Ping	A utility that tests for network connectivity.
Arp	A utility that lets you view (and possibly modify) the ARP cache of a local or remote computer. The ARP cache contains the physical address to IP address mappings. (See Hour 4, "The Internet Layer.")
Traceroute	A utility that traces the path of a datagram through the internetwork.
Route	A utility that lets you view, add, or edit entries in a routing table. (See Hour 9, "Network Hardware.")
Netstat	A utility that displays IP, UDP, TCP, and ICMP statistics.
NBTstat	A utility that displays statistics on NetBIOS and NBT.
Hostname	A utility that returns the hostname of the local host.
File Transfer Utilities	
Ftp	A basic file transfer utility that uses TCP.
Tftp	A basic file transfer utility that uses UDP. Tftp offers very little security and is used for tasks such as downloading code to network devices.
Rcp	A simple remote file transfer utility.
Remote Utilities	
Telnet	A remote terminal utility.
Rexec	A utility that runs commands on a remote computer through the rexecd daemon.
Rsh	A utility that invokes the shell on a remote computer to execute a command.
Finger	A utility that displays user information.
Internet Utilities	

TABLE 7.1 continued

Utility	Description
Browsers	Utilities that provide access to World Wide Web HTML content.
Newsreaders	Utilities that connect with Internet newsgroups.
E-mail readers	Utilities that provide a means of sending and receiving e-mail.
Archie	A legacy Internet utility that provides access to indexes of anonymous FTP sites.
Gopher	A legacy menu-based Internet information utility.
Whois	A utility that provides access to directories with personal contact information, similar to Internet white pages.

Summary

This hour introduced TCP/IP's Application layer and described some of the applications and services the Application layer supports. You learned about network services and TCP/IP's native utilities. You also learned about some of the ways in which TCP/IP supports network environments such as NetBIOS and NetWare.

Q&A

Q A computer that is acting as a file server is running and is connected to the network, but the users can't access files. What could be wrong?

A Any number of things could be wrong, and a closer look at the particular operating system and configuration will yield a more detailed analysis. For purposes of understanding this hour, the first step is be to check to see if the computer's file server service is running. A file server is not just a computer; it is a service running on that computer that fulfills file requests.

Q The DNS service is running properly on my network, but the names of other computers don't appear in Windows 98 Network Neighborhood. What could be wrong?

A Microsoft computer names are NetBIOS names, and DNS does not provide name service for NetBIOS names. You'll need to provide a means of resolving NetBIOS names using NetBIOS over TCP/IP. See Hour 11 for more on NetBIOS name resolution.

Q Why does IPX tunneling use the UDP Transport protocol rather than the

7

more reliable TCP protocol?

A   IPX essentially grafts the IPX/SPX stack onto TCP/IP. IPX/SPX has its own error
control and flow control features, so the error control and flow control provided by
TCP aren't necessary.

Key Terms

Review the following list of key terms:

File service—A service that fulfills network requests to write or read files to or from
storage.

IPX tunneling—A method of supporting IPX/SPX on TCP/IP networks by interfacing
IPX with TCP/IP's Transport layer.

Name resolution service—A service that maps user-friendly names with network
addresses.

NetBIOS—A collection of network services and an interface to those services used on
some computer-based networks.

NetBIOS over TCP/IP (NBT)—A component that enables NetBIOS to function on
TCP/IP networks.

Print service—A service that fulfills network requests to print documents.

Redirector—A service that checks local resource requests and forwards them to the network if necessary.

Sockets—A network API originally developed for BSD Unix that provides applications
with access to TCP/IP.

WinSock—A Windows programming interface that provides access to TCP/IP.

HOUR **8**

Dial-Up TCP/IP

One of the most popular methods for connecting to a TCP/IP network is a
dial-up connection through a telephone line. This hour introduces modems
and TCP/IP modem connectivity. You'll also learn about the two most popular TCP/IP dial-up networking protocols: Serial Line Internet Protocol
(SLIP) and Point-to-Point Protocol (PPP).

At the completion of this hour, you'll be able to

- Describe what a point-to-point connection is
- Describe why dial-up protocols are different from LAN-based network
  protocols
- Describe the difference between early host dial-up access and today's
  SLIP and PPP access
- Describe the SLIP data format
- Describe SLIP's characteristics
- List the components that make up PPP
- Describe PPP data format
- Describe PPP characteristics

A Look at Modems

One of the most common methods for connecting to the TCP/IP network (the Internet) is through a phone line. Telephone access is now an everyday feature of home and traveling computers. Dial-up access is also an option on many office networks, where dial-up service can offer inexpensive Internet access or provide a link for a worker who travels or has an office at home. In most cases this dial-up access is accomplished using a modem.

A *modem* provides network access through a phone line. The term is short for MOdulate/ DEModulate. Engineers created modems because the industry saw the enormous benefit of providing a way for computers to communicate over the world's most accessible transmission medium: the global telephone system. Telephone lines have grown more sophisticated in recent years. Some lines are now capable of transmitting digitized data; other lines are not. In any case, even digital telephone systems are not designed to automatically handle a network protocol like TCP/IP. The purpose of a modem is to transform the digital protocol transmissions from a computer into an analog signal that can pass through the interface with the phone system and to transform incoming analog signals from the phone line into a digital signal that the receiving computer understands.

Point-to-Point Connections

As you learned in Hour 3, "The Network Access Layer," local networks such as ethernet and token ring employ elaborate access strategies for enabling the computers to share the network medium. By contrast, the two computers at either end of a phone line do not have to compete for the transmission medium with other computers—they have to share it only with each other. This type of connection is called a point-to-point connection (see Figure 8.1).

FIGURE 8.1

A point-to-point connection.

A point-to-point connection is simpler than a LAN-based configuration because it doesn't have to provide a means for multiple computers to share the transmission medium. At the same time, a connection through a phone line has some limitations. One of the biggest limitations is that transmission rates over a phone connection are much slower than rates over a LAN-based network such as ethernet. This reduced transmission speed argues for a protocol that minimizes the data overhead of the protocol itself—less is better. As you'll learn in this hour, as modems have become faster, modem protocols have taken on additional responsibilities.

Another challenge of dial-up protocols is the great diversity of hardware and software configurations they must support. On a local network, a system administrator oversees and controls the configuration of each computer, and the protocol system depends on a high degree of uniformity among the communicating devices. A dial-up connection, on the other hand, can occur from almost anywhere in the world. Dial-up protocols must contend with a wider and more varied range of possibilities regarding the hardware and software of the communicating machines.

Modem Protocols

You might wonder why this point-to-point connection, with its two computers, even needs the complication of the TCP/IP stack to make a connection. The simple answer is that it doesn't.

Early modem protocols were merely a method for passing information across the phone line, and in that situation, the logical addressing and internetwork error control of TCP/IP were not necessary or even desirable. Later, with the arrival of local networks and the Internet, engineers began to think about using a dial-up connection as a means of providing network access. The first implementations of this remote network access concept were an extension of earlier modem protocols. In these first *host dial-up* schemes, the computer attached to the network assumed all responsibility for preparing the data for the network. Either explicitly or implicitly, the remote computer acted more like a terminal (see Figure 8.2), directing the networked host to perform networking tasks and sending and receiving data across the modem line through an entirely separate process.

FIGURE 8.2

An early host-dial-up configuration.

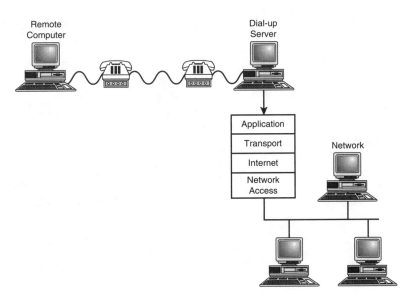

However, these early host dial-up schemes had some limitations. They reflected an earlier, centralized model of computing that placed huge demands on the computer providing the network access. (Imagine the configuration in Figure 8.2 with several computers simultaneously connected to the dial-up server.) They also made inefficient use of the processing power of the remote computer.

As TCP/IP and other routable protocols began to emerge, designers began to imagine another solution in which the remote computer would take more responsibility for networking tasks, and the dial-up server would act more like a router. This solution (shown in Figure 8.3) was more consistent with the newer, less centralized paradigm of computer networks and also closer to the true nature of TCP/IP. In this arrangement, the remote computer operates its own protocol stack, with the modem protocol(s) acting at the Network Access layer. The dial-up server accepts the data and routes it to the greater network.

FIGURE 8.3

A true TCP/IP dial-up connection.

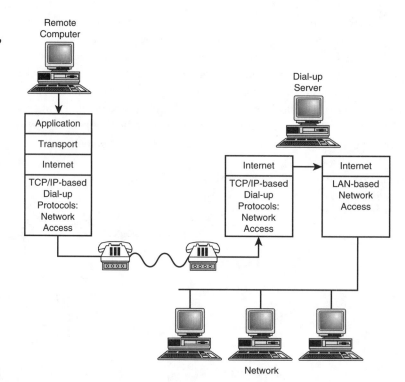

8

Dial-up protocols, therefore, began to work directly with TCP/IP and became an integral part of the stack. This hour covers the two most common TCP/IP modem protocols:

- Serial Line Internet Protocol (SLIP)—An early TCP/IP-based modem protocol, SLIP was simple and therefore had some limitations, some of which you'll learn about later in this hour.
- Point-to-Point Protocol (PPP)—Currently the most popular protocol for modem connections, PPP began as a refinement of SLIP. It offers many important features that weren't available with its predecessor.

PPP has replaced SLIP as the method of choice for dial-up Internet connections. The remainder of this hour takes a closer look at SLIP and PPP.

 Both SLIP and PPP are built on lower-level serial communication protocols that see to the details of actually modulating and demodulating the signal. These serial communication protocols provide what would be considered OSI Physical layer functions.

Serial Line Internet Protocol (SLIP)

SLIP was an early attempt at directly integrating modem protocols with TCP/IP. SLIP began with 3COM's UNET TCP/IP. It was later implemented on Berkeley Unix systems and since then has become widely available, both within the Unix world and in the world of computer compatibles.

SLIP's technology is now considered somewhat obsolete. There is no question, however, that it works, and in some situations SLIP's simplicity is a benefit. Two reasons SLIP survives to this day are its ties to Unix and the large investment that some institutions made in SLIP several years ago when they began to go online.

What SLIP Does

The purpose of SLIP is to transmit IP datagrams across a modem line. SLIP provides no physical addressing or error control and depends on upper-layer protocols for error control functions. SLIP simply sends the data and then sends a signal marking the end of the data.

The SLIP data format is shown in Figure 8.4. A special END character (equivalent to decimal 192) marks the end of the data. If an END character occurs naturally in the data, SLIP includes a special ESC character before the END character so that the receiving computer doesn't prematurely stop receiving the packet.

FIGURE 8.4

The SLIP data format.

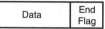

The ESC character used in SLIP is unrelated to the Esc button on your computer keyboard.

The RFCs do not specify a standard maximum size for a packet of SLIP data, but RFC 1055 recommends a maximum size of 1006 bytes, excluding the characters that mark the end of the frame, when using a Berkeley Unix SLIP driver.

SLIP implementation developers can set a maximum size and define other configuration settings. Unlike PPP, SLIP does not enable the communicating computers to negotiate connection configuration settings dynamically. Therefore, SLIP configurations are not always compatible.

Characteristics

SLIP has survived beyond its years and, although it was an innovation in its time, in the context of today's technology a list of SLIP's characteristics looks similar to a list of its shortcomings.

RFC 1055 identifies the following SLIP characteristics and deficiencies:

- Addressing—Both computers have to know each other's IP address. SLIP is incapable of supporting dynamic IP address assignment. This makes SLIP impractical for dial-up accounts with Internet service providers (ISPs), which typically lease IP addresses to dial-up users (using DHCP) for the duration of the session. SLIP is incapable of receiving this leased address.

- Type identification—As RFC 1055 puts it, "SLIP has no Type field." Because SLIP offers no means of specifying a protocol type, it is incapable of supporting multiple protocols simultaneously. Unlike PPP, SLIP cannot multiplex/demultiplex other protocol systems with TCP/IP.

- Error correction/detection—SLIP does not provide error correction. As you learned in previous hours, various forms of error checking occur at upper layers, so error checking through the modem protocols is not absolutely essential. However, some services are designed with the assumption that network access protocols will check for transmission errors on the physical network. Depending solely on an upper-layer error recovery scheme such as TCP's (refer to Hour 6, "The Transport Layer") can result in a significant amount of retransmission, reducing efficiency over the already slow modem link.

8

- Compression—Because transmission over a phone line is so slow, any means of reducing the quantity of data is beneficial. Successive TCP and IP headers often contain redundant information, and there are several strategies for compressing header information. SLIP does not support header compression.

The networking industry addressed some of the shortcomings of SLIP through the development of PPP, which you'll learn more about in the following sections.

Point-to-Point Protocol (PPP)

When industry experts began to design the PPP standard, they had a much better idea of what features would be useful for the emerging Internet. They also knew that modems and phone lines were getting faster and could support a greater amount of protocol overhead. PPP was an effort to address some of the shortcomings of SLIP.

The designers of PPP also wanted PPP to be capable of dynamically negotiating configuration settings at the beginning of a connection and to be capable of managing the link between the communicating computers throughout the session.

How PPP Works

PPP is really a collection of protocols that interact to supply a full complement of modem-based networking features. The design of PPP evolved through a series of RFCs. The current PPP standard is RFC 1661; subsequent documents have clarified and extended PPP components. RFC 1661 divides the components of PPP into three general categories:

- A method for encapsulating multiprotocol datagrams. SLIP and PPP both accept datagrams and prepare them for the Internet. But PPP, unlike SLIP, must be prepared to accept datagrams from more than one protocol system.

- A Link Control Protocol (LCP) for establishing, configuring, and testing the connection. PPP negotiates configuration settings and thus eliminates compatibility problems encountered with SLIP connections.

- A family of Network Control Protocols (NCPs) supporting upper-layer protocol systems. PPP can include separate sublayers that provide separate interfaces to TCP/IP and to alternative suites, such as IPX/SPX.

The following sections discuss these components of PPP.

PPP Data

The primary purpose of PPP (and also SLIP) is to forward datagrams. One challenge of PPP is that it must be capable of forwarding more than one type of datagram. In other words, the datagram could be an IP datagram, or it could be some OSI network-layer datagram.

> The PPP RFCs use the term *packet* to describe a bundle of data transmitted in a PPP frame. A packet can consist of an IP (or other upper-layer protocol) datagram, or it can consist of data formatted for one of the other protocols operating through PPP. The word "packet" is an often-imprecise term used throughout the networking industry for a package of data transmitted across the network; for the most part, this book has attempted to use a more precise term, such as "datagram." Not all PPP data packages, however, are datagrams, so in keeping with the RFCs, this hour uses the term *packet* for data transmitted through PPP.

PPP must also forward data with information relating to its own protocols: the protocols that establish and manage the modem connection. Communicating devices exchange several types of messages and requests over the course of a PPP connection. The communicating computers must exchange LCP packets, used to establish, manage, and close the connection; authentication packets, which support PPP's optional authentication protocols; and NCP packets, which interface PPP with various protocol suites. The LCP data exchanged at the beginning of the connection configures the connection parameters that are common to all protocols. NCP protocols then configure suite-specific parameters relating to the individual protocol suites supported by the PPP connection.

The data format for a PPP frame is shown in Figure 8.5. The fields are as follows:

- Protocol—A one- or two-byte field providing an identification number for the protocol type of the enclosed packet. Possible types include an LCP packet, an NCP packet, an IP packet, or an OSI Network layer protocol packet. ICANN maintains a list of standard identification numbers for the various protocol types.

- Enclosed data (zero or more bytes)—The control packet or upper-layer datagram being transmitted with the frame.

- Padding (optional and variable length)—Additional bytes as required by the protocol designated in the protocol field. Each protocol is responsible for determining how it will distinguish padding from the enclosed datagram.

FIGURE 8.5
The PPP data format.

Protocol 1-2 Byte	Enclosed Data	Padding

8

If the enclosed data is a datagram of some other protocol suite, it isn't related to TCP/IP, and you won't find it discussed in this book.

PPP Connections

The lifecycle of a PPP connection is as follows:

1. The connection is established using the LCP negotiation process, as described later in this hour.

2. If the negotiation process in step 1 specifies a configuration option for authentication, the communicating computers enter an authentication phase. RFC 1661 offers the authentication options Password Authentication Protocol (PAP) and Challenge Handshake Authentication Protocol (CHAP). Additional authentication protocols are also supported, as specified in the Assigned Numbers Standard, RFC 1340.

3. PPP uses NCP packets to specify protocol-specific configuration information for each supported protocol suite (for example, TCP/IP or IPX/SPX).

4. PPP transmits datagrams received from upper-layer protocols. If the negotiation phase in step 1 includes a configuration option for link quality monitoring, then monitoring protocols will transmit monitoring information. NCP might transmit information regarding specific protocols.

5. PPP closes the connection through the exchange of LCP termination packets.

Link Control Protocol (LCP)

Much of PPP's power and versatility comes from the LCP functions that establish, manage, and terminate connections. RFC 1661 identifies three types of LCP packets:

- Link configuration packets
- Link termination packets
- Link maintenance packets

Many PPP features that aren't available with SLIP are a result of LCP. Figure 8.6 describes how LCP configuration packets enable the communicating computers to establish a connection. In Figure 8.6, Computer A sends an LCP Configure-Request packet to Computer B. The Configure-Request packet includes a proposal for any connection parameters Computer A would like to negotiate for the connection. These parameters include the Maximum Receive Unit (MRU), the maximum length for the data enclosed in a PPP frame; the authentication protocol; and the quality control protocol, which defines how the connection monitors for reliable delivery, compression protocol settings, and other configuration choices.

FIGURE 8.6

An LCP connection configuration.

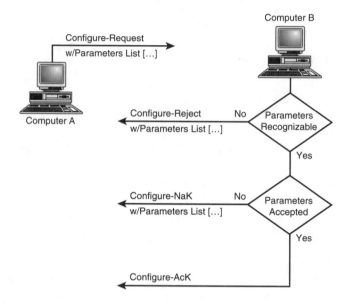

If Computer B accepts all configuration options submitted in the Configure-Request packet, Computer B responds with a Configure-AcK packet (AcK stands for *acknowledged*). If all configuration options transmitted with the Configure-Request packet are recognizable but some are not acceptable to Computer B, then Computer B responds with a Configure-NaK packet (NaK stands for *not acknowledged*) and returns a list of unacceptable parameters with alternative values. Computer A then responds to the Configure-NaK with a new configuration request using adjusted values. This process continues until all values are accepted.

If the Configure-Request packet includes unrecognizable options, Computer B returns a Configure-Reject packet, which lists any unacceptable options.

Figure 8.7 shows the format for an LCP packet. Several other types of LCP packets assist with overseeing the modem connection. The Code field in Figure 8.7 identifies the LCP packet type. The Identifier field identifies the packet and helps to match up requests with acknowledgments. The Length field is the length of the packet. The data transmitted with the packet depends on the type of packet. A list of LCP packet type codes is shown in Table 8.1.

FIGURE 8.7
LCP packet format.

Code (1-Byte)	Identifier (1-Byte)	Length (2-Byte)	Data (Varies)...

TABLE 8.1   LCP Packet Type Codes

Code	Description
1	Configure-Request
2	Configure-AcK
3	Configure-NaK
4	Configure-Reject
5	Terminate-Request
6	Terminate-AcK
7	Code-Reject
8	Protocol-Reject
9	Echo-Request
10	Echo-Reply
11	Discard-Request

As mentioned earlier, LCP tends to maintenance and termination tasks as well as configuration tasks. The Terminate-Request and Terminate-AcK packets are used to request and acknowledge termination of the connection. Code-Reject and Protocol-Reject reject requests for an unknown code or protocol. Echo-Request, Echo-Reply, and Discard-Request provide maintenance, quality assurance, and troubleshooting capabilities.

PPP: A View from the Client

As mentioned earlier, a dial-up connection is essentially a network connection with PPP at the Network Access layer of the protocol stack. The PPP server computer "answers the phone" and listens for requests from PPP clients. The PPP client computer initiates the call and requests a connection with the server. When you initiate a dial-up connection to your Internet service provider from a home computer, your home computer is acting as a PPP client (if your dial-up software uses PPP, which is very likely).

The digital details of the sending and receiving computers are almost totally invisible to the user. The dial-up software handles nearly all of the details described in this hour. Still, a look at a typical dial-up configuration offers a useful vantage point from which to consider the concepts discussed in this hour.

Figure 8.8 shows the properties dialog box for a Windows NT 4.0 Dial-Up Networking phonebook entry. (In Windows, a set of configuration parameters for initiating a connection is called a *phonebook entry*.) The Basic tab gives the name of the entry. You can also specify the telephone number the modem will dial. The Dial Using field tells which modem to use for the call. This setting may seem superfluous, since most dial-up clients have only one modem. In fact, there are other options for this field, such as a null modem cable or a multilink connection, but for our purposes, the important thing to notice is that the computer must access the network through some kind of device. As a practical matter, the device driver for the network device forms the base of the protocol stack (see Hour 2, "How TCP/IP Works"). When you choose a different modem from the drop-down list, you essentially are replacing this layer of the protocol stack with a different layer. The advantage of a layered architecture such as TCP/IP is that you can (theoretically) change one layer without affecting the rest of the stack.

FIGURE 8.8

Windows NT's Dialup Properties Basic tab.

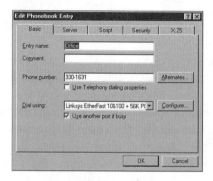

The Server tab for the phonebook entry (see Figure 8.9) tells the dial-up client what to expect from the server on the other end of the connection. Actually, the primary purpose of this tab is to specify the protocols to use for the dial-up connection. The Dial-Up Server Type field lets you specify whether to use PPP, SLIP, or another dial-up protocol. As you learned earlier in this hour, PPP supports other network protocols in addition to TCP/IP. The Server tab lets you choose a network protocol: TCP/IP, IPX/SPX (a protocol used on Novell NetWare networks), or NetBEUI (an alternative Microsoft network protocol). If you change the Dial-Up Server Type setting from PPP to SLIP, you'll see that the IPX/SPX and NetBEUI settings are inactivated. (As you learned earlier, SLIP does not support alternative protocol suites.)

The Server tab also includes a pair of check boxes. As you learned in a previous section, the slow data transmission speed of a modem often causes a bottleneck. Compression reduces the amount of data that must be transmitted and therefore increases the effective data transmission rate. Checking the Enable PPP LCP Extensions check box turns on advanced features for the Link Control Protocol (LCP). LCP, as you learned earlier in this hour, manages PPP connections.

FIGURE 8.9

The Dial-Up Properties Server tab.

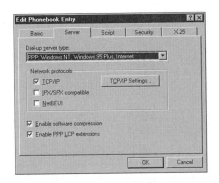

The TCP/IP Settings button in the Server tab invokes the PPP TCP/IP Settings dialog box (see Figure 8.10). This dialog box lets you specify an IP address for the connection. If you read the previous hours carefully, you may wonder why you would configure an IP address along with PPP, since PPP inhabits the Network Access layer and IP address information is handled at the Internet layer. This IP configuration feature underscores the difference between an implementation of TCP/IP, such as Microsoft's TCP/IP implementation for Windows NT, and the TCP/IP ideal discussed in this book. Although it is possible for multiple devices to share the same Internet layer (and the same IP address), as a practical matter, your computer needs a different IP address for each network it connects to, since each network has a different network number and subnet address. In Windows, the IP address for the local area network typically is configured through the Network Control Panel and associated with the TCP/IP software and the network adapter. Each dial-up connection, on the other hand, receives a separate IP address configuration. You'll learn about some of the other TCP/IP Settings configuration options (such as DNS servers, WINS servers, and server-assigned IP addresses) in later hours.

The PPP TCP/IP Settings dialog box also lets you specify compression for the IP header. Compression requires processor time but speeds up transmission time. The cost-effectiveness of IP header compression (or the software compression offered in Figure 8.9) depends upon the properties of the dial-up server, and thus these compression settings are configured separately for each phonebook entry. The check box labeled Use Default Gateway on Remote Network (refer to Figure 8.10) illustrates the role of the PPP connection as a doorway to another network. When this check box is enabled, the dial-up client will have access to addresses beyond the immediate subnet through the server's default gateway.

FIGURE 8.10

The PPP TCP/IP Settings dialog box.

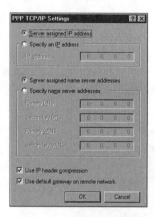

The option labeled Use Default Gateway on Remote Network is important for dial-up connections to Internet service providers. If this box wasn't checked, you'd still be able to connect to the dial-up server, but you wouldn't be able to access any sites beyond the server's subnet.

The Security tab of the Dial-Up Networking Configuration dialog box (see Figure 8.11) illustrates another important facet of dial-up configuration. As stated earlier, PPP offers a number of authentication options. Some of these options are more secure than others. It is possible that PPP might support some authentication formats that you do not want to allow. The Security tab lets you specify which authentication options you'll accept. Note that if you set up the connection to accept only the strictest possible security, you will not be able to connect to computers that do not support this strict security. If two computers cannot connect using the encryption options, a common troubleshooting technique is to enable temporarily the policy labeled Accept Any Authentication Including Clear Text. If the computers can connect using clear text authentication, it is likely that the problem originated from incompatibility of encryption formats.

FIGURE 8.11

The Dial-Up Properties Security tab.

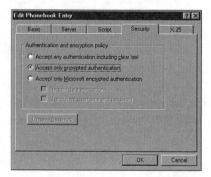

New Uses for PPP

As residential broadband and wireless technologies rise to prominence, it is clear that the traditional dial-up modem will not be as critical in the next decade as it was in the last. PPP, however, shows no sign of fading and in fact is undergoing something of a rebirth. Engineers have adapted the concept of a point-to-point connection to the open Internet, providing a private tunnel for secure communication through what is known as a Virtual Private Network (VPN). In a common VPN scenario, a PPP packet is encapsulated in an Internet-ready TCP/IP packet. PPP, with its versatile authentication and encryption features, can offer security and privacy even over a public network.

Summary

This hour covered some of the basics of dial-up networking. You learned about modems, point-to-point connections, and host dial-up access. This hour also discussed the two most important TCP/IP dial-up protocols: SLIP and PPP. You learned about SLIP data format and some of SLIP's weaknesses. You also learned about the newer and more powerful PPP protocol, which provides dynamic configuration and supports multiple protocol suites.

Q&A

Q Why don't SLIP and PPP require a complete physical addressing system such as the system used with ethernet?

A A point-to-point connection doesn't require an elaborate physical addressing system such as ethernet's because only the two computers participating in the connection are attached to the line. However, SLIP and PPP do provide full support for logical addressing using IP or other Network layer protocols.

Q Why does PPP use NCP protocols to configure protocol-specific settings instead of configuring protocol-specific settings during the LCP connection establishment phase?

A LCP undertakes only configuration tasks that are common to all protocols. Individual protocols are then configured through NCP packets. This modular arrangement minimizes startup time because only the protocol settings that are necessary will be configured.

Q Why wouldn't SLIP be a good choice for a typical dial-up Internet service connection?

A Most ISPs assign temporary IP addresses at connect time. SLIP doesn't support dynamic IP address assignment, so it wouldn't be a good choice for a typical dial-up account.

Key Terms

Review the following list of key terms:

Link Control Protocol (LCP)—A protocol used by PPP to establish, manage, and terminate dial-up connections.

Maximum Receive Unit (MRU)—The maximum length for the data enclosed in a PPP frame.

Modem—A device that translates a digital signal to or from an analog signal.

Network Control Protocol (NCP)—One of a family of protocols designed to interface PPP with specific protocol suites.

Point-to-Point Connection—A connection consisting of exactly two communicating devices sharing a transmission line.

Point-to-Point Protocol (PPP)—A dial-up protocol. PPP supports TCP/IP and also other network protocol suites. PPP is newer and more powerful than SLIP.

Serial Line Internet Protocol (SLIP)—An early TCP/IP-based dial-up protocol.

PART III
Networking with TCP/IP

Hour

HOUR 9

Network Hardware

All but the smallest networks are more than computers and wires. Most networks include extra devices that provide connectivity, reduce traffic, and enhance performance. Some of these devices, such as routers and bridges, are designed to subdivide the network. Other devices, such as hubs, support cleaner and more convenient connectivity under everyday ethernet. A switch is a useful device that looks like a hub but has some of the features of a bridge. This hour discusses some important network devices and shows how these devices function on TCP/IP networks.

At the completion of this hour, you'll be able to

- Explain why network administrators subdivide networks
- Describe a bridge
- Describe a router
- Describe a hub
- Describe a switch
- Explain the differences between static and dynamic routing

Divided Networks

As previous hours have mentioned, network access methods such as CSMA/CD (ethernet) and token passing (token ring) are designed to serve limited numbers of computers.
A large network must provide some means of filtering and directing network traffic to
prevent an overload of the transmission medium. Large networks, therefore, are divided
into smaller segments. Each segment is isolated from the rest of the network by some
filtering device.

If the source and the destination of a transmission are within the segment, the filtering
device stops the transmission from passing to the greater network (see Figure 9.1). In a
practical sense, this segmenting concept stops a considerable amount of traffic, because
computers that are in close proximity (and thus on the same segment) are in many cases
the most likely to be sharing information over the network. Two computers in the same
office suite, for example, might regularly exchange files and share a printer and might
only occasionally communicate with a third computer on the other end of the building.

FIGURE 9.1

A filtering device.

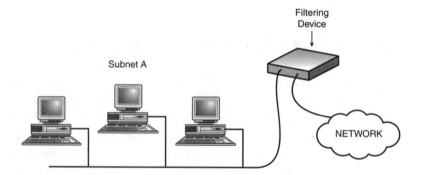

A device that filters traffic (as shown in Figure 9.1) is sometimes called a *connectivity
device*, although the term is sometimes used more generally to include a device such as
a repeater, which doesn't provide filtering capabilities.

The primary uses for connectivity devices are as follows:

- **Traffic control**   As mentioned previously, a large network needs a means of
  filtering and isolating network traffic.
- **Connectivity**   Connectivity devices can connect dissimilar physical networks (for
  example, an ethernet and a token ring). Some protocol-translating gateway devices
  can even connect a network using one protocol suite (such as a NetWare network
  using IPX/SPX) with a network using another protocol suite (such as the Internet,
  which uses TCP/IP).

- **Hierarchical addressing**   A logical addressing scheme such as the IP addressing system (see Hour 4, "The Internet Layer," and Hour 5, "Subnetting") provides for a hierarchical delivery system in which the network ID is analogous to a street and the host ID is a house on that street. Segmenting the network provides a physical manifestation of this logical addressing concept.
- **Signal regeneration**   Connectivity devices can regenerate a network signal and thus extend the maximum cabling distance for a network.

Many types of connectivity devices exist, and they all play a role in managing traffic on TCP/IP networks. The following sections examine the these devices:

- Bridges
- Hubs
- Switches
- Routers

Bridges

A *bridge* is a connectivity device that filters and forwards packets by physical address. Bridges operate at the OSI Data Link layer (which, as described in Hour 3, "The Network Access Layer," falls within the TCP/IP Network Access layer).

Though a bridge is not a router, a bridge still uses a routing table as a source for delivery information. This physical address–based routing table is considerably different from and less sophisticated than the routing tables described later in this hour.

A modern bridge listens to each segment of the network it is connected to and builds a table showing which physical address is on which segment. When data is transmitted on one of the network segments, the bridge checks the destination address of the data and consults the routing table. If the destination address is on the segment from which the data was received, the bridge ignores the data. If the destination address is on a different segment, the bridge forwards the data to the appropriate segment. If the destination address isn't in the routing table, the bridge forwards the data to all segments except the segment from which it received the transmission.

It is important to remember that the hardware-based physical addresses used by a bridge are different from the logical IP addresses. See Hours 1–4 for more on the difference between physical and logical addresses.

Bridges are commonly used on LANs as an inexpensive means of filtering traffic and, therefore, increasing the number of computers that can participate in the network. Because bridges use only Network Access layer physical addresses and do not examine logical addressing information available in the IP datagram header, bridges are not very useful for connecting dissimilar networks. Bridges also cannot assist with the IP routing and delivery schemes used to forward data on large networks such as the Internet.

Hubs

Up until a few years ago, most ethernet networks used a scheme that connected the computers with a single, continuous coaxial cable. In recent years, 10BASE-T–style hub-based ethernet has become the dominant form. Almost all ethernet networks today use a central hub or switch to which the computers on the network connect (see Figure 9.2).

FIGURE 9.2

A hub-based ethernet network.

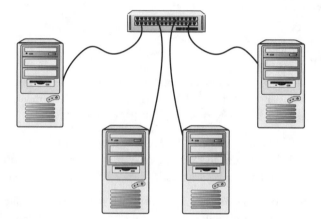

As you'll recall from Hour 3, the classic ethernet concept calls for all computers to share the transmission medium. Each transmission is heard by all network adapters. An ethernet hub receives a transmission from one of its ports and echoes that transmission to all of its other ports (refer to Figure 9.2). In other words, the network behaves as if all computers were connected using a single continuous line. The hub does not filter or route any data. Instead, the hub just receives and retransmits signals.

One of the principal reasons for the rise of hub-based ethernet is that in most cases a hub simplifies the task of wiring the network. Each computer is connected to the hub through a single line. A computer can easily be detached and reconnected. In an office setting where computers are commonly grouped together in a small area, a single hub can serve a close group of computers and can be connected to other hubs in other parts of the network. With all cables connected to a single device, vendors soon began to realize the opportunities for innovation. More sophisticated hubs, called *intelligent hubs,* began to appear. Intelligent hubs provided additional features, such as the capability to detect a line problem and block off a port.

Switches

A hub-based ethernet network still faces the principal liability of ethernet: Performance degrades as traffic increases. No computer can transmit unless the line is free. Furthermore, each network adapter must receive and process every frame placed on the ethernet. A smarter version of a hub, called a *switch,* was developed to address these problems with ethernet. A switch looks very similar to the hub shown in Figure 9.2. Each computer is attached to the switch through a single line. However, the switch is smarter about where it sends the data received through one of its ports. Most switches associate each port with the physical address of the adapter connected to that port (see Figure 9.3). When one of the computers attached to the port transmits a frame, the switch checks the destination address of the frame and sends the frame to the port associated with that destination address. In other words, the switch sends the frame only to the adapter that is supposed to receive it. Every adapter does not have to examine every frame transmitted on the network. The switch reduces superfluous transmissions and therefore improves the performance of the network.

FIGURE 9.3

A switch associates each port with a physical address.

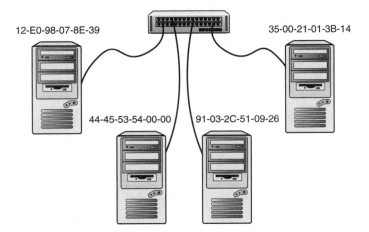

12-E0-98-07-8E-39   35-00-21-01-3B-14

44-45-53-54-00-00   91-03-2C-51-09-26

Note that the switch operates with physical addresses (see Hour 3) and not IP addresses. The switch is not a router. Actually, a switch is more like a bridge—or, more accurately, like several bridges in one. The switch isolates each of its network connections so that only data coming from or going to the computer on the end of the connection enters the line (see Figure 9.4).

FIGURE 9.4
A switch isolates each computer to reduce traffic.

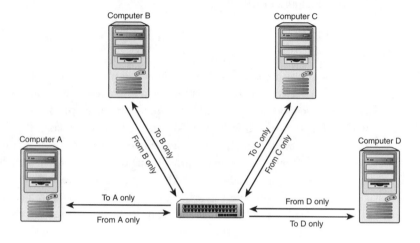

Several types of switches are now available. Two of the most common switching methods are

- **Cut-through**   The switch starts forwarding the frame as soon as it obtains the destination address.
- **Store and forward**   The switch receives the entire frame before retransmitting. This method slows down the retransmission process, but it can sometimes improve overall performance because the switch filters out fragments and other invalid frames.

Switches have become increasingly popular in recent years. Corporate LANs often use a collection of layered and interconnected switches for optimum performance.

Not all switches forward by physical address. Some vendors offer switches that operate at higher protocol layers.

Routers

A *router* is a device that filters traffic by logical address. Routers operate at the Internet layer (OSI Network layer) using IP addressing information in the Internet layer header.

Routers are an essential part of any large TCP/IP network. Without routers the Internet could not function. In fact, the Internet never would have grown to what it is today without the development of network routers and TCP/IP routing protocols.

A large network such as the Internet contains many routers that provide redundant pathways from the source to the destination nodes. The routers must work independently, but the effect of the system must be that data is routed accurately and efficiently through the internetwork.

Routers are far more sophisticated than bridges. Routers replace Network Access layer header information as they pass data from one network to the next, so a router can connect dissimilar network types. Many routers also maintain detailed information describing the best path based on considerations of distance, bandwidth, and time. (You'll learn more about route-discovery protocols later in this hour.)

Routing in TCP/IP

Routing in TCP/IP is a subject that has filled 162 RFCs (at last count) and could easily fill a dozen books. What is truly remarkable about TCP/IP routing is that it works so well. An average homeowner can call up an Internet browser and connect with a computer in China or Finland without a passing thought to the many devices forwarding the request around the world. Even on smaller networks, routers play a vital role in controlling traffic and keeping the network fast. The following sections discuss some of the concepts you'll need to be familiar with in order to understand routing in TCP/IP. The next hour discusses these concepts in greater detail.

What Is a Router?

The best way to describe a router is to describe how it looks. In its simplest form (or, at least, in its most fundamental form) a router looks like a computer with two network adapters. The earlier routers were actually computers with two or more network adapters (called *multihomed* computers). Figure 9.5 shows a multihomed computer acting as a router.

The first step to understanding routing is to remember that the IP address belongs to the adapter and not to the computer. The computer in Figure 9.5 has two IP addresses—one for each adapter. In fact, it is possible for the two adapters to be on completely different IP subnets corresponding to completely different physical networks (as shown in Figure 9.5). In Figure 9.5, the protocol software on the multihomed computer can receive the data from segment A, check the IP address information to see if the data belongs on segment B, replace the Network Access layer header with a header that provides physical address information for segment B (if the data is addressed to segment B), and transmit the data onto segment B. In this simple scenario, the multihomed computer acts as a router.

FIGURE 9.5

A multihomed computer acting as a router.

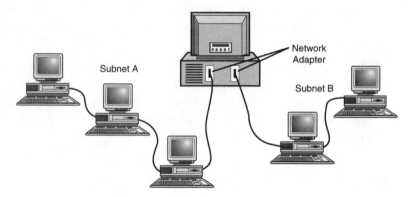

If you really want to understand the scope of what the world's networks are doing, imagine the scenario in the preceding paragraph with the following complications:

- The router has more than two ports (adapters) and can therefore interconnect more than two networks. The decision of where to forward the data then becomes more complicated, and the possibility for redundant paths increases.

- The networks that the router interconnects are each interconnected with other networks. In other words, the router sees network addresses for networks to which it is not directly connected. The router must have a strategy for forwarding data addressed to networks to which it is not directly attached.

- The network of routers provides redundant paths, and each router must have a way of deciding which path to use.

The simple configuration in Figure 9.5, combined with the preceding three complications, offers a more detailed view of the router's role (see Figure 9.6).

On today's networks, most routers are not multihomed computers. It is more cost effective to assign routing responsibilities to a specialized device. The routing device is specifically designed to perform routing functions efficiently, and the device does not include all the extra features found in a complete computer.

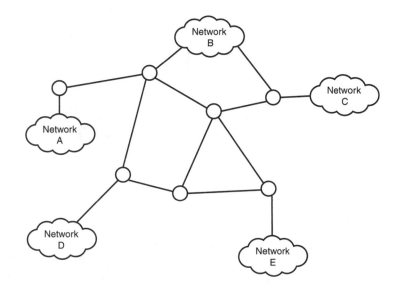

FIGURE 9.6
Routing on a complex network.

9

Introduction to Routing

Building on the discussion of the simple router described in the preceding section, a more general description of the router's role is as follows:

1. The router receives data from one of its attached networks.

2. The router passes the data up the protocol stack to the Internet layer. In other words, the router discards the Network Access layer header information and reassembles (if necessary) the IP datagram.

3. The router checks the destination address in the IP header. If the destination is on the network from whence the data came, the router ignores the data. (The data presumably has already reached its destination because it was transmitted on the network of the destination computer.)

4. If the data is destined for a different network, the router consults a routing table to determine where to forward the data.

5. After the router determines which of its adapters will receive the data, it passes the data down through the appropriate Network Access layer software for transmission through the adapter.

The routing process is shown in Figure 9.7. It might occur to you that the routing table described in step 4 is a rather crucial element. In fact, the routing table and the protocol that builds the routing table are distinguishing characteristics of the router. Most of the discussion of routers is about how routers build routing tables and how the route protocols that assemble routing table information cause the collection of routers to serve as a unified system.

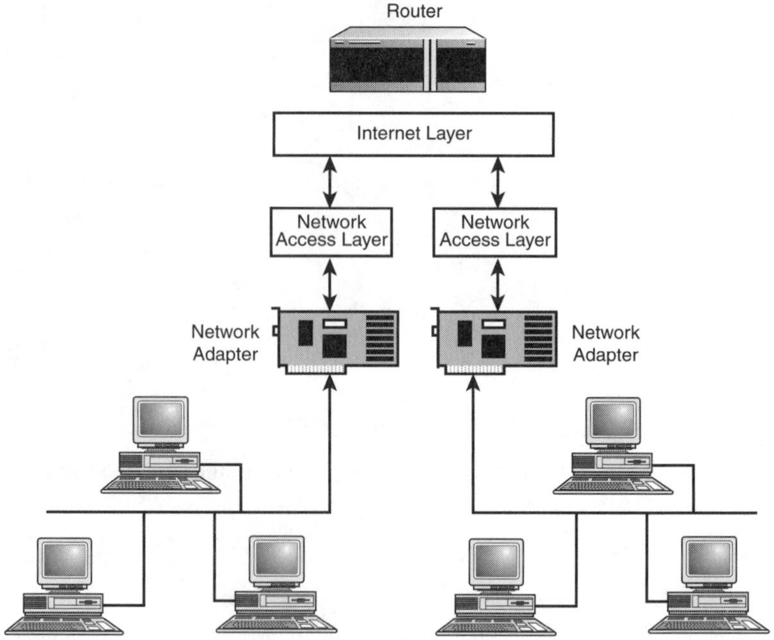

FIGURE 9.7
FIGURE **9.7**
The routing process.

The two primary types of routing are named for where they get their routing table information:

- **Static routing**   Requires the network administrator to enter route information manually.
- **Dynamic routing**   Builds the routing table dynamically based on routing information obtained using routing protocols.

Static routing can be useful in some contexts, but as you might guess, a system that requires the network administrator to enter routing information manually has some severe limitations. First, static routing does not adapt well to large networks with hundreds of possible routes. Second, on all but the simplest networks, static routing requires a disproportionate investment of time from the network administrator, who must not only create but also continually update the routing table information. Also, a static router cannot adapt as quickly to changes in the network, such as a downed router.

Individual static routes are sometimes used on dynamic networks to troubleshoot problems or preference desirable links. See Hour 10, "Routing."

Routing Table Concepts

It is best to focus on a few important concepts before continuing with the discussion of dynamic routing protocols. The role of the routing table and other Internet layer routing elements is to deliver the data to the proper local network. After the data reaches the local network, network access protocols will see to its delivery. The routing table, therefore, does not need to store complete IP addresses and can simply list addresses by network ID. (See Hours 4 and 5 for a discussion of the host ID and network ID portions of the IP address.)

Conceptually, the contents of a typical routing table are as shown in Figure 9.8. A routing table essentially maps destination network IDs to the IP address of the next hop—the next stop the datagram makes on its path to the destination network. Note that the routing table makes a distinction between networks directly connected to the router itself and networks connected indirectly through other routers. The next hop can be either the destination network (if it is directly connected) or the next downstream router on the way to the destination network. The Router Port Interface in Figure 9.8 refers to the router port through which the router forwards the data.

FIGURE 9.8

The routing table.

Destination	Next Hop	Router Port Interface
129.14.0.0	Direct Connection	1
150.27.0.0	131.100.18.6	3
155.111.0.0	Direct Connection	2
165.48.0.0	129.14.16.1	1

The next hop entry in the routing table is the key to understanding dynamic routing. On a complex network, several paths to the destination might exist, and the router must decide which of these paths the next hop will follow. A dynamic router makes this decision based on information obtained through routing protocols.

A host computer, like a router, can have a routing table; because the host does not have to perform routing functions, its routing table usually isn't as complicated. Hosts often make use of a *default router* or *default gateway.* The default gateway is the router that receives the datagram if it can't be delivered on the local network or to another router.

Network Address Translation (NAT)

As you have probably noticed, network devices are constantly becoming more sophisticated. One advance is the appearance of routers that perform network address translation.

A network address translation device obscures all details of the local network and hides the very existence of the local network. Figure 9.9 shows a network address translation device on the Internet. The NAT device serves as a gateway for computers on the local network to access the Internet. Behind the NAT device, the local network can use any network address space. The network does not have to use specially assigned Internet addresses because the local network is not even part of the Internet. The NAT device instead acts as a proxy for the local network on the Internet. When a local computer attempts to connect to an Internet resource, the NAT device makes the connection instead. Any packets received from the Internet resource are translated into the address scheme of the local network and forwarded to the local computer that initiated the connection.

FIGURE 9.9
A network address
translation (NAT)
device.

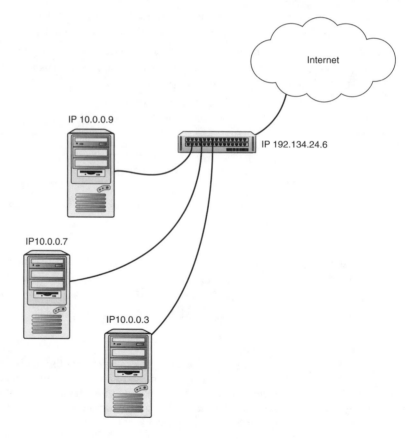

A NAT device improves security because it can prevent an outside attacker from even finding out about the local network. To the outside world, the NAT device looks like a single host connected to the Internet. Even if an attacker knew the address of a computer on the local network, she would not be able to open a connection with the local network because the local addressing scheme is not contiguous with the Internet address space.

> A NAT device is one form of what is called a *proxy server*. A proxy server is a computer that acts on behalf of other computers. The other computers can thus be isolated from the Internet. The proxy server assumes the role of communicating with the outside world and transmits any reply to the appropriate computer on the local network.

9

Summary

This hour discussed some common network devices. You learned about routers, bridges, hubs, and switches. The next hour takes a deeper look at routing on TCP/IP networks.

Q&A

Q What's the difference between a bridge and a router?

A A bridge forwards data by physical address. A router forwards data by logical (IP) address.

Q Why does core Internet primarily use dynamic routing?

A It wouldn't be practical for a network administrator to type in static routing table information for a core router on the wildly complex and amorphous Internet.

Key Terms

Review the following list of key terms:

bridge—A connectivity device that forwards data based on physical address.

cut-through switching—A switching method that causes the switch to start forwarding the frame as soon as it obtains the destination address.

dynamic routing—A routing method in which routing information is supplied dynamically through routing protocols.

hub—A connectivity device to which network cables are attached to form a network segment. Hubs typically do not filter data and instead retransmit incoming frames to all ports.

intelligent hub—A hub capable of performing additional tasks such as blocking off a port when a line problmd is detected.

multihomed computer—A computer with multiple network adapters.

router—A connectivity device that forwards data based on logical address (IP address, in the case of TCP/IP).

routing table—A table within the router that relates network IDs to network paths.

static routing—A routing method in which the routing information is input manually by the network administrator.

store and forward switching—A switching method that causes the switch to receive the entire frame before retransmitting.

switch—A connectivity device. A switch is aware of the address associated with each of its ports and forwards each incoming frame to the correct port.

HOUR 10

Routing

Introduction to Routing in TCP/IP

The infrastructure that supports global networks such as the Internet could not function without routers. TCP/IP was designed to operate through routers, and no discussion of TCP/IP is complete without a discussion of what the routers are doing. As you'll learn in this hour, a router participates in a complex process of communication with other routers on the network to determine the best path to each destination. In this hour, you'll learn about routers, routing tables, and routing protocols.

At the end of this hour, you'll know how to

- Describe what IP forwarding is and how it works
- Distinguish between distance vector routing and link state routing
- Discuss the roles of core, interior, and exterior routers
- Describe the common interior routing protocols RIP and OSPF

Recapping Routers

Hours 1, "What Is TCP/IP?," and 9, "Network Hardware," introduced you to the essential networking device known as a router. You learned that the role of the router is to forward datagrams by IP address. A router, therefore, is a network hardware device that implements the IP addressing scheme discussed in Hour 4, "The Internet Layer." As you'll recall, a router is similar to a computer with multiple network cards connected to multiple network segments (refer to Figure 9.2). When a router receives a datagram through one of its ports, it inspects the datagram to determine the destination IP address. If the destination address is located on the network segment from which the message came, there is no need to forward the datagram, and the router ignores it. If the destination address is located on a different network segment, the router forwards the datagram according to the information located in its routing table.

Routers are necessary for the following reasons:

- Routers provide the delivery mechanism necessary for IP addressing (see Hour 4 and Hour 5, "Subnetting"). The elegant and efficient hierarchy of networks and subnets requires network devices that can direct a datagram by IP address.
- Routers filter traffic so that every host does not have to listen to messages addressed to every other host. As you learned in Hour 9, switches also filter traffic, but most switches use physical addresses rather than hierarchical IP addresses and therefore are not as effective on large networks.
- Routers hide the details of the physical network. Because IP forwarding occurs above the Network Access layer, routers can connect dissimilar network types. A computer on an ethernet LAN in Connecticut can communicate with a computer on a token ring LAN in Istanbul even though token ring and ethernet network adapters aren't compatible.

Unfortunately, it is difficult to discuss some of the topics in this hour on a small scale. The figures and descriptions are sometimes simplified to make the concepts more manageable, but the real benefit of routers can best be seen on large, diverse, and dynamic networks where a group of routers must constantly share information in order to keep the lines alive.

A Look at IP Forwarding

Both hosts and routers have routing tables. A host's routing table can be much simpler than a router's routing table. The routing table for a single computer may contain only two lines: an entry for the local network and a default route for packets that can't be delivered on the local segment. This rudimentary routing information is enough to point a datagram toward its destination. You'll learn later in this hour that a router's role is a bit more complex.

As you learned in Hour 4, the TCP/IP software uses ARP to resolve an IP address to a physical address on the local segment. But what if the IP address isn't on the local segment? As Hour 4 explains, if the IP address isn't on the local segment, the host sends the datagram to a router. You may have noticed by now that the situation is actually a bit more complicated. The IP header (refer to Figure 4.3) lists only the IP address of the source and destination. The header doesn't have room to list the address of every intermediate router that passes the datagram toward its destination. As you read this hour, it is important to remember that the IP forwarding process does not actually place the router's address in the IP header. Instead, the host passes the datagram and the router's IP address down to the Network Access layer, where the protocol software uses a separate lookup process to enclose the datagram in a frame for local delivery to the router. In other words, the IP address of a forwarded datagram refers to the host that will eventually receive the data. The physical address of the frame that relays the datagram to a router on the local network is the address of the local adapter on the router.

10

A brief description of this process is as follows (see Figure 10.1):

1. A host wants to send an IP datagram. The host checks its routing table.

2. If the datagram cannot be delivered on the local network, the host extracts from the routing table the IP address of the router associated with the destination address. (In the case of a host on a local segment, this router IP address will most likely be the address of the default gateway.) The router's IP address is then resolved to a physical address using ARP.

3. The datagram (addressed to the remote host) is passed to the Network Access layer along with the physical address of the router that will receive the datagram.

4. The network adapter of the router receives the frame because the destination physical address of the frame matches the router's physical address.

5. The router unpacks the frame and passes the datagram up to the Internet layer.

6. The router checks the IP address of the datagram. If the IP address matches the router's own IP address, the data is intended for the router itself. If the IP address does not match the router's IP address, the router attempts to forward the datagram by checking its own routing table to find a route associated with the datagram's destination address.

7. If the datagram cannot be delivered on any of the segments connected to the router, the router sends the datagram to another router, and the process repeats (go to step 1) until the last router is able to deliver the datagram directly to the destination host.

FIGURE **10.1**
*The IP forwarding
process.*

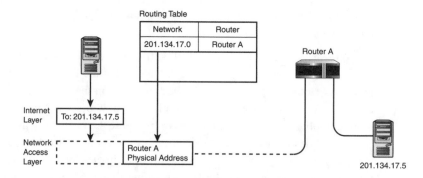

The IP forwarding process described in step 6 of the preceding procedure is an important
characteristic of a router. It is important to remember that a device will not act like a
router just because it has two network cards. Unless the device has the necessary software to support IP forwarding, data will not pass from one interface to another. When a
computer that is not configured for IP routing receives a datagram addressed to a different computer, the datagram is simply ignored.

Direct Versus Indirect Routing

If a router just connects two subnets, that router's routing table can be very simple. The
router in Figure 10.2 will never see an IP address that isn't associated with one of its
ports, and the router is directly attached to all subnets. In other words, the router in
Figure 10.2 can deliver any datagram through direct routing.

FIGURE **10.2**
*A router connecting
two segments can
reach each segment
directly.*

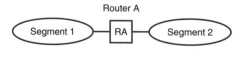

Consider the slightly more complex network shown in Figure 10.3. In this case, router A
is not attached to segment 3 and does not have a way of finding out about segment 3
without some help. This situation is called *indirect* routing. Most routed networks depend
to some degree on indirect routing. Large corporate networks may have dozens of
routers, with no more than one or two connected directly to each network segment.
You'll learn more about these larger networks later in this hour. For now, the important
questions to ask about Figure 10.3 are How does router A find out about segment 3? and
How does router A know that datagrams addressed to segment 3 should be sent to router
B and not to router C?

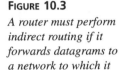

FIGURE 10.3
A router must perform indirect routing if it forwards datagrams to a network to which it isn't directly attached.

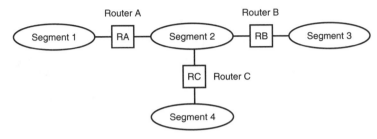

There are two ways that routers learn about indirect routes:

- From a system administrator
- From other routers

These two options correspond (respectively) to the static routing and dynamic routing methods described in Hour 9. A system administrator can enter network routes directly into the routing table. This approach is known as *static routing*. The other option is for router B to tell router A about segment 3. This method is called *dynamic routing*. Dynamic routing offers several advantages. First, it does not require human intervention. Second, it is responsive to changes in the network. If a new network segment is attached to router B, router B can inform router A about the change.

As it turns out, static routing is sometimes an effective approach for small, simple, and permanent networks. Static routing would probably be acceptable on the simple network shown in Figure 10.3, but as the number of routers increases, static routing becomes inadequate. The number of possible routes multiplies as you add segments to the network, creating additional work for the administrator. More importantly, the interaction of static routes on a large network can lead to inefficiencies and to quirky behavior, such as routing loops (described in Hour 9).

It is worth noting that it would also be possible to configure routing on the network shown in Figure 10.3 using defaults. In that case, router A would not really have to find out about segment 3. It could just route to router B any datagram with an unknown address and let router B figure out what to do next. Once again, this scenario might work on the small network shown in Figure 10.3. But a default route is a static route, and configuring the routers themselves to route by default on a complex network can lead to the same inefficiencies and quirky behavior associated with static routing.

For these reasons, most modern routers use some form of dynamic routing. The routers communicate with each other to share information on network segments and network paths, and each router builds its routing table using the information obtained through this communication process. The following sections describe how dynamic routing works.

10

Routers sometimes use a combination of static and dynamic routing. A system administrator may configure a few static paths and let others be assigned dynamically. Static routes are sometimes used to force traffic over a specific path. For example, a system administrator may want to configure the routers so that traffic is funneled to a high-bandwidth link.

Dynamic Routing Algorithms

The routers in a router group exchange enough information about the network so that each router can build a table that describes which way to send datagrams addressed to any particular segment. What exactly do the routers communicate? How does a router build its routing table? As you have probably figured out by now, the behavior of a router depends entirely upon the routing table. Several routing protocols are currently in use. Many of those routing protocols are designed around one of two routing methods:

- Distance vector routing
- Link state routing

These methods are best understood as different approaches to the task of communicating and collecting routing information. The following sections discuss distance vector and link state routing. Later in this hour, you'll take a closer look at a pair of routing protocols that use these methods: RIP (a distance vector routing protocol) and OSPF (a link state routing protocol).

Distance vector and link state are *classes* of routing protocols. The implementations of actual protocols include additional features and details. Also, many routers support startup scripts, static routing entries, and other features that complicate any idealized description of distance vector or link state routing.

Distance Vector Routing

Distance vector routing (also called *Bellman-Ford* routing) is an efficient and simple routing method employed by many routing protocols. Distance vector routing once dominated the routing industry, and it is still quite common, although recently more sophisticated routing methods (such as link state routing) have been gaining popularity.

Distance vector routing is designed to minimize the required communication among routers and to minimize the amount of data that must reside in the routing table. The underlying philosophy of distance vector routing is that a router does not have to know the complete pathway to every network segment—it only has to know in which direction to send a datagram addressed to the segment (hence the term *vector*). The distance between network segments is measured in the number of routers a datagram must cross to travel from one segment to the other. Routers using a distance vector algorithm attempt to optimize the pathway by minimizing the number of routers that a datagram must cross. This distance parameter is referred to as the *hop count*.

> You'll notice that the routing method discussed in the introduction to routing in Hour 9 is a distance vector routing method.

Distance vector routing works as follows:

1. When router A initializes, it senses the segments to which it is directly attached and places those segments in its routing table. The hop count to each of those directly attached segments is 0 (zero), since a datagram does not have to pass through any routers to travel from this router to the segment.

2. At some periodic interval, the router receives a report from each neighboring router. The report lists any network segments the neighboring router knows about and the hop count to each of those segments.

3. When router A receives the report from the neighboring router, it integrates the new routing information into its own routing table as follows:

   a. If router B knows about a network segment that router A doesn't currently have in its routing table, router A adds the segment to its routing table. The route for the new segment is router B, meaning that if router A receives a datagram addressed to the new segment, it will forward that datagram to router B. The hop count for the new segment is whatever router B listed as the hop count plus 1 (one), because router A is one hop farther away from the segment than router B was.

   b. If router B lists a segment that is already in router A's routing table, router A adds 1 to the hop count received from B and compares the revised hop count to the value stored in its own routing table. If the path through B is more efficient (fewer hops) than the path router A already knows about, router A revises its routing table to list router B as the route for datagrams addressed to this segment.

    c. If the revised hop count for the path to the segment through router B (the hop count received from B plus 1) is greater than the hop count currently listed in router A's routing table, the route through B is not used. Router A continues to use the route already stored in its routing table.

With each round of routing table updates, the routers receive a more complete picture of the network. Information about routes slowly disseminates across the network. Assuming nothing changes on the network, the routers will eventually learn the most efficient path to every segment.

An example of a distance vector routing update is shown in Figure 10.4. Note that at this point other updates have already taken place because both router A and router B know about networks to which they are not directly attached. In this case, router B has a more efficient path to network 14, so router A updates its routing table to send data addressed to network 14 to router B. Router A already has a better way to reach network 7, so the routing table is not changed.

FIGURE 10.4

A distance vector routing update.

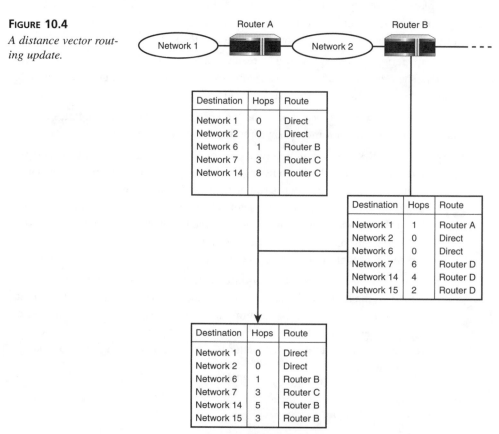

Destination	Hops	Route
Network 1	0	Direct
Network 2	0	Direct
Network 6	1	Router B
Network 7	3	Router C
Network 14	8	Router C

Destination	Hops	Route
Network 1	1	Router A
Network 2	0	Direct
Network 6	0	Direct
Network 7	6	Router D
Network 14	4	Router D
Network 15	2	Router D

Destination	Hops	Route
Network 1	0	Direct
Network 2	0	Direct
Network 6	1	Router B
Network 7	3	Router C
Network 14	5	Router B
Network 15	3	Router B

Router A Table

The destinations listed in Figure 10.4 (network 1, network 2, and so on) are either whole IP networks or IP subnets, depending on the context.

Link State Routing

Distance vector routing is a worthy approach if you assume that the efficiency of a path coincides with the number of routers a datagram must cross. This assumption is a good starting point, but in some cases it is an oversimplification. Also, distance vector routing does not scale well to large groups of routers. Each router must maintain a routing table entry for every destination, and the table entries are merely vector and hop-count values. The router cannot economize its efforts through some greater knowledge of the network's structure. Furthermore, complete tables of distance and hop count values must pass among routers even if most of the information isn't really necessary. Computer scientists began to ask if they could do better, and link state routing evolved from this discussion. Link state routing is now the primary alternative to distance vector routing.

The philosophy behind link state routing is that every router attempts to build its own internal map of the network topology. Each router periodically sends status messages to the network. These status messages list the network's other routers to which the router is directly connected and also the status of the link (whether the link is currently operational). The routers use the status messages received from other routers to build a map of the network topology. When a router has to forward a datagram, it chooses the best path to the destination based on the existing conditions.

Link state protocols require more processing time on each router, but the consumption of bandwidth is reduced because every router is not required to propagate a complete routing table. Also, it is easier to trace problems through the network because the status message from a given router propagates unchanged through the network. (The distance vector method, on the other hand, increments the hop count each time the routing information passes to a different router.)

Routing on Complex Networks

So far this hour has focused on a single router or single group of routers. In fact, some large networks may contain hundreds of routers. The Internet contains thousands of routers. On very large networks such as the Internet, it is not feasible for all routers to share all the information necessary to support the routing methods described in previous sections. If every router had to compile and process routing information for every other router on the Internet, the volume of router protocol traffic and the size of the routing tables would soon overwhelm the infrastructure. But it isn't really necessary for every router on the Internet to know about every other router. A router in a dentist's office in Istanbul could operate for years without ever having to learn about another router in an office pool at a paint factory in Lima, Peru. If the network is organized efficiently, most routers need to exchange routing protocol information only with other nearby routers.

In the ARPAnet system that led to the Internet, a small group of core routers served as a central backbone for the internetwork, linking individual networks that were configured and managed autonomously. The core routers knew about every network, though they did not have to know about every subnet. As long as any datagram could find a path to a core router, it could reach any point in the system. The routers in the tributary networks beneath the core didn't have to know about every network in the world, they just had to know how to send data among themselves and how to reach the core routers.

This system evolved into the system depicted in Figure 10.5. The core routers in the backbone network pass messages among the networks. Attached to the core are independently managed networks called *autonomous systems*. An autonomous system might represent a corporate network or, more commonly in recent times, a network associated with an Internet service provider (ISP). The owner of the autonomous system manages the details of configuring individual routers. Interior routers within the autonomous system share information and build fairly complete routing tables that describe the internal design of the network. A message addressed to another network is forwarded to the core. Also important are exterior routers. An *exterior router* is designated to exchange information with other networks. The volume of internetwork router communication is thus reduced because only the exterior routers communicate routing information across network boundaries.

Each router type uses different protocols and algorithms to build the routing table. You'll learn about some of these routing protocols in later sections. Keep in mind this quick summary of the router types:

- Core routers—Core routers have complete information about other core routers. The routing table is basically a map of where autonomous systems tie into the core. Core routers do not possess detailed information about routes within the autonomous networks. Examples of core router routing protocols include Gateway-to-Gateway Protocol (GGP) and a more recent routing protocol called SPREAD.

- Exterior routers—Exterior routers are non-core routers that communicate routing information between autonomous networks. They maintain routing information about their own and neighboring autonomous networks but do not have a map of the complete internetwork. Exterior routers traditionally have used a protocol called Exterior Gateway Protocol (EGP). The actual EGP protocol is now outdated, but newer routing protocols that serve exterior routers are commonly referred to as EGPs. A popular exterior gateway protocol now in use is Border Gateway Protocol (BGP). Often an exterior router is also participating as an interior router within its autonomous system.

- Interior routers—Routers within an autonomous region that share routing information are called *interior gateways*. These routers use a class of routing protocols called Interior Gateway Protocol (IGP). Examples of interior routing protocols include Routing Information Protocol (RIP) and Open Shortest Path First (OSPF). You'll learn more about RIP and OSPF later in this hour.

FIGURE 10.5
Internet router architecture.

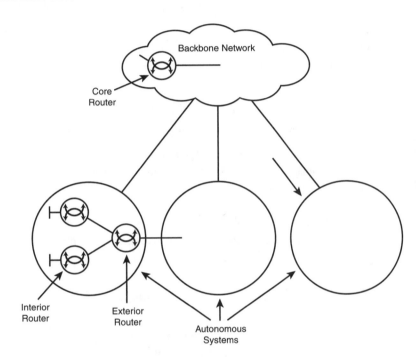

10

It is important to note that the routers within one of the autonomous networks might also have a hierarchical configuration. A large autonomous system might consist of multiple groups of interior routers with exterior routers passing routing information between the interior groups. Managers of the autonomous network are free to design a router configuration that works for the network and to choose routing protocols accordingly.

The Internet is now so complex that the tidy ARPAnet core system described in this section is something of an oversimplification. The Internet core is usually depicted as an impenetrable cloud with an autonomous network on one end and another autonomous network branching out elsewhere.

Examining Interior Routers

As you learned earlier in this hour, interior routers operate within an autonomous network. An interior router should have complete knowledge of any network segments attached to other routers within its group, but it does not need complete knowledge of networks beyond the autonomous system.

Several interior routing protocols are available. A network administrator must choose an interior routing protocol appropriate for the conditions of the network and compatible with the network hardware. The following sections discuss the important interior routing protocols:

- Routing Information Protocol (RIP)
- Open Shortest Path First (OSPF)

RIP is a distance vector protocol, and OSPF is a link state protocol. In each case, the real protocol must address details and problems that weren't discussed in the broad methodologies described earlier.

Most routers available today support multiple routing protocols.

Routing Information Protocol (RIP)

RIP is a distance vector protocol, which means that it determines the optimum route to a destination by hop count. (See the section "Distance Vector Routing," earlier in this hour.) RIP was developed at University of California, Berkeley, and originally gained popularity through the distribution of the Berkeley Systems Design (BSD) versions of Unix. RIP became an extremely popular routing protocol, and it is still used widely, though it is now considered somewhat outdated. The appearance of the RIP II standard cleared up some of the problems associated with RIP I. Many routers now support RIP I and RIP II.

RIP is implemented on Unix and Linux systems through the routed daemon.

As described earlier in this hour, RIP (as a distance vector protocol) requires routers to listen for and integrate route and hop count messages from other routers. RIP participants are classified as either active or passive. An active RIP node is typically a router participating in the normal distance vector data exchange process. The active RIP participant sends its routing table to other routers and listens for updates from other routers. A passive RIP participant listens for updates but does not propagate its own routing table.

A passive RIP node is typically a host computer. (Recall that a host needs a routing table also.)

When you read the previous discussion of distance vector routing, you may have wondered what happens when a hop count received and incremented is exactly equal to the hop count already present in the routing table. That is the kind of detail that is left to the individual protocol. In the case of RIP, if two alternative paths to the same destination have the same hop count, the route that is already present in the routing table is retained. This prevents the superfluous route oscillation that would occur if a router continually changed a routing table entry whenever there was a tie in the hop count.

A RIP router broadcasts an update message every 30 seconds. It also can request an immediate update. Like other distance vector protocols, RIP works best when the network is in equilibrium. If the number of routers becomes too large, problems can occur because of the slow convergence of the routing tables. For this reason, RIP sets a limit on the maximum number of router hops from the first router to the destination. The hop count limit in RIP is 15. This threshold limits the size of a router group, but if the routers are arranged hierarchically, it is possible to encompass a very large group in 15 hops.

Although the distance vector method does not specifically provide for considerations of line speed and physical network type, RIP lets the network administrator influence route selection by manually entering artificially large hop counts for inefficient pathways.

The venerable RIP protocol is gradually being replaced by newer routing protocols, such as OSPF, which you'll learn about in the next section.

Open Shortest Path First (OSPF)

OSPF is a more recent interior routing protocol that is gradually replacing RIP on many networks. OSPF is a link state routing protocol. OSPF first appeared in 1989 with RFC 1131. Several updates have occurred since then. The latest update of OSPF version 2 is described in RFC 2328.

Each router in an OSPF router group is assigned a *router ID*. The router ID is typically the numerically highest IP address associated with the router. (If the router uses a loopback interface, the router ID is the highest loopback address. See Hour 4 for more on loopback addresses.)

As you learned earlier in this hour, link state routers build an internal map of the network topology. Other routers use the router ID to identify a router within the topology. Each router organizes the network into a tree format with itself at the root. This network tree is known as the *Shortest Path Tree (SPT)*. Pathways through the network correspond to branching pathways through the SPT. The router computes the cost for each route. The cost metric can include parameters for the number of router hops and other considerations, such as the speed and reliability of a link.

Summary

This hour took a close look at routing. You learned about the distance vector and link state routing methods. You also learned about IP forwarding, core routers, interior routers, and exterior routers. Finally, this hour described a pair of common interior routing protocols: RIP and OSPF.

Q&A

Q Why must a computer be configured for IP forwarding in order to act as a router?

A A router receives datagrams that have addresses other than its own. Typically, the TCP/IP software will ignore a datagram if it is addressed to a different host. IP forwarding provides a means for accepting and processing datagrams that must be forwarded to other networks.

Q Why is link state routing better for larger networks?

A Distance vector routing is not efficient for large numbers of routers. Each router must maintain a complete table of destinations. Network data is altered at each step in the propagation path. Also, entire routing tables must be sent with each update even though most of the data may be unnecessary.

Q What is the purpose of the exterior router?

A The exterior router is designated to exchange routing information about the autonomous system with other autonomous systems. Assigning this role to a specific router protects the other routers in the system from having to get involved with determining routes to other networks.

Q Why does RIP set a maximum hop count of 15?

A If the number of routers becomes too large, problems can result from the slow convergence of the routers to an equilibrium state.

Key Terms

Review the following list of key terms:

autonomous system—A network participating in a larger network that is maintained by an autonomous entity.

exterior router—A router in an autonomous system that passes routing information to other autonomous systems.

interior router—A router within an autonomous system that exchanges routing information with other computers in the autonomous system.

IP forwarding—The process of passing an IP datagram from one network interface to another network interface of the same device.

OSPF—A common link state interior routing protocol.

RIP—A common distance vector interior routing protocol.

routing protocol—Any of several protocols used by routers to assemble route information.

SPT (Shortest Path Tree)—A tree-like map of the network assembled by an OSPF router.

10

HOUR 11

Name Resolution

In Hour 2, "How TCP/IP Works," you learned about name resolution, a powerful technique that associates an alphanumeric name with the 32-bit IP address. The name resolution process accepts a name for a computer and attempts to resolve the name to the corresponding address. In this hour you will learn about hostnames, domain names, and fully qualified domain names (FQDNs). You will also learn about the alternative NetBIOS name resolution system commonly used on Microsoft networks.

At the completion of this hour, you will be able to

- Explain how name resolution works
- Explain the differences between hostnames, domain names, and FQDNs
- Describe hostname resolution
- Describe DNS name resolution
- Describe NetBIOS name resolution

What Is Name Resolution?

When the early TCP/IP networks went online, users quickly realized that it was not healthy or efficient to attempt to remember the IP address of every computer on the network. The people at the research center were much too busy to have to remember whether Computer A in Building 6 had the address `100.12.8.14` or `100.12.8.18`. Computer professionals are always looking for new ways to automate tasks. Each time a programmer had to write out a note by hand, you can bet he was wondering if there was a way he could simply enter the name directly and let the computer take care of associating the name with an address.

The hostname system was developed early in the history of TCP/IP. In this system, each computer is assigned an alphanumeric name called a *hostname*. If the operating system encounters an alphanumeric name where it is expecting an IP address, the operating system consults a *hosts file* (see Figure 11.1). The hosts file contains a list of hostname-to-IP-address associations. If the alphanumeric name is on the list of hostnames, the computer reads the IP address associated with the name. The computer then replaces the hostname in the command with the corresponding IP address and executes the command.

FIGURE 11.1
Hostname resolution.

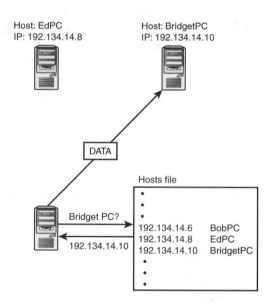

The hosts file system worked well (and still does) on small local networks. However, this system becomes inefficient on larger networks. The host-to-address associations have to reside in a single file, and the search efficiency of that file diminishes as the file expands. In ARPAnet days, a single master file called `hosts.txt` maintained a list of name-to-address associations, and local administrators had to continually update `hosts.txt` to stay current. Furthermore, the hosts name space was essentially flat. All nodes were equal, and the name resolution system could not make use of the efficient, hierarchical structure of the IP address space.

Even if the ARPAnet engineers could have solved these problems, the hosts file system could never work with a huge network with millions of nodes like the Internet. The engineers knew they needed a hierarchical name resolution system that would

- Distribute the responsibility for name resolution among a group of special name resolution servers. The name resolution servers maintain the tables that define name-to-address associations. Other computers on the network query the name resolution servers for IP address information.
- Grant authority for local name resolution to a local administrator. In other words, instead of maintaining a centralized, master copy of all name-to-address pairs, let an administrator on Network A be responsible for name resolution on Network A and let an admin of Network B configure name resolution for Network B. That way, the individuals responsible for any changes on a network are also responsible for making sure those changes are reflected in the name resolution infrastructure.

These priorities led to the development of the domain name system (DNS). DNS is the name resolution method used on the Internet and is the source of common Internet names such as `www.unixreview.com` and `www.usobi.org`. As you will learn later in this hour, DNS divides the namespace into hierarchical entities called *domains*. The domain name can be included with the hostname in what is called a *fully qualified domain names (FQDN)*. For instance, a computer with the hostname `maybe` in the domain `whitehouse.gov` would have the FQDN `maybeW.whitehouse.gov`.

This hour describes hostname resolution and DNS name resolution. You'll also learn about NetBIOS, another popular name resolution system used on Microsoft networks.

Name Resolution Using Hosts Files

As you learned earlier in this hour, a hosts file is a file containing a table that associates hostnames to IP addresses. Hostname resolution was developed before the more sophisticated DNS name resolution, but hostname resolution is still used on some networks, especially smaller networks that do not require the overhead and expense of operating DNS. Some networks may use a hosts file for local lookups and still use DNS for remote queries.

Configuring hostname resolution on a small network is usually very simple. Operating systems that support TCP/IP recognize the hosts file and use it for name resolution with

11

little or no intervention from the user. The details for configuring hostname resolution vary, depending on the implementation. The steps are roughly as follows:

1. Assign an IP address and hostname to each computer.
2. Create a hosts file that maps the IP address to the hostname of each computer. The hosts file is often named `hosts`, although some implementations use the filename `hosts.txt`.
3. Place the hosts file in the designated location on each computer. The location varies, depending on the operating system. Unix systems typically place the file in the `/etc` directory.

The hosts file contains entries for hosts that a computer needs to communicate with, allowing you to enter an IP address with a corresponding hostname, an FQDN, or other aliases statically. Also, the file usually contains an entry for the loopback address, `127.0.0.1`. The *loopback address* is used for TCP/IP diagnostics and represents "this computer."

NEW TERM To *statically* enter an IP address means that after it is entered the address must be changed manually.

The following is an example of what a hosts file might look like (the IP address of the system is on the left, followed by the hostname and an optional comment about the entry):

```
127.0.0.1               localhost               #this machine
198.1.14.2              bobscomputer            #Bob's workstation
198.1.14.128            r4downtown              #gateway
```

When an application on a computer needs to resolve a name to an IP address, the system first compares its own name to the name being requested. If there is no match, the system then looks in the hosts file (if one is present) to see if the computer name is listed.

If a match is found, the IP address is returned to the local computer and, as you learned in earlier hours, is used with ARP to obtain the hardware address of the other system. Now communication between the two can take place.

If you're using hosts files for name resolution, a change to the network forces you to edit or replace the hosts file on every computer. You can use a number of text editors to edit the hosts file. On a Unix system, use a text editor such as vi, Pico, or Emacs; on Windows, use Notepad; on DOS-based computers, use Edit. Some systems also provide TCP/IP configuration tools that act as a user interface to configure the hosts file.

When you create or edit the hosts file, be sure to keep the following points in mind:

- The IP address must be left justified and separated from the hostname by one or more spaces.
- Names must be separated by at least one space.
- Additional names on a single line become aliases for the first name.
- The file is *parsed* (that is, read by the computer) from top to bottom. The IP address associated with the first match is used. When the match is made, parsing stops.
- Because it is parsed from top to bottom, you should put the most commonly used names at the top of the list. This can help speed up the process.
- Comments might be placed to the right of a # symbol.
- Remember that the hosts file is static; you must manually change it when IP addresses change.
- Incorrectly configured hosts files (that is, typographic errors within hosts files) can cause problems with name resolution. If the wrong address is returned to the requesting application during the resolution process, the application might not function properly.
- Although FQDNs are allowed and work in hosts files, their use in hosts files is discouraged and can lead to problems that are difficult for an administrator to diagnose. The local administrator who controls the hosts file does not have any control over the allocation of IP addresses and hostnames on a remote network. Therefore, if a server on the remote network is assigned a new IP address, and the FQDN in the local hosts file is not updated, the hosts file continues to point to the old IP address.

A hosts file is a very efficient and simple way to provide name resolution for a small, isolated TCP/IP network. Some of the implementation details differ, depending on the operating system. Consult your vendor documentation.

DNS Name Resolution

The designers of DNS wanted to avoid having to keep an up-to-date name resolution file on each computer. DNS instead places name resolution data on one or more special servers. The DNS servers provide name resolution services for the network (see Figure 11.2). If a computer on the network encounters a hostname where it is expecting an IP address, it sends a query to the server asking for the IP address associated with the hostname. If the DNS server has the address, it sends the address back to the requesting computer. The computer then invisibly substitutes the IP address for the hostname and executes the command. When a change occurs on the network (such as a new computer or a change to a hostname), the network administrator only has to change the DNS configuration once (on the DNS server). The new information will then be available to any computer that initiates a DNS query to the server. Also, the DNS server can be optimized for search speed and can support a larger database than would be possible with each computer searching separately through the cumbersome hosts file.

FIGURE 11.2

A DNS server provides name resolution services for the network.

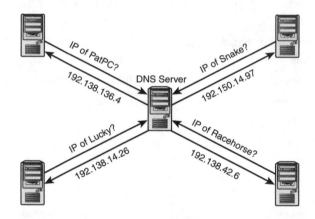

The DNS server shown in Figure 11.2 provides several advantages over hosts filename resolution. It offers a single DNS configuration point for a local network and provides more efficient use of network resources. However, the configuration shown in Figure 11.2 still does not solve the problem of providing decentralized management of a vast network infrastructure. Like the hosts file, the configuration in Figure 11.2 would not scale well to a huge network like the Internet. The name server in Figure 11.2 could not operate efficiently with a database that included a record for every host on the Internet. Even if it could, the logistics of maintaining an all-Internet database would be prohibitive. Whoever configured the server would have to know about every change to any Internet host anywhere in the world.

A better solution, reasoned the designers, was to let every office or institution configure a local name server to operate as shown in Figure 11.2 and then to provide a means for all the name servers to talk to each other (see Figure 11.3). In this scenario, when a DNS client sends a name resolution request to a name server, the name server does one of the following:

- If the name server can find the requested address in its own address database, it immediately sends the address to the client.

- If the name server cannot find the address in its own records, it queries other name servers to find the address and then sends the address to the client.

You may be wondering how the first name server knows which name server to contact when it begins the query process that will lead to the address.

FIGURE 11.3

On large networks, DNS servers communicate with each other to provide name resolution services.

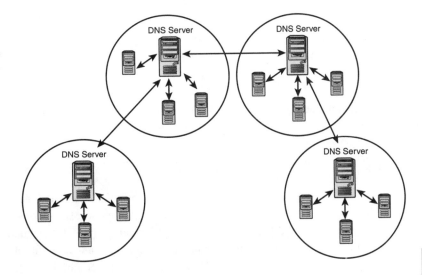

Actually, this query process is closely associated with the design of the DNS namespace. Keep in mind that DNS is not working strictly with a hostname. As described earlier in this hour, DNS works with :fully qualified domain names (FQDNs). An FQDN consists of both a hostname and a name specifying the domain.

The DNS namespace is a multitiered arrangement of domains (see Figure 11.4). A domain is a collection of computers under a single authority sharing a common portion of the namespace (that is, bearing the same domain name). At the top of the DNS tree is a single node known as *root*. Root is sometimes shown as a period (.), although the actual symbol for root is a null character. Beneath root is a group of domains known as *top level domains (TLDs)*. Figure 11.4 shows some of the TLDs for the world's most famous DNS namespace: the Internet. Top level domains include the familiar .com, .org, and .edu domains, as well as domains for national governments, such as .us (United States), .uk (United Kingdom), .fr (France), and .jp (Japan).

A new crop of top level domains was recently announced, including .biz, .coop, .info, and .museum.

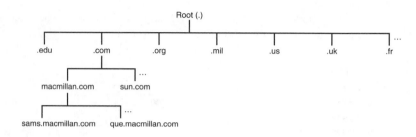

Beneath each of these top level domains is another tier of domains that (in the case of the Internet) are operated by companies, institutions, or organizations. The institutional name is prefixed to the top level domain name. For instance, in Figure 11.5, DeSade College has the domain name `DeSade.edu`. The organization with authority over a domain can create one or more additional tiers of subdomains. At each level, the name of the local domain is prefixed to the parent domain name. For example, the department of recreational pyrotechnics at DeSade has the domain name `flames.DeSade.edu` (refer to Figure 11.5), and the department's popular lounge (which the students affectionately call "the dungeon") has the name `dungeon.flames.DeSade.edu`. In all, DNS system supports up to 127 levels of domains, although a name of that length would evoke agony.

FIGURE 11.5

An appropriate DNS scenario.

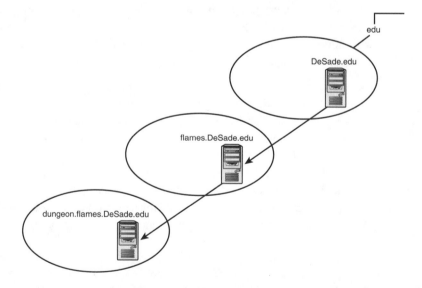

If you've worked much with the Internet, you have probably noticed that extended domain names with several levels (such as the scenario shown in Figure 11.5) are relatively uncommon. Web sites, especially in the crowded .com TLD, are typically referenced as the institutional domain name with the www prefix: www.ibm.com. However, keep in mind that a Web site might be served from a single server or group of servers at a single location. Multitiered domain names are encountered more commonly by network admins accessing resources on a large corporate network that spans several locations. TLDs in the public sector (such .gov) tend to make more use of multitiered names.

The domain name shows the chain of domains from the top of the tree. The name server in the domain sams.com holds name resolution information for hosts located in sams.com. The authoritative name server for a domain can delegate name resolution for a subdomain to another server. For instance, the authoritative name server in sams.com can delegate authority for the subdomain edit.sams.com to another name server. The name resolution records for the subdomain edit.sams.com are then located on the name server that has been delegated authority for the subdomain. Authority for name resolution is thus delegated throughout the tree, and the administrators for a given domain can have control of name-to-address mappings for the hosts in that domain.

When a host on the network needs an IP address, it usually sends what is called a *recursive* query to a nearby name server. This query tells the name server, "either give me the IP address associated with this name or else tell me that you can't find it." If the name server cannot find the requested address among its own records, it initiates a process of querying other name servers to obtain the address. This process is shown in Figure 11.6. Name server A is using what is called an iterative query to find the address. An *iterative* query tells the next name server "either send me the IP address or give me a clue to where I might find it."

The process for DNS name resolution is as follows (refer to Figure 11.6):

1. Host1 sends a query to name server A asking for the IP address associated with the domain name trog.DogInStarlight.marines.mil.

2. Name server A checks its own records to see if it has the requested address. If server A has the address, it returns the address to Host1.

3. If name server A does not have the address, it initiates the process of finding the address. Name server A sends an iterative request for the address to name server B, a top level name server for the .mil domain, asking for the address associated with the name trog.DogInStarlight.marines.mil.

FIGURE 11.6

The name resolution process.

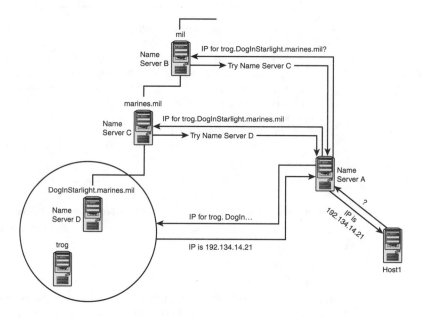

4. Name server B is not able to supply the address, but it is able to send name server A the address of name server C, the name server for marines.mil.

5. Name server A sends a request for the address to name server C. Name server C is not able to supply the address, but it is able to send the address of name server D, the name server for DogInStarlight.marines.com.

6. Name server A sends a request for the IP address to name server D. Name server D looks up the address for the host trog.DogInStarlight.marines.mil and sends the address to name server A. Name server A then sends the address to Host1.

7. Host1 initiates a connection to the host trog.DogInStarlight.marines.mil.

This process occurs thousands (if not millions) of times a day on the Internet. This tidy scenario is complicated somewhat by some additional features of the modern network, including address caching, DHCP, and dynamic DNS. However, the functionality of most TCP/IP networks depends on this form of DNS name resolution.

It is also important to note that the network is not required to have a separate name server for each node on the domain tree. A single name server can handle multiple domains. It is also common for multiple name servers to serve a single domain.

Registering a Domain

The Internet is only one example of a DNS namespace. You do not have to be connected to the Internet to use DNS. If you are not connected to the Internet, you do not have to worry about registering your domain names. However, organizations that want to use their own domain names (such as BuddysCars.com) must register that name with the proper registration authority.

ICANN oversees the task of domain name registration but delegates registration for particular TLDs to other groups. Registration services for a number of commonly used TLDs are listed here.

- **.com, .org, and .net** A number of companies are authorized to provide domain name resolution services for the popular .com, .org, and .net TLDs. See the ICANN Web site at www.icann.com.
- **.gov** The .gov domain is reserved for the U.S. federal government. State and local government names branch from the U.S. TLD. Registration services for the .gov domain are located at www.registration.fed.gov.
- **.mil** The .mil domain is reserved for the United States military. Registration services are located at www.nic.mil.

Managing DNS

When implementing DNS on your network, you need to choose at least one server to be responsible for maintaining your domain. This is referred to as your *primary name server*, and it gets all the information about the zones it is responsible for from local files. Any changes you make to your domain are made on this server.

Many networks also have at least one more server as a backup, or *secondary name server*. If something happens to your primary server, this machine can continue to service requests. The secondary server gets its information from the primary server's zone file. When this exchange of information takes place, it is referred to as a *zone transfer*.

A third type of server is called a *caching-only* server. A *cache* is part of a computer's memory that keeps frequently requested data ready to be accessed. As a caching-only server, it responds to queries from clients on the local network for name resolution requests. It queries other DNS servers for information about domains and computers that offer services such as Web and FTP. When it receives information from other DNS servers, it stores that information in its cache in case a request for that information is made again.

11

Caching-only servers are used by client computers on the local network to resolve names. Other DNS servers on the Internet will not know about them and therefore will not query them. This is desirable if you want to distribute the load your servers are put under. A caching-only server is also simple to maintain, if for instance you have a remote site where client computers need name resolution services and nothing more.

The cache is preconfigured with the IP addresses of nine root-level DNS servers. If this computer has access to the Internet via a router, it is ready to work. Client computers could include the IP address of this DNS server in their search order list, and this DNS server would begin to service requests by contacting other DNS servers and automatically adding entries to its cache.

> DNS must be implemented as a service or daemon running on the DNS server machine. Windows NT and Windows 2000 have a DNS service, though some Microsoft admins prefer to use third-party DNS implementations. The Unix world has a number of DNS implementation options, but the most popular choice is Berkeley Internet Name Domain (BIND).

Configuring the DNS Server

Zone files contain the information that tells the DNS service how to respond to queries from local clients and other DNS servers. You use the zone file to define the server's zone of authority. A *zone file* is a text file with a standardized structure that contains records for all the computers and services that server is responsible for. You also use this file to add entries in order to make new computers available to the DNS.

In a domain with a small number of computers, the zone file probably contains all the entries for the domain. This is often the case, so it can be easy to confuse a zone and a domain for the same thing. However, the computers in a domain could be separated into two zones, with each zone residing on a different DNS server.

For example, say Lasting Impressions is a large company with offices in New York and Los Angeles. The computers in both cities would be in the lastingimpressions.com domain, but their DNS entries need to be managed locally. The solution would be a zone file managed by a DNS server in New York with records for all the computers in that office and a zone file on a DNS server in Los Angeles with entries for that office's computers. Each DNS server would then respond only to requests for computers within its zone.

Resource Records

The entries contained in a zone file are known as *resource records*. Different resource records are used to identify what type of computer or service an entry represents. Each resource record type has a specific purpose. For example, an A type resource record indicates the IP address associated with the hostname. A CNAME record is an alias. (*CNAME* stands for canonical name.) If a user enters `Web server.lastingimpressions.com`, your DNS server will supply the correct IP address. However, you don't want users to have to know the names of your servers, so aliases are often used that point to the actual server. In this case you want users to enter `www.lastingimpressions.com` but to be directed to `Web server.lastingimpressions.com`. Other important resource record types include those associated with name server (NS), e-mail exchange (MX records), and the responsible person (RP record) for this DNS server.

One resource record that every DNS server contains is a *Start of Authority (SOA)* record. This record, which is always first in a zone file, defines what entity is responsible from that point in the hierarchy downward. Figure 11.7 shows three resource records as created on a Windows NT DNS server. The NS resource record identifies the computer located at `dnsserver.lastingimpressions.com` as a DNS server. The SOA resource record identifies your name server to be authoritative for the `lastingimpressions.com` domain. The A resource record supplies the IP address for the hostname `dnsserver`.

11

FIGURE 11.7

Resource records created during zone creation.

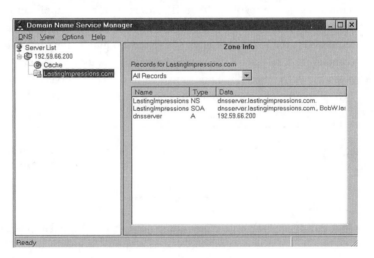

The Reverse Lookup Zone File

One type of zone file used on DNS servers is the reverse lookup file. This file is used when a client provides an IP address and requests the corresponding hostname. In IP addresses, the leftmost portion is general, and the rightmost portion is specific. However, in domain names the opposite is true: The left portion is specific, and the right portion, such as com or edu, is general. To create a reverse lookup zone file you must reverse the order of the network address so the general and specific portions follow the same pattern used within domain names. For example, the zone for the 192.59.66.0 network would have the name 66.59.192.in-addr.arpa.

Every resource record in this file always has the host ID followed by .in-addr.arpa. The in-addr portion stands for *inverse address*, and the arpa portion is another top level domain and is a holdover from the original ARPAnet that preceded the Internet.

> Class A and B networks have shorter reverse lookup zone names due to the fact that they contain fewer network bits. For example, in the Class A network 43.0.0.0, the reverse lookup zone must have the name 43.in-addr.arpa. In the Class B network 172.58.0.0, the reverse lookup zone must have the name 58.172.in-addr.arpa.

Configuring the DNS Client

Another important aspect of DNS is the process of enabling a client computer to use it.

When a user enters a name in an application such as a Web browser or an FTP client, the name needs to be resolved to an IP address before the application can continue. By default this name is first compared to the local hostname to determine if the destination requested is the local computer. If there is no match, the hosts file (if present) is then scanned for a match on the name entered by the user. If the name doesn't match any hosts file entry, then the names are sent to the DNS servers for resolution, but only if TCP/IP on the client computer has been configured to use DNS.

> When a client is configured to use DNS to resolve names, it becomes a *resolver.* A resolver passes name resolution requests between applications on a system and DNS servers.

Configuring TCP/IP on a client computer to use DNS is simply the process of adding the IP addresses of one or more DNS servers in the proper location. The following is an example of how to configure a computer to use a DNS server. This example is on a computer running Windows NT:

1. Choose the Network icon from Control Panel. From the Networks dialog box, choose the Protocols tab, then the TCP/IP Protocol, and then Properties. Finally, choose the DNS property sheet from the Microsoft TCP/IP Properties dialog box.

2. The DNS property sheet appears as shown in Figure 11.8. If you have not already done so, you should enter the hostname and domain name in the two fields provided for that purpose.

FIGURE 11.8

The DNS property sheet on Windows NT.

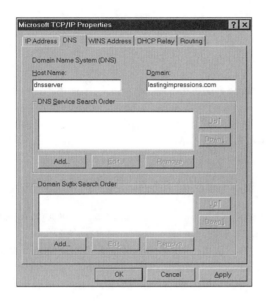

3. To add the IP addresses for one or more DNS servers, choose the Add button in the DNS Service Search Order frame.

   The dialog box shown in Figure 11.9 is presented; enter an IP address and add it to the existing list of DNS servers. When two or more DNS servers are referenced, you can arrange their order.

   When a client uses DNS to resolve a name to an address, the top DNS server is searched first, then the second DNS server is searched, and so on until either a match is found or all DNS servers have been searched.

FIGURE 11.9

TCP/IP DNS Server dialog box.

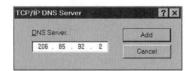

On Unix computers, the client application initiates the process of name resolution on the client computer. To configure a Unix DNS client, you must create a file called /etc/resolv.conf. The resolv.conf file contains the name of the local domain and the

IP addresses of any available DNS servers. The domain name is prefaced with the word domain, and the IP address of a name server is prefaced with the word nameserver. An example of a resolv.conf file is

```
domain whitehouse.gov

nameserver 114.12.120.6

nameserver 114.12.120.8
```

When a client application needs an IP address, it consults the resolv.conf file to get the address of a name server that will supply the necessary information. The domain entry in resolv.conf (showing the local domain name) is used as the default domain name. If a hostname is given in unqualified form (without the domain name), the default domain name is appended to the hostname for DNS name resolution.

DNS Utilities

You can use any network utility that supports name resolution to test whether your network is resolving names properly. A Web browser, an FTP client, a Telnet client, or the Ping utility can tell you whether your computer is succeeding with name resolution. If you can connect to a resource using its IP address but you cannot connect to the resource using a hostname or FQDN, there is a good chance the problem is a name resolution problem.

If your computer uses a hosts file and also uses DNS, keep in mind that you need to disable or rename the hosts file temporarily when you test DNS. Otherwise it will not be easy to determine whether the name was resolved through the hosts file or DNS. The following section describes how to use ping to test DNS. A later section describes the NSLookup utility, which provides a number of DNS configuration and troubleshooting features.

Checking Name Resolution with Ping

The simple and useful ping utility is a good candidate for testing your DNS configuration. Ping sends a signal to another computer and waits for a reply. If a reply arrives, you know that the two computers are connected. If you know the IP address of a remote computer, you can ping the computer by IP address:

```
ping 198.1.14.2
```

If this command succeeds, you know your computer can connect to the remote computer by IP address.

Now try to ping the remote computer by DNS name:

```
ping williepc.remotenet.com
```

If you can ping the remote computer by IP address but not by DNS name, you may have a name resolution problem. If you can ping by DNS name, name resolution is working properly.

You'll learn more about ping in Hour 13, "Connectivity Utilities."

Checking Name Resolution with NSLookup

The NSLookup utility enables you to query DNS servers and view information such as their resource records, and it is useful when troubleshooting DNS problems. The NSLookup utility operates in two modes:

- **Batch mode**   In Batch mode you start NSLookup and provide input parameters. NSLookup performs the functions requested by the input parameters, displays the results, and then terminates.

- **Interactive mode**   In Interactive mode you start NSLookup without supplying input parameters. NSLookup then prompts you for parameters. When you enter the parameters, NSLookup performs the requested actions, displays the results, returns to a prompt, and waits for the next set of parameters. Most administrators use Interactive mode because it is more convenient when performing a series of actions.

NSLookup has an extensive list of options. A few basic options covered here give you a feel for how NSLookup works.

To run NSLookup in Interactive mode, enter the name `nslookup` from a command prompt.

As shown in Figure 11.10, each NSLookup response starts with the name and IP address of the DNS server that NSLookup is currently using, for example

```
Default Server:    dnsserver.Lastingimpressions.com
Address:    192.59.66.200
>
```

The chevron character (>) is NSLookup's prompt.

11

FIGURE **11.10**

NSLookup responses.

NSLookup has about 15 settings that you can change to affect how NSLookup operates. A few of the most commonly used settings are listed here:

- **?; help**   These commands are used to view a list of all NSLookup commands.

- **server**   This command specifies which DNS server to query.

- **ls**   This command is used to list the names in a domain, as shown near the middle of Figure 11.10.

- **ls -a**   This command lists canonical names and aliases in a domain, as shown in Figure 11.10.

- **ls -d**   This command lists all resource records, as shown near the bottom of Figure 11.10.

- **set all**   This command displays the current value of all settings.

NSLookup is not restricted to viewing information from your DNS server; you can view information from virtually any DNS server. If you have an Internet service provider (ISP), you should have IP addresses for at least two DNS servers. NSLookup can use either IP addresses or domain names. You can switch NSLookup to another DNS server by entering the server command followed by either the IP address or the FQDN. For instance, to connect NSLookup to the E root server, you can enter server 192.203.230.10. Then you can enter virtually any domain name, such as samspublishing.com, and see the IP addresses registered for that domain name. Be aware that most commercial DNS servers and root servers will refuse ls commands because they can generate a tremendous amount of traffic and may pose a security leak.

Dynamic DNS

DNS, as it has been described so far, is designed for situations in which there is a permanent (or at least semi-permanent) association of a hostname with an IP address. In today's networks (as you'll learn in the next hour), IP addresses are often assigned dynamically. In other words, a new IP address is assigned to a computer through Dynamic Host Configuration Protocol (DHCP) each time the computer starts. This means that if the computer is to be registered with DNS and accessible by its hostname, the DNS server must have some way to learn the IP address the computer is using.

The recent popularity of dynamic IP addressing has forced DNS vendors to adapt. Some IP implementations (including BIND) now offer dynamic update of DNS records. In a typical scenario (see Figure 11.11), the DHCP server assigns an IP address to the client and then updates the DNS server with the client's address.

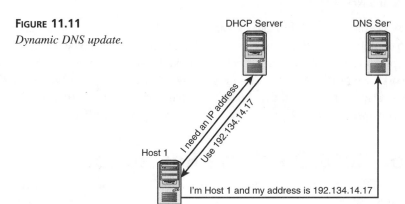

FIGURE 11.11
Dynamic DNS update.

Microsoft Windows 2000 Server also offers dynamic DNS. In fact, dynamic DNS is an essential feature in Windows 2000's DNS-based Active Directoryenvironment.

NetBIOS Name Resolution

As you Learned in Hour 7, "The Application Layer," NetBIOS is an API and name resolution system originally developed by IBM that is common on Microsoft Windows networks. The NetBIOS name is the computer name you assign to your Windows computer. The NetBIOS computer name is used to identify the computer in Explorer and My Computer. NetBIOS was developed for networks that don't use TCP/IP. The NetBIOS name system is actually a little redundant on TCP/IP networks because the NetBIOS name serves a role that is similar to the role of the hostname. Microsoft has de-emphasized NetBIOS in

Windows 2000 and will probably continue to favor native TCP/IP name resolution in the future. NetBIOS, however, is still extremely popular on Microsoft networks. The principal reasons for this continued popularity are as follows:

- **Built-in support**   Windows utilities such as Explorer are designed to work with NetBIOS names. Other built-in Windows features, such as file and print sharing, are designed around NetBIOS.
- **Dynamic update**   NetBIOS performs dynamic name resolution. Name resolution tables are updated for the current state of the network. As you learned in a previous section, dynamic DNS is now available also, but dynamic DNS is relatively new. You do not need a server for dynamic NetBIOS name resolution. The computers on a single network segment can resolve NetBIOS names through broadcast.
- **Interoperablility**   NetBIOS can be used with other network protocol suites, such as IPX/SPX and NetBEUI.

Because NetBIOS operates through broadcasts, the user on a small network doesn't have to do anything to configure NetBIOS name resolution (other than setting up networking and assigning a computer name). On a larger network, though, NetBIOS is more complex. Large networks use NetBIOS name servers called WINS servers for NetBIOS name resolution. You can also configure a static LMHosts file (similar to the hosts file) for name resolution lookups. The following sections take a closer look at NetBIOS.

Methods for NetBIOS Name Resolution

On TCP/IP networks, the ultimate goal of NetBIOS name resolution is to provide an IP address for a given NetBIOS name.

NetBIOS names are single names up to 15 characters in length, such as Workstation1, HRServer, and CorpServer. NetBIOS does not allow for duplicate computer names on a network.

> Technically there are 16 characters in a NetBIOS name. However, the sixteenth character is used by the underlying application and in general is not directly configurable by the user. These characters are discussed later in this hour.

NetBIOS names, like hostnames, are said to be in a flat namespace, because there is no hierarchy or capability to qualify the names. In the following sections you will examine several ways to resolve NetBIOS names to their corresponding IP addresses:

- Broadcast-based name resolution
- LMHosts filename resolution
- WINS name resolution

Broadcast-Based Name Resolution

One way for name resolution to take place is through broadcasts. A *broadcast* occurs when a computer announces to all the other machines on its network segment that it needs the address of a particular computer. All the computers on the segment hear the broadcast, but only the machine specified in the broadcast responds to the request.

This method of name resolution, also known as *B-Node name resolution*, works well in a LAN environment but does not work in networks that extend beyond the LAN, due to the fact that routers, by design, block broadcasts.

> Broadcasts can produce a great deal of network traffic, which can be disruptive to the network. Routers limit this disruption by not forwarding broadcasts to the rest of the network.

11

The broadcast name resolution process is simple and requires no extra configuration to set up or use. Simply installing a network card and TCP/IP networking software onto a Windows for Workgroups, Windows 95/98, Windows NT, or Windows 2000 operating system enables these systems to use broadcasts to locate other computers through NetBIOS name resolution.

LMHosts Files Name Resolution

Windows systems can also resolve NetBIOS names to IP addresses using the LMHosts file. The LMHosts file is similar to the hosts file (described earlier in this hour). An LMHosts file associates NetBIOS names to IP addresses. The IP address is listed in the left column of the file with the corresponding computer name to the right separated by at least one space; comments can be put in the file by placing them after a # character. LMHosts requires a static mapping of IP addresses to NetBIOS names. A separate LMHosts file resides on each computer. You have to manually configure the LMHosts file. If a new computer is added to the network, the other computer will not be able to find it through LMHosts until an entry for that computer is manually added to each LMHosts file.

On a network consisting of a single segment, an LMHosts file is usually not necessary, because computers on the network can resolve NetBIOS names through broadcast. (In some cases, LMHosts can be used for efficiency or for compatibility with older, non-broadcasting systems.) On larger networks consisting of more than one segment, broadcast cannot be used to resolve names beyond the router. In that case, computers must perform NetBIOS name resolution using either LMHosts or a WINS server (described in the next section). In some cases, LMHosts is useful for pointing the way to a domain controller on a different network segment. (A domain controller is necessary for authentication in a domain-based Windows environment.)

On Windows systems, the LMHosts file is included with Microsoft TCP/IP. Microsoft also includes a sample LMHosts file named LMHosts.sam. You can edit the LMHosts.sam file, but you must drop the .sam extension before the file is usable.

> The LM in LMHosts is a holdover from Microsoft's LAN Manager, a networking product that predates Windows NT.

The following is an example of what a basic LMHosts file looks like:

```
192.59.66.205     marketserv     #file server for marketing department
192.59.66.206     marketapp      #application server for marketing
192.59.66.207     bobscomputer    #bob's workstation
```

Recently resolved NetBIOS names are stored in the NetBIOS name cache. A cache is part of a computer's memory that keeps frequently requested data in memory and ready to be accessed. Whenever a user attempts to locate a specific computer, the system always consults the NetBIOS name cache before searching the LMHosts file. If no match is found, the entries within the LMHosts file can then be scanned for the requested name. This can be a time-consuming process if there are many entries in the LMHosts file, so to speed up the process you can designate certain high-use entries to be preloaded into the NetBIOS name cache by including the #PRE keyword (see Figure 11.12). The LMHosts file is scanned once in its entirety when networking starts, so for efficiency the lines that include #PRE keywords are usually placed toward the bottom of the LMHosts file. These lines need to be read only once, and placing them later in the file lessens the chance that they will be reread.

> You can use the NBTStat utility to view and manipulate the NetBIOS name cache. To view the contents of the cache, type **nbtstat -c** at the command prompt.

Maintaining static files such as hosts and LMHosts is difficult because these files are located on each individual computer and therefore are not centralized. The LMHosts file addresses this problem by using the keyword #INCLUDE followed by an entry for the path to LMHosts files on other machines. With this keyword, the local LMHosts file can include the location of a server-based LMHosts file for use by the local machine. This enables edits to be performed on the server-based LMHosts file, but the changes are accessible from the user's computer.

If there is more than one #INCLUDE entry, they need to be placed between the keywords #BEGIN ALTERNATE and #END ALTERNATE, as shown in Figure 11.12.

FIGURE 11.12

Contents of an LMHosts file.

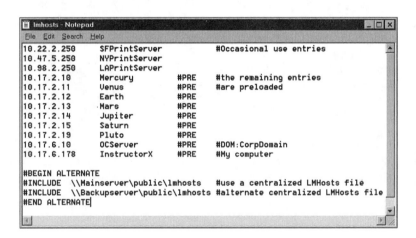

As mentioned previously, LMHosts can be used to locate a Windows domain controller on a different network segment. The #DOM keyword identifies an LMHosts entry that represents a domain controller.

Windows Internet Name Service (WINS) Name Resolution

Windows Internet Name Service (WINS) was created to address the same types of short-comings in LMHosts that DNS was created to address regarding hosts files. When a client needs to get the IP address for a computer, it can query the WINS server for the information.

> WINS is the name assigned to Microsoft's implementation of what is generically known as a NetBIOS name server or NBNS. NetBIOS name servers are described in RFCs 1001 and 1002.

WINS maintains a database of registered NetBIOS names for a variety of objects, including users, computers, services running on those computers, and workgroups. However, instead of the entries in this database coming from manually edited text files, as in most DNS implementations, a client computer registers its name and IP address with the WINS server dynamically when it starts up.

The WINS server receives and responds to NetBIOS name resolution requests (see Figure 11.13). If the WINS server in Figure 11.13 looks similar to the DNS server in Figure 11.2, that is because it is. A WINS server does for NetBIOS name resolution what the DNS server does for domain name resolution. However, the flat NetBIOS namespace provides no equivalent to the hierarchical name resolution techniques available through DNS.

FIGURE **11.13**
WINS NetBIOS name
resolution.

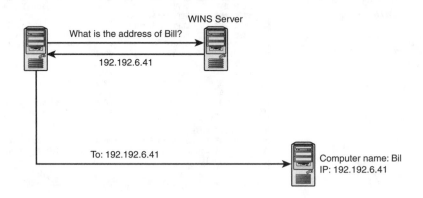

Microsoft introduced a form of DNS/WINS integration with Windows NT 4 that provided DNS name resolution over a larger network combined with automatic NetBIOS resolution. The further integration of DNS with NetBIOS in the Windows 2000 Active Directory environment makes this feature largely unnecessary.

To configure a Windows computer to use WINS, you enter the IP address of one (or two) WINS server in the WINS Address Property tab or the TCP/IP Properties dialog box. After this is finished and the computer has rebooted, it is now considered a WINS client.

When a WINS client computer boots after being configured to use WINS, the following process occurs:

1. **Service startup**   As the computer boots, various services are started, some of which need to be made known to other computers.

2. **Registration request**   To be known to other computers on the network, the service must register itself. A WINS client computer packages the NetBIOS name and the computer's IP address inside a name registration request, and the registration request is sent to the WINS server. Upon receiving the registration request, WINS checks its database to see if the name is already registered.

   If the name does not exist, WINS adds the NetBIOS name and IP address pair to its database and sends a name registration response indicating the name was successfully registered. If the requested NetBIOS name already exists in the WINS database, WINS challenges the computer currently registered by sending a message to the registered IP address. If the currently registered computer responds, a negative acknowledgement is sent to the computer attempting to register the name. If the computer being challenged doesn't respond, WINS allows the registration to occur and overwrites the previous registration.

3. **Lease**   Assuming the computer is successful in registering its NetBIOS names and services with WINS, these names are considered leased. In essence, the computer is allowed to use the NetBIOS name for a specified period of time—for instance six days—but the client can renew the lease before it expires. The client typically renews the lease at 50% of the total lease time or in this case every three days.

Earlier I noted that the sixteenth character of a NetBIOS name is not configurable by the user. During the WINS registration process, the sixteenth character is appended to the name by the WINS server based on what type of service the computer is trying to register before it is placed in the database. Between computer names, workgroup names, and a number of services, it is not unusual for a single computer to have 5 to 10 registration entries in the WINS database.

As another example of the WINS name resolution process, suppose a user on a computer uses a utility such as Network Neighborhood to connect to another computer on the network. A name query request, which includes the desired NetBIOS name, is constructed by the application and sent to the WINS server. When WINS receives the request, it queries its database for a matching registration. If the requested name is found, WINS returns the corresponding IP address in the response packet. After the client computer has the IP address for the requested computer, the client can then communicate directly.

11

One nice feature of WINS is that it works well in both local and remote networks and can be integrated with DNS. However, that discussion is beyond the scope of this book. What I have done here is given you a basic overview of WINS as it relates to name resolution.

Testing NetBIOS Name Resolution

You can test NetBIOS name resolution using NetBIOS-based utilities. One typical test of name resolution is using the `net view` command, which enables you to view the share point names on a server. (Remember that a *share point* is a directory where client computers can connect with another computer to view or exchange files.) To perform this test, choose a computer that has one or more share points. At a command prompt, type

`net view \\computername`

where `computername` is the name of the computer you selected. If `net view` is capable of resolving the computer name to an IP address, you should see the names of share points listed in the first command and response.

You can also use the ubiquitous Ping utility to test NetBIOS name resolution. On most Windows systems, if NetBIOS name resolution is working properly, you should be able to ping a computer by its NetBIOS computer name. For instance, if a computer has the computer name `Shirley`, you should be able to type

`ping Shirley`

and receive a response.

Summary

Name resolution enables the use of meaningful, easy-to-remember names for computers instead of the IP address assigned to a computer. This hour described name resolution by hostname and also through DNS. You also learned about the NetBIOS name resolution system used on Microsoft networks.

Q&A

Q What is a domain name?

A It is a name that is administered by a central authority to ensure the name's uniqueness. The first part of the name identifies or is related to a company or organization. The second portion of a domain name is a suffix such as `com`, `gov`, or `edu` that provides a means of classification.

Q What is a hostname?

A It is a single name that is assigned to a particular host. Usually the hostname has some meaning such as location, usage, or ownership.

Q What is an FQDN?

A A combination of a hostname concatenated to a domain name by the addition of a dot character. For example, a hostname `bigserver` and a domain name `mycompany.com` when combined become the FQDN `bigserver.mycompany.com`.

Q What are DNS resource records?

A Resource records are the entries contained in a DNS zone file. Different resource records are used to identify different types of computers or services.

Q What type of resource record is used for an alias? Why are aliases used?

A CNAME; it is used to represent the real name of a computer on a network.

Q What is a caching-only server?

A A caching-only server responds to queries from clients on the local network for name resolution requests and stores that information in its cache in case a request for that information is made again. Caching-only servers are not registered as DNS servers, so other DNS servers don't know about them and therefore won't query them.

Q What is the role of a resolver?

A A resolver passes name resolution requests between the applications on a system and DNS servers.

Q How do you centrally administer entries in an LMHosts file?

A You can implement centralized administration by adding several lines to the LMHosts files found on each local computer. A line that starts with `#INCLUDE` and contains a UNC name of an LMHosts file located on a server provides a link to the central file.

Q How can you create static NetBIOS entries in the NetBIOS name cache?

A By using the keyword `#PRE` on the line of the desired entry in an LMHosts file.

Workshop

- At the command line of your computer, enter the command `ping localhost` and write down the IP address that you see.

- At the command line of your computer, enter the command `hostname` and write down the hostname that is returned. On Windows 95/98, the hostname does not work, but it is visible from WinIPCfg.

11

- Enter a `ping` command followed by the hostname for your computer.
- If you computer has a domain name, ping your FQDN.
- Enter the commands - `ping router`, - `ping gateway`, - `ping exit ramp`.
- Determine if IP is configured to use a DNS server. If so try the following pings:
  ```
  ping www.internic.net
  ping www.whitehouse.gov
  ```
- Use NSLookup to connect to one of your ISP's DNS servers.

Key Terms

Review the following list of key terms:

DNS (domain name system)—A system for naming resources on TCP/IP networks.

domain name—A name assigned to a hierarchical partition of the DNS namespace.

FQDN (fully qualified domain names)—The name generated by concatenating a hostname with a domain name.

hostname—A single name used to identify a computer (host).

LMHosts—A file that associates IP addresses to NetBIOS names.

resource record—An entry added to zone files. There are a number of resource record types, and each type has a specific purpose.

WINS (Windows Internet Naming Service)—A WINS server is a Microsoft implementation of a NetBIOS name server.

zone file—The configuration files used by DNS servers. These text files are used to configure DNS servers. One zone file is created for each domain name. A single DNS server can support multiple domains and therefore multiple zone files simultaneously.

Hour 12

Dynamic Host Configuration Protocol (DHCP)

The Dynamic Host Configuration Protocol (DHCP) enables computers to receive TCP/IP configuration settings automatically. A DHCP server computer can configure a DHCP client with an IP address and a subnet mask. The DHCP client also can receive other settings from DHCP, such as IP addresses for the default gateway, DNS servers, and WINS servers.

In this hour you will learn what DHCP is, how DHCP works, why it is important, and in what situations DHCP is most useful.

At the completion of this hour, you will be able to

- Describe what DHCP is and what benefits it provides
- Describe the process involved when a DHCP client leases an IP address
- Explain what a DHCP scope is
- Describe the process of configuring a DHCP server

The Case for Server-Supplied IP Addresses

Every computer, as you learned in a previous hour, must have an IP address in order to operate on a TCP/IP network. The IP addressing system was originally designed for the very logical condition in which each computer is preconfigured with an IP address. This condition is known as *static* IP addressing. Each computer knows its IP address from the moment it boots and is able to use the network immediately. Static IP addressing works well for small, permanent networks, but on larger networks that are subject to reconfiguration and change (such as new computers coming and going from the network), static IP addressing has some limitations.

The principal shortcomings of static IP addressing are

- More configuration: Each client must be configured individually. A change to the IP address space or to some other parameter (such as the DNS server address) means that each client must be reconfigured separately.

- More addresses: Each computer uses an IP address whether it is currently on the network or not.

- Reduced flexibility: A computer must be manually reconfigured each time it accesses a different network.

As an answer to these limitations, an alternative IP addressing system has evolved in which IP addresses are assigned upon request using the DHCP protocol. DHCP was developed from an earlier protocol called BOOTP, which was used primarily to boot diskless computers. (A diskless computer receives a complete operating system over the network as it boots.) DHCP has become increasingly popular in recent years because of the dwindling supply of IP addresses and the growth of large, dynamic networks.

What Is DHCP?

DHCP is a protocol used to automatically assign TCP/IP configuration parameters to computers. DHCP is a standard described in RFC 1531. Three other RFCs—1534, 2131, and 2132—address enhancement and specific vendor implementations of DHCP. A DHCP server can supply a DHCP client with a number of TCP/IP settings, such as an IP address, subnet mask, and DNS server.

Because the DHCP server is assigning the IP addresses, only the DHCP server must be configured with IP address information. The only parameter you need to configure on the client end is an option for the client to receive IP address information from the server. The rest of the configuration takes place on the server side. If some aspect of the TCP/IP configuration changes on the network, the network administrator needs only to update the DHCP server, rather than updating each client manually.

Furthermore, each client receives a lease of finite duration for the address. If the client is no longer using the address when the lease expires, the address can be assigned to another client. The effect of DHCP's leasing feature is that, typically, a network will not need as many IP addresses as it has clients.

DHCP is especially important in today's environment, in which many employees carry notebook computers between offices of a large corporation. If a laptop computer is configured with a static IP address, it must be reconfigured each time the traveling employee plugs into a different network. If the computer is configured to receive an IP address through DHCP, the laptop automatically receives a complete TCP/IP configuration each time the user attaches to a network with a DHCP server.

How DHCP Works

When a DHCP client computer is started, the TCP/IP software is loaded into memory and starts to operate. However, because TCP/IP has not been given an IP address yet, it is incapable of sending or receiving directed datagrams. TCP/IP can, however, transmit and listen for broadcasts. This capability to communicate via broadcasts is the basis for how DHCP works. The process of leasing an IP address from the DHCP server involves four steps:

1. **DHCPDISCOVER** The DHCP client initiates the process by broadcasting a datagram destined for UDP port 68 (used by BOOTP and DHCP servers). This first datagram is known as a DHCP Discover message, which is a request to any DHCP server that receives the datagram for configuration information. The DHCP discover datagram contains many fields, but the one that is most important contains the physical address of the DHCP client.

2. **DHCPOFFER** A DHCP server configured to lease addresses for the network on which the client computer resides constructs a response datagram known as a DHCP offer and sends it via broadcast to the computer that issued the DHCP discover. This broadcast is sent to UDP port 67 and contains the physical address of the DHCP client. Also contained in the DHCP offer are the physical and IP addresses of the DHCP server, as well as the values for the IP address and subnet mask that are being offered to the DHCP client.

At this point it is possible for the DHCP client to receive several DHCP offers, assuming there are multiple DHCP servers with the capability to offer the DHCP client an IP address. In most cases, the DHCP client accepts the first DHCP offer that arrives.

12

3. **DHCPREQUEST**   The client selects an offer and constructs and broadcasts a DHCP request datagram. The DHCP request datagram contains the IP address of the server that issued the offer and the physical address of the DHCP client. The DHCP request performs two basic tasks. First it tells the selected DHCP server that the client requests it to assign the DHCP client an IP address (and other configuration settings). Second, it notifies all other DHCP servers with outstanding offers that their offers were not accepted.

4. **DHCPACK**   When tthe DHCP server from which the offer was selected receives the DHCP request datagram, it constructs the final datagram of the lease process. This datagram is known as a *DHCP ack* (short for *acknowledgement*). The DHCP ack includes an IP address and subnet mask for the DHCP client. Optionally, the DHCP client is often also configured with IP addresses for the default gateway, several DNS servers, and possibly one or two WINS servers. In addition to IP addresses, the DHCP client can receive other configuration information such as a NetBIOS node type, which can change the order of NetBIOS name resolution.

    Three other key fields are contained in the DHCP ack, all of which indicate time periods. One field identifies the length of the lease. Two other time fields, known as T1 and T2, are used when the client attempts to renew its lease. The use of these three time fields is explained later in this hour.

Relay Agents

If both the DHCP client and the DHCP server reside on the same network segment, the process proceeds exactly as previously indicated. If the DHCP client and DHCP server reside on different networks separated by one or more routers, the process becomes more complicated. Routers typically do not forward broadcasts to other networks. For DHCP to work, a middleman must be configured to assist the DHCP process. The middleman can be another host on the same network as the DHCP client, but often it is the router itself. In any case, the process that performs this middleman function is called either a *BOOTP relay agent* or a *DHCP relay agent*.

A relay agent is configured with a fixed IP address and also contains the IP address of the DHCP server. Because relay agents have configured IP addresses, they can always send and receive directed datagrams to the DHCP server. Because the relay agent resides on the same network as the DHCP client, it can communicate with the DHCP client via broadcasts.

Relay agents listen for broadcasts destined for UDP port 68; when the relay agent detects a DHCP request, it retransmits the request to the DHCP server. When the agent receives a response from the DHCP server, the response is rebroadcast on the local segment. This explanation has eliminated a few details for brevity but conveys the essence of the function performed by a relay agent. For more on relay agents, you can read RFC 1542.

Not all routers are capable of providing BOOTP/DHCP relay agent services. Routers that do have this capability are said to be RFC 1542 compliant.

DHCP Time Fields

DHCP clients lease IP addresses from DHCP servers for a fixed period of time, with the actual lease length being configured on the DHCP server. The T1 and T2 time values sent with the DHCP ack message are used during the lease renewal process. The T1 value indicates to the client when it should begin the process of renewing its lease. T1 is typically set to one-half of the actual lease time. Assume in the following example that leases are issued for a period of eight days.

Four days into the lease, the client sends a DHCP request to attempt to renew its IP address lease with the DHCP server that issued the lease. Assuming the DHCP server is online, the lease typically is renewed using a DHCP ack. Unlike the DHCP request and ack explained earlier in the four-step process, these two datagrams are not broadcast but are sent as directed datagrams. This is possible because both computers at this time contain valid IP addresses.

If the DHCP server is not available when the DHCP client issues the first request at 50% (four days), the client waits and attempts to renew the lease at 75% of the lease period, or six days into the lease. If this request also fails, the DHCP client tries a third time at 87.5%, or seven-eighths of the lease. Up to this point the DHCP client has attempted to renew its lease with the DHCP server that issued the lease by sending directed datagrams. If the DHCP client is incapable of renewing its lease by 87.5% of the total lease, the T2 time period comes into effect. The T2 time allows the DHCP client to begin broadcasting requests for any DHCP server. If the DHCP client is incapable of either renewing its lease or obtaining a new lease from another DHCP server by the time the lease expires, the client must stop using the IP address and stop using TCP/IP for normal network operations.

Configuring DHCP

The DHCP client receives a bundle of configuration information from the DHCP server. That information includes the IP address and other configuration settings. You must manually configure the DHCP server with the TCP/IP address information it will need for the clients. You configure DHCP with blocks or ranges of IP addresses that it can use to satisfy lease requests. Each block of IP addresses is called a *DHCP scope*. Each DHCP scope contains the block of addresses that will be used to configure DHCP clients on a given network segment.

12

DHCP Server Configuration in Windows

A tour through a DHCP server configuration gives a glimpse of the kind of information you need in order to set up DHCP. Windows NT Server provides a good example for DHCP server configuration. The following is a description of how to set up a Windows NT DHCP server. It is important to note that Windows NT isn't the only DHCP server. In fact, you are more likely to find a Unix-based DHCP server leasing addresses for your Internet service provider. This example is provided only for illustration purposes. DHCP configuration in Windows 2000 Server is similar.

To configure the DHCP server in Windows NT, follow these steps:

1. Install the DHCP service. (See your Windows NT documentation.)

2. Launch the DHCP Manager utility by choosing Start, Programs, Administrative Tools, DHCP Manager.

    The DHCP Manager (Local) utility appears. There is a single entry labeled Local Machine; if you double-click this entry, a character at the far left toggles between + and -. Make sure that the Local Machine entry displays the - symbol, which indicates it is currently expanded.

3. Choose Scope, Create from the menu.

    You are presented with the Create Scope - (Local) dialog box, as depicted in Figure 12.1. The Start Address and End Address fields define the two ends of the block of IP addresses you will allow the DHCP server to control. In Figure 12.1 you can see that the starting address in the range is 192.59.66.10 and the ending address is 192.59.66.254. If any statically assigned IP addresses fall within this range, you must exclude those addresses from the scope so that they are not assigned to other computers, which would cause networking problems. In this example, the DHCP server itself is statically configured with an IP address of 192.59.66.200; therefore, you can see that this address has been excluded from the scope.

> It is not required and probably not desirable to configure a scope with the full range of allowable IP addresses on a network or a subnetwork. If you do so, be sure to exclude the IP address of any configured routers and other nodes with static IP addresses.

4. Configure the Subnet Mask field with the proper subnet mask. If you want, you can alter the length of the lease and make entries into the Name and Comment fields. The text you enter in these two fields is used only for administrative purposes.

When you are finished, choose OK to close the Create Scope - (Local) dialog box and display the DHCP Manager dialog box. The DHCP Manager dialog box indicates that the scope has been successfully created but is not yet active. This dialog box asks if you want to activate the scope at this time. You can choose either the Yes or No button. Typically, you would choose not to activate the scope at this time if you want to add options such as the IP addresses of the default gateway or DNS servers and so on.

FIGURE 12.1
The DHCP Manager's Create Scope dialog box.

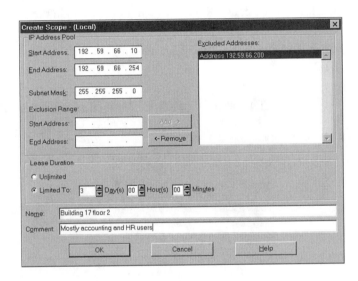

Often two (or possibly more) DHCP servers are configured with scopes to service a network. The additional DHCP server(s) provides fault tolerance and allows a DHCP client to acquire a lease successfully when a DHCP server is offline. However, be aware that each DHCP server operates independently and does not share information regarding leased IP addresses. For this reason, do not configure multiple DHCP servers with scopes that contain overlapping addresses. Otherwise it is just a matter of time until two DHCP clients are configured with the same IP address, which can cause network problems. Some operating systems, such as Windows, will tell you when they detect a duplicate address error.

Usually you want the DHCP server to configure DHCP clients with more configuration parameters than the IP address and subnet mask. In Windows NT, the DHCP Options menu allows you to add a number of other configuration options. These options are typically configured at two levels. One configuration level establishes scope options, which are used to configure parameters that change from scope to scope. The other establishes global options, which are used to configure parameters that apply to all scopes.

To configure scope options in Windows NT, follow these steps:

1. Choose DHCP Options, Scope from the DHCP Manager menu. The DHCP Options: Scope dialog box appears.

2. From the Unused Options list, select the options that you want applied at the scope level. In this case, 003 Router, which now appears in the Active Options list, is selected and added.

3. Click the Value button to expand the dialog box so it appears as depicted in Figure 12.2.

FIGURE 12.2

The DHCP Options: Scope dialog box.

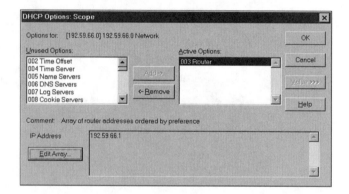

4. After the dialog box is expanded, choose the Edit Array button and add the IP address for the default gateway using the dialog box provided. Once all scope-level options for the currently selected scope have been entered and configured, you can choose OK to close the DHCP Options: Scope dialog box.

You use global options to configure parameters that remain constant from scope to scope. For instance, computers on every network segment typically use the same DNS server IP addresses. For this reason the DNS server IP addresses are typically configured using a global option.

To configure global options in Windows NT, follow these steps:

1. Choose DHCP Options, Global from the DHCP Manager menu. The DHCP Options: Global dialog box appears.

2. From the Unused Options list, select the options that you want applied at the scope level. In this case, 006 DNS Servers is selected and added and appears in the Active Options list.

3. Click the Value button to expand the dialog box so that it appears as depicted in Figure 12.3.

FIGURE 12.3

The DHCP Options: Global dialog box.

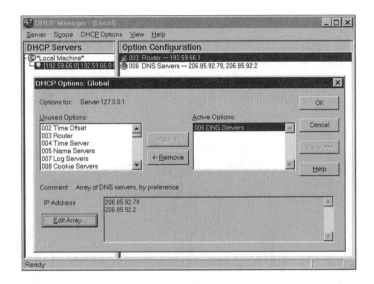

4. After the dialog box is expanded, choose the Edit Array button. The IP Address Array Editor dialog box appears, as shown in Figure 12.4. The IP Address Array Editor is used to enter several IP addresses, as in the case of DNS servers.

FIGURE 12.4

The IP Address Array Editor dialog box.

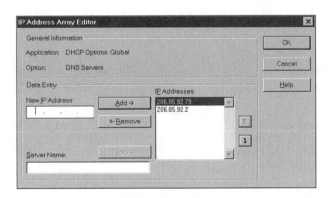

12

5. Add the IP addresses for the DNS servers. After all global-level options have been entered and configured, you can choose OK to close the DHCP Options: Global dialog box.

At this point you have configured one DHCP scope with options. If you have not done so previously, you must activate the scope before the DHCP server can begin leasing IP addresses to DHCP clients on that network.

To activate a scope, select the scope to be activated, choose Scope, and then choose Activate from the menu, as shown in Figure 12.5. DHCP is configured and active and should successfully lease IP addresses to DHCP clients. You can determine if the server is performing its leasing task successfully by booting a DHCP client computer and using the ipconfig or winipcfg command with the Release and Renew options, as described in Hour 13, "Connectivity Utilities."

FIGURE 12.5

The Scope menu.

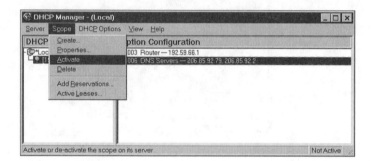

DHCP Server Configuration in Linux

Linux systems provide DHCP services through dhcpd, the DHCP daemon. Instructions for installing dhcpd vary according to the vendor. DHCP configuration information is stored in the configuration file /etc/dhcpd.conf.

The /etc/dhcpd.conf file contains the IP address configuration information that the DHCP daemon will assign to clients. /etc/dhcpd.conf also contains optional settings such as the broadcast address, domain name, DNS server address, and the addresses of routers. A sample /etc/dhcpd.conf file follows:

```
default-lease-time 600;
max-lease-time 7200;
option domain-name "macmillan.com";
option subnet-mask 255.255.255.0;
option broadcast-address 185.142.13.255;
subnet 185.142.13.0 netmask 255.255.255.0 {
range 185.142.13.10 185.142.13.50;
range 185.142.13.100 185.142.13.200;
}
```

Summary

DHCP provides an easy way to configure IP addresses and other configuration settings for client computers. It is especially useful when changes occur; for instance, if you change ISPs, you will need to change the DNS server entries. If your company has 5,000 manually configured computers spread over 10 states, making this change can be an expensive and time-consuming process. However, with a DHCP server you can effect this change by simply changing a Global Scope option. The next time each DHCP client renews its IP address, it will receive the IP addresses for the new DNS servers.

In this hour you learned how DHCP works. You also learned about configuring scopes and how to install and configure DHCP on a Windows NT server.

Q&A

Q How does a DHCP client communicate with a DHCP server when it is first started?

A By broadcasting and receiving broadcasted datagrams.

Q What is required to enable a DHCP client on one network to lease an IP address from a DHCP server on another network?

A A DHCP relay agent

Q Can a router be a relay agent? Can any router be a relay agent?

A Yes. A router can be a relay agent. No. Not all routers can be relay agents, only routers that are RFC 1542 compliant.

12

Key Terms

Review the following list of key terms:

BOOTP—A protocol used primarily to assign addresses to diskless clients.

DHCP—Dynamic Host Configuration Protocol. A protocol that provides dynamic assignment of IP addresses.

DHCP client—A computer that contains TCP/IP software and is not manually config-ured with TCP/IP parameters.

DHCP server—A computer that is capable of configuring DHCP client computers with an IP address, a subnet mask, and other TCP/IP configuration parameters.

Scope—A range of IP addresses controlled by a DHCP server. These IP addresses are intended for lease to DHCP client computers.

PART IV
TCP/IP Utilities

Hour

HOUR 13

Connectivity Utilities

This hour introduces utilities you can use to troubleshoot and configure TCP/IP. You will find these tools indispensable when you need to identify connectivity problems, test communication between network nodes, and check the TCP/IP settings of computers on your network.

The section "Using Connectivity Utilities to Troubleshoot Problems," later in this hour, introduces several techniques to help you zero in on problems.

 Companies that write TCP/IP software might implement the utilities presented in this hour differently or not at all. Generally speaking, these utilities are not covered by RFC specifications, which explains the latitude in implementation. Check your TCP/IP documentation for more information on how your system implements these utilities.

At the completion of this hour, you will be able to

- Identify and describe common TCP/IP connectivity utilities
- Use connectivity utilities to troubleshoot problems

Connectivity Problems

A protocol, as described in earlier hours, is a standard for communication. That standard is then implemented by a software vendor into a software module that performs the operations described in the standard. A human installs and configures the protocol software, either directly or by installing an operating system that supports the protocol software. As you might guess, once the software is up and running, the network still might not work. Sometimes certain services function and others do not. Other times, a computer can connect to one remote PC and not to another. Once in a while, a computer appears to have no network access at all, as if it weren't even connected.

Network dysfunction typically results from one of a handful of common problems. The TCP/IP community has developed a number of utilities for uncovering these problems and tracing a problem to its source. This hour discusses some of the common network problems and the tools you can use to solve them.

The top four network connectivity problems are typically some variation of the following:

- Protocol dysfunction or misconfiguration: The protocol software doesn't work or (for whatever reason) isn't configured to operate properly on the network.
- Line problems: A cable isn't plugged in or isn't working. A hub, router, or switch isn't working.
- Faulty name resolution: DNS or NetBIOS names can't be resolved. Resources are accessible by IP address but not by hostname or DNS name (www.sun.com).
- Excessive traffic: The network appears to be working, but it is working very slowly.

The following sections discuss tools and techniques for addressing these common connectivity problems.

Protocol Dysfunction and Misconfiguration

Like any software, TCP/IP protocol software sometimes doesn't get installed properly. Even after it is installed, it might stop working because of a corrupt file or some change to the system configuration. For example, even if the software is working, the computer may not be able to connect to other computers because its IP address and subnet mask are incorrect.

The TCP/IP protocol suite provides a number of useful utilities that help you determine if TCP/IP is functioning and properly configured, such as

- Ping: This utility is an extremely useful diagnostic tool that initiates a simple test of network connectivity and reports on whether the other computer responds.
- Configuration information utilities: Each OS vendor provides some form of utility that displays TCP/IP configuration information and lets you check whether the IP address, subnet mask, DNS server, and other parameters are configured properly.
- arp: This lets you view and configure the contents of the ARP cache (see Hour 4, "The Internet Layer"), which associates IP addresses with physical addresses.

The following sections discuss these important TCP/IP configuration utilities.

Ping

If you notice that your computer can't complete a network operation, the first question you should ask is whether it can complete any other network operation. In other words, is your computer currently functioning as a member of the network? The ping utility initiates the most minimal test of network connectivity. It sends a message to another computer that says "Are you there?" and waits for the other computer to respond.

> The name *ping* is based on the sonar technology used by submarines and ships to locate other objects. Ping is an acronym for Packet Internet Groper.

The basic form of a `ping` command is

```
ping <IP_address>
```

where `IP_address` is the address of the computer to which you'd like to connect. Like other utilities, ping offers a number of additional command-line options. These options differ, depending on the implementation.

The ping utility sends a message to the recipient computer using the ICMP echo request command. (For more information on ICMP, see Hour 4.) If the recipient computer is present and operational, it responds using the ICMP Echo Reply message.

When the sending computer receives the reply, it outputs a message stating that the ping was successful.

Successful completion of the `ping` command verifies that both the pinging and the pinged computers are on the network and able to communicate. However, keep in mind that ping is a very minimal application. It requires only that the bottom two layers of the

13

TCP/IP stack are operational. You could have problems with TCP, UDP, or applications in the upper two layers and ping would still operate. If ping operates correctly, you can largely rule out problems with items such as the Network Access layer, the network adapter, cabling, and even routers.

Ping offers a number of options that make it particularly useful for troubleshooting network problems. You can

- Ping the local IP software using a special IP address called the loopback address: 127.0.0.1. If the command ping 127.0.0.1 is successful, your TCP/IP protocol software is functioning properly.

- Ping your own IP address (in other words, ping yourself). If you can ping the IP address assigned to your network adapter, you know that the adapter is properly configured and interfaced with the TCP/IP software.

- Ping by hostname. Most systems let you substitute a hostname for the IP address in the ping command. If you can ping a computer by IP address, but you can't ping the same computer by its hostname, you know that the problem is related to name resolution.

In a typical troubleshooting scenario, a network administrator performs the following ping commands (in this order):

1. Ping the loopback address (127.0.0.1) to verify that TCP/IP is working properly on the local computer.

2. Ping the local IP address to verify that the network adapter is functioning and the local IP address is configured.

3. Ping the default gateway to verify that the computer can communicate with the local subnet and to verify that the default gateway is online.

4. Ping an address beyond the default gateway to verify that the gateway is successfully forwarding packets beyond the local network segment.

5. Ping the local host and remote hosts by hostname to verify that name resolution is functioning.

The preceding steps are a good beginning for searching out a network problem. You may not find an answer, but at least you'll get a clue about where to look.

Looking Closer at Ping Output

The output for the `ping` command varies according to the implementation. In some systems, such as Solaris 8, the output is a single line stating `<ip_address>` is alive. Some versions of Linux (by default) send ICMP packets and output packet response information continuously until you press Ctrl+C. Windows NT and Windows 2000 (by default) send four ICMP echo requests and output four responses. It is not uncommon to receive three or even fewer responses to those four echo requests. You should not consider the occasional dropped datagram a failure, though, since the IP protocol does not guarantee delivery. However, missing responses could be an indication of an overcrowded network. Dropped packets notwithstanding, the most common responses to a ping are that all requests were successful (indicating that the connection is working) or that all requests were unsuccessful (indicating that the connection isn't working).

Some versions of the ping utility display the time in milliseconds from the time the Echo Request message is sent until the Echo Reply message is returned. Short response times indicate that a datagram does not have to pass through too many routers or through slow networks. If `ping` responses are returning with a TTL value near zero, it might be an indication that the connection is near the TTL threshold and some packets are getting lost or re-sent.

Configuration Information Utilities

All modern operating systems offer a utility that lets you view the current TCP/IP configuration. These utilities output information such as the IP address, subnet mask, and default gateway for the local computer. You can use these utilities to verify that the IP address information for the computer is what you expect. With the recent popularity of DHCP, you can't always determine the IP address information from configuration files or setup dialog boxes. The configuration information utilities tell you the address that the computer is actually using. If your computer is configured for DHCP, you might even discover that the computer has no IP address at all, indicating a problem with the DHCP server connection.

Of course, these utilities don't tell what your IP address and subnet mask should be. They just tell what address and mask your computer is using. It is then up to you to verify that the address parameters are consistent with the IP addressing scheme for your network (see Hours 5, "Subnetting," and 6, "The Transport Layer").

Unix and Linux systems use the `ifconfig` command to display address information. As you will recall from earlier hours, the IP address is actually associated with a network interface (such as a network adapter card) rather than with the computer itself. If a computer has two network interfaces, it will have two IP addresses. The `ifconfig` command displays address information associated with each network interface.

13

To display IP address information using `ifconfig`, enter

`ifconfig <interface_name>`

where `<interface_name>` is the name of the network interface for which you'd like to display address information. (In Unix and Linux, each network interface is assigned a name by the configuration file that defines the interface and is referenced by that name.) For example

`ifconfig eth0`

displays the current IP address and netmask (and other parameters depending on the Unix/Linux version) for the interface called `eth0`.

`ifconfig` also lets you directly configure IP address information for a network interface by typing the IP address and netmask directly at the command line:

`ifconfig eth0 <IP_Address> netmask <netmask>`

where `<IP_Address>` is the address of the interface and `<netmask>` is the network mask of the interface.

The `ifconfig` up and down options let you enable and disable the network interface. For example

```
ifconfig eth0 up
ifconfig eth0 down
```

Other `ifconfig` options are also available. Options vary with the version. Consult the `ifconfig` man page on your Unix/Linux system for more on `ifconfig`:

`man ifconfig`

Windows NT and Windows 2000 use the `ipconfig` command to display local TCP/IP configuration settings.

`ipconfig` options include the following:

- **Default (no options)**   When `ipconfig` is used without options, it displays the IP address, subnet mask, and default gateway values for each configured interface, as shown in the upper portion of Figure 13.1.
- **all**   When the `all` option (`ipconfig /all`) is used, `ipconfig` displays additional information such as the IP addresses for the DNS and WINS server(s) it is configured to use, as well as the physical address burned into local network adapters. If addresses were leased from a DHCP server, `ipconfig` displays the IP address of the DHCP server and the date the lease is scheduled to expire. (Setting up a DHCP server is an advanced topic that is covered in Hour 12, "Dynamic Host Configuration Protocol (DHCP).")

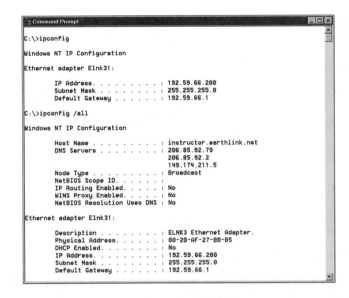

FIGURE 13.1

The ipconfig *and* ipconfig /all *commands and responses.*

```
Command Prompt

C:\>ipconfig

Windows NT IP Configuration

Ethernet adapter Elnk31:

        IP Address. . . . . . . . . : 192.59.66.200
        Subnet Mask . . . . . . . . : 255.255.255.0
        Default Gateway . . . . . . : 192.59.66.1

C:\>ipconfig /all

Windows NT IP Configuration

        Host Name . . . . . . . . . : instructor.earthlink.net
        DNS Servers . . . . . . . . : 206.85.92.79
                                      206.85.92.2
                                      149.174.211.5
        Node Type . . . . . . . . . : Broadcast
        NetBIOS Scope ID. . . . . . :
        IP Routing Enabled. . . . . : No
        WINS Proxy Enabled. . . . . : No
        NetBIOS Resolution Uses DNS : No

Ethernet adapter Elnk31:

        Description . . . . . . . . : ELNK3 Ethernet Adapter.
        Physical Address. . . . . . : 00-20-AF-27-BB-B5
        DHCP Enabled. . . . . . . . : No
        IP Address. . . . . . . . . : 192.59.66.200
        Subnet Mask . . . . . . . . : 255.255.255.0
        Default Gateway . . . . . . : 192.59.66.1
```

- **releaserenew**   These optional parameters work only on computers that lease their IP address from a DHCP server. If you enter ipconfig /release, the leased IP addresses for all interfaces are released back to the DHCP server(s). Conversely, if you enter ipconfig /renew, the local computer attempts to contact a DHCP server and lease an IP address. Be aware that in many cases the network adapter(s) will be reassigned the same IP addresses previously assigned.

> A variation on the release and renew options can be used to release or renew one adapter at a time in a computer that contains multiple network adapters. Assuming one of the computer adapters is named Elnk31, this one adapter can be released or renewed by using the command ipconfig /release Elnk31 or ipconfig /renew Elnk31.

13

If you are using Windows 95 or 98, you use the command winipcfg instead of ipconfig. Winipcfg displays a graphical interface with the same information as displayed by ipconfig, and it provides the same options for releasing and renewing IP addresses. (See Figure 13.2.)

FIGURE 13.2
Output from the Windows winipcfg utility.

Address Resolution Protocol (ARP)

ARP is a key TCP/IP protocol used to determine the physical address that corresponds to an IP address. Each home on a TCP/IP network maintains an ARP cache—a table used to connect IP addresses to physical addresses. The arp command enables you to view the current contents of the ARP cache of either the local computer or another computer. In most cases, the protocol software takes care of updating the ARP cache, and cases in which you need to use the arp command to troubleshoot a network connection are rare. However, the arp command is occasionally useful for tracing subtler problems related to the association of IP addresses with physical addresses. Some Unix and Linux systems, for instance, still require manual configuration of the physical address.

The arp command also enables you to enter desired physical/IP address pairs manually. You might want to do this for commonly used hosts such as the default gateway and local servers. This helps reduce traffic on the network.

Entries in the ARP cache are dynamic by default. Entries are automatically added to the cache whenever a directed datagram is sent and a current entry does not exist in the cache of the destination computer. The cache entries start to expire as soon as they are entered. Therefore, don't be surprised if there are few or no entries in the ARP cache. Entries can be added by performing pings of another computer or router. The following arp commands can be used to view cache entries:

- **arp -a** Use this command to view all ARP cache entries.
- **arp -g** Use this command to view all ARP cache entries.

You can use either arp -a or arp -g. The -g option has for many years been the option used on Unix platforms to display all ARP cache entries. Windows NT/2000 uses arp -a (think of -a as *all*), but it also accepts the more traditional -g option.

- **arp -a <*IP address*>** If you have multiple network adapters, you can see just the ARP cache entries associated with one interface by using arp -a plus the IP address of the interface, for example arp -a 192.59.66.200.

- **arp -s** You can add a permanent static entry to the ARP cache manually. This entry remains in effect across boots of the computer or is updated automatically if errors occur using manually configured physical addresses. For example, to add an entry for a server manually using IP address 192.59.66.250 with a physical address of 0080C7E07EC5, enter arp -s 192.59.66.250 00-80-C7-E0-7E-C5.

- **arp -d <*IP address*>** Use this command to delete a static entry manually. For example, enter arp -d 192.59.66.250.

See Figure 13.3 for examples of arp commands and responses.

FIGURE 13.3

arp *commands and responses.*

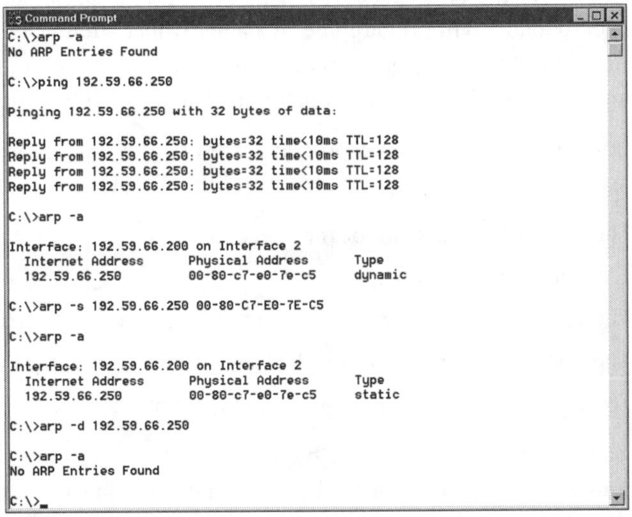

```
Command Prompt                                                     _ □ ×
C:\>arp -a
No ARP Entries Found

C:\>ping 192.59.66.250

Pinging 192.59.66.250 with 32 bytes of data:

Reply from 192.59.66.250: bytes=32 time<10ms TTL=128
Reply from 192.59.66.250: bytes=32 time<10ms TTL=128
Reply from 192.59.66.250: bytes=32 time<10ms TTL=128
Reply from 192.59.66.250: bytes=32 time<10ms TTL=128

C:\>arp -a

Interface: 192.59.66.200 on Interface 2
  Internet Address      Physical Address      Type
  192.59.66.250         00-80-c7-e0-7e-c5     dynamic

C:\>arp -s 192.59.66.250 00-80-C7-E0-7E-C5

C:\>arp -a

Interface: 192.59.66.200 on Interface 2
  Internet Address      Physical Address      Type
  192.59.66.250         00-80-c7-e0-7e-c5     static

C:\>arp -d 192.59.66.250

C:\>arp -a
No ARP Entries Found

C:\>_
```

13

Line Problems

A problem with a network hub or cable is not really a TCP/IP problem. However, you can still use TCP/IP diagnostic utilities such as ping to diagnose line problems. In general, if the network used to work and has stopped working suddenly, a line problem is often the cause. Make sure all network cables are properly plugged in. Most network cards, hubs, and routers have display lights that indicate whether the unit is on and ready to receive data. Several tools exist for testing network cabling. If you don't have access to a cable testing tool, you can always unplug a suspicious cable and plug a new cable into its place to see if that solves the problem.

You can use ping (described in an earlier section) to isolate line problems. If a computer can ping its own address but cannot ping any other addresses on the network, the trouble may be in the cable segment that connects the computer to the local subnet.

Name Resolution Problems

A name resolution problem occurs when a hostname to which a message is addressed cannot be resolved on the network. A name resolution problem is (arguably) not a connectivity problem, because it doesn't necessarily mean that the source computer cannot connect with the target. In fact, as was mentioned in an earlier section, the most common symptom of a name resolution problem is that the source computer can reach the target by IP address but can't reach the target hostname. Even though a name resolution problem isn't a connectivity problem in the strictest sense, as a practical matter, resources on today's networks are referenced by hostname or NetBIOS name, and your first attempt to connect to a host will probably be by name. If that attempt fails, you can begin the problem-solving steps discussed in the "Ping" section, earlier in this hour. If you can still connect by IP address, you probably have a problem with name resolution.

Many common name resolution problems are obvious when you consider the process of name resolution (see Hour 11, "Name Resolution"). Some common causes are

- The hosts file is missing or incorrect.
- The name server is offline.
- The name server is referenced incorrectly in the client configuration.
- The host you are trying to reach does not have an entry in the name server.
- The hostname used in the command is incorrect.

If you can't connect to a computer by hostname, try connecting to a different computer. If you can connect to Computer A by hostname and you can't connect to Computer B, chances are the problem has something to do with Computer B and how it is referenced by the name service. If you can't connect to either Computer A or Computer B, chances are the problem is a more general failure of the name service infrastructure.

Keep in mind that your computer may also be resolving names by the hosts file (see Hour 11). If a DNS server fails, your computer will continue to resolve the names entered explicitly in the hosts file. The hosts file may therefore provide a clue about why some names are resolved and some are not.

If you are experiencing name resolution problems on a network that uses a name server, it is a good idea to ping the name server to make sure it is online. If the name server is beyond the local subnet, ping the gateway to ensure that name resolution requests can reach the name server. Double-check the name you entered to ensure that it is the correct name for the resource. If none of these measures lead you to a solution, you can use the nslookup utility to query the name server about specific entries. See Hour 11 for more on nslookup.

If you are working at a computer and you don't know its hostname, use the `hostname` command. `hostname` is a simple command that returns the hostname of the local computer. There are no options or parameters to `hostname`. Simply enter the command `hostname` and view the one-word response.

Network Performance Problems

Network performance problems are problems that cause your network to respond slowly. Because TCP/IP protocols commonly use TTL (Time to Live) settings limiting the age of a packet on the network, slow performance can cause lost packets and therefore loss of connectivity. Even if you don't lose connectivity, slow network performance can be an irritation and a source of lost productivity. A common cause for poor network performance is excessive traffic. Your network may be experiencing heavy traffic because there are too many computers on the network, or the cause might be a malfunctioning device such as a network adapter creating unnecessary traffic on the network in what is known as a "broadcast storm." Sometimes the cause for poor network performance is a downed router that has stopped forwarding traffic and caused a bottleneck somewhere else in the network.

TCP/IP offers a number of utilities that let you see where packets are going and display statistics related to network performance. The following sections discuss these utilities, which will help you find answers to problems related to network performance.

13

Traceroute

The traceroute utility is used to trace the path taken by datagrams as they travel from your computer through multiple gateways to their destinations. The path traced by this utility is just one path between the source and destination; there is no guarantee or assumption that datagrams will always follow this path. If you are configured to use DNS, you can often determine the names of cities, regions, and common carriers from the responses. traceroute is a slow command; you need to give it approximately 10–15 seconds per router.

Traceroute (or tracert if you are using Windows NT/2000) makes use of the ICMP protocol to locate each router that stands between your client computer and the destination computer. The TTL value tells you the number of routers or gateways that a packet has passed through. By manipulating the TTL value that is used in the original outgoing ICMP Echo message, traceroute is able to find each router along the path, as follows:

1. An ICMP Echo message is sent to the destination IP address with a TTL value set to 1. The first router subtracts 1 from the TTL value, which results in a new TTL value of 0.

2. Since the TTL value is now set to 0, the router knows that it should not make any attempt to forward the datagram and simply discards it. The datagram's Time to Live value has expired. The router sends an ICMP Time Exceeded—TTL Expired In Transit message back to the client computer.

3. The client computer that issued the traceroute command displays the name of this router and then sends out another ICMP Echo message with the TTL value set to 2.

4. The first router subtracts 1 from the TTL value and, if it can, forwards the datagram to its next hop along the path. When the datagram reaches the second router, the TTL value is again decremented by 1, resulting in a 0 value.

5. The second router, like the first, simply discards the packet and returns an ICMP message to the sender in the same way the first router did.

6. This process continues, with traceroute incrementing the TTL value and routers decrementing this value until the datagram finally reaches its intended destination.

7. When the destination computer receives the ICMP Echo message, it sends back an ICMP Echo Reply message.

In addition to locating each router or gateway the datagram travels through, the traceroute utility also records the round-trip time that it takes to reach each router. Depending on the implementation, traceroute may actually send more than a single Echo message to each router. For example, in the Windows 2000 version of this utility (tracert), two additional Echo messages are sent to each router so that it can better judge the round-trip time. However, you shouldn't use this round-trip time value to judge your network's performance precisely. Many routers simply give a lower priority to ICMP traffic and spend most of their processing time forwarding more important datagrams.

The syntax for the `traceroute` command is simply `traceroute` followed by an IP address, a DNS name, or even a URL:

```
traceroute 198.137.240.-91
traceroute www.whitehouse.gov.
```

Traceroute is useful for showing you the path a datagram traverses on the way to its destination. Traceroute can also provide some diagnostic capabilities.

route

As you learned in Hours 9, "Network Hardware," and 10, "Routing," each computer and each router contains a routing table. Most routers use special routing protocols to exchange routing information and dynamically update their tables periodically. However, there are many times when it is necessary to add entries manually to route tables on routers and host computers.

The `route` command has many uses in TCP/IP networking. You can use `route` to display the routing table in cases where packets from a host are not being routed efficiently. If the `traceroute` command reveals an abnormal or inefficient path, you may be able to use `route` to determine why that path is being used and possibly to configure a more efficient route.

The `route` command is also used to add, delete, and change entries in routing tables manually. Some options include

- `route print`   This form of the route command displays the current entries in the routing table. See Figure 13.4 for an example of output from a `route print` command. As you can see, several entries refer to various networks, for example `0.0.0.0`, `127.0.0.0`, and `192.59.66.0`; some are used for broadcasting `255.255.255.255` and `207.168.243.255`, and others are for multicasting `224.0.0.0`. All of these entries were added automatically as a result of configuring network adapters with IP addresses.

13

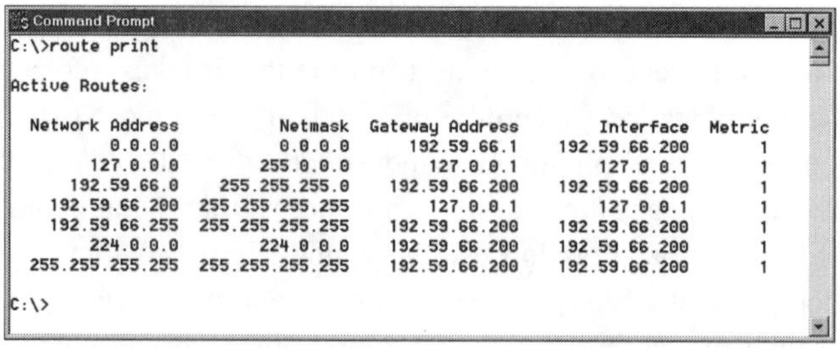

FIGURE 13.4

A route print *command displays the current information in the routing table.*

```
Command Prompt                                                    _ □ ×
C:\>route print

Active Routes:

Network Address          Netmask  Gateway Address      Interface  Metric
      0.0.0.0            0.0.0.0      192.59.66.1   192.59.66.200       1
    127.0.0.0            255.0.0.0      127.0.0.1       127.0.0.1       1
   192.59.66.0      255.255.255.0   192.59.66.200   192.59.66.200       1
 192.59.66.200    255.255.255.255      127.0.0.1       127.0.0.1       1
 192.59.66.255    255.255.255.255   192.59.66.200   192.59.66.200       1
    224.0.0.0          224.0.0.0   192.59.66.200   192.59.66.200       1
255.255.255.255  255.255.255.255   192.59.66.200   192.59.66.200       1

C:\>
```

- route add   Use this form of the route command to add a new routing entry to a routing table. For example, to specify a route to a destination network 207.34.17.0 that is five router hops away and passing first through a router with an IP address on the local network of 192.59.66.5 and the subnet mask of 255.255.255.224, you would enter the following command:

  route add 207.34.17.0 mask 255.255.255.224 192.59.66.5 metric 5

The route information added in this way is volatile and is lost if the computer or router reboots. Often a series of route add commands is contained in startup scripts so that it is reapplied every time the computer or router boots.

- route change   You can use this syntax to change entries in the routing table. The following example changes the routing of the data to a different router that has a more direct three-hop path to the destination:

  route change 207.34.17.0 mask 255.255.255.224 192.59.66.7 metric 3

- route delete   Use this command syntax to delete an entry from the routing table:

  route delete 207.34.17.0

Netstat

The netstat utility displays statistics related to the IP, TCP, UDP, and ICMP protocols. The statistics display numerical counts for items such as datagrams sent, datagrams received, and a wide variety of errors that could have occurred.

You should not be surprised if your computer occasionally receives datagrams that cause errors, discards, or failures. TCP/IP is tolerant of these types of errors and automatically resends the datagram. Discards occur when a datagram is delivered to the wrong location. If your computer acts as a router, it will also discard datagrams when TTL reaches zero on a routed datagram. Reassembly failures occur when all the fragments fail to arrive within a time period based on the TTL value in received fragments. Again, like errors and discards, occasional reassembly failures should not be a reason for concern. In all three cases, accumulated counts that are a significant percentage of the total IP packets received or that rapidly accumulate should cause you to investigate why this is occurring.

The following list describes various `netstat` command options:

- `netstat -s`   This option displays statistics on a protocol-by-protocol basis. If user applications such as Web browsers seem unusually slow or are incapable of displaying data such as Web pages, you might want to use this option to see what information is displayed. You can look through the rows of statistics for the words `error`, `discard`, or `failure`. If the counts in these rows are significant relative to the IP packets received, this should prompt further investigation.

- `netstat -e`   This option displays statistics about ethernet. Items listed include total bytes, errors, discards, number of directed datagrams, and number of broadcasts. These statistics are provided for datagrams both sent and received.

- `netstat -r`   This option displays routing table information similar to what is seen with the `route print` command. In addition to the active routes, current active connections are also displayed.

- `netstat -a`   This option displays the list of all active connections, including both established connections and those that are listening for a connection request.

The following three options provide subset information of what is displayed with the `-a` option:

- `netstat -n`   This option displays all established active connections.
- `netstat -p TCP`   This option displays established TCP connections.
- `netstat -p UDP`   This option displays established UDP connections.

See Figure 13.5 for an example of the statistics displayed by `netstat -s`.

Nbtstat

The nbtstat (NetBIOS over TCP/IP statistics) utility provides statistics about NetBIOS over TCP/IP (see Hour 7). Nbtstat allows you to view the NetBIOS name table on the local computer or on a remote computer.

13

FIGURE 13.5

Netstat displays protocol-by-protocol statistics.

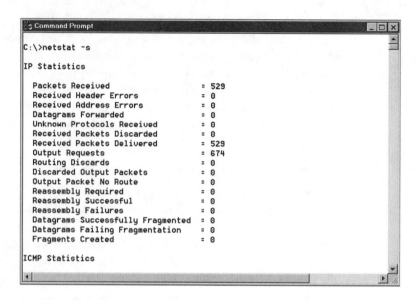

The following command options are used in relation to the local computer:

- `nbtstat -r`   This command causes the NetBIOS name cache to be purged and reloaded. This is done to load recently added entries from the LMHosts file. (LMHosts entries are covered in Hour 11.)
- `nbtstat -n`   This command displays the names and services registered on the local computer.
- `nbtstat -c`   This command displays the contents of the NetBIOS name cache that holds the NetBIOS names to IP address pairs of other computers with which this computer has had recent communication.
- `nbtstat -r`   This command lists the count of registrations and resolved names of other computers and whether they were registered or resolved by broadcast or by a name server.

See Figure 13.6 for examples of these outputs.

The `nbtstat` command can also be used to view the NetBIOS name table of remote computers. The output is similar to `nbtstat -n` on the local computer.

- `nbtstat -A <IP address>`   Displays the name table including physical addresses from another computer by using its IP address.
- `nbtstat -a <NetBIOS name>`   Displays the name table including physical addresses from another computer by using its NetBIOS name.

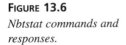

Figure 13.6

Nbtstat commands and responses.

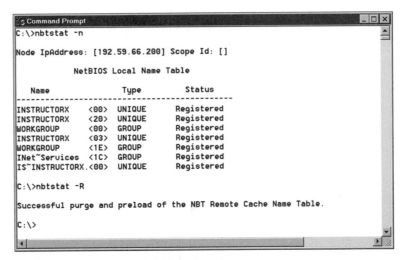

```
Command Prompt                                                _ □ ×
C:\>nbtstat -n

Node IpAddress: [192.59.66.200] Scope Id: []

            NetBIOS Local Name Table

    Name              Type        Status
---------------------------------------------
INSTRUCTORX    <00>  UNIQUE      Registered
INSTRUCTORX    <20>  UNIQUE      Registered
WORKGROUP      <00>  GROUP       Registered
INSTRUCTORX    <03>  UNIQUE      Registered
WORKGROUP      <1E>  GROUP       Registered
INet~Services  <1C>  GROUP       Registered
IS~INSTRUCTORX.<00>  UNIQUE      Registered

C:\>nbtstat -R

Successful purge and preload of the NBT Remote Cache Name Table.

C:\>
```

Similarly, two other `nbtstat` command options enable you to view the list of NetBIOS connections that a remote computer has open. This list is called a connections table:

- `nbtstat -S <IP address>` Displays the NetBIOS connections table of another computer using its IP address.

- `nbtstat -s <NetBIOS name>` Displays the NetBIOS session table of another computer using its NetBIOS name.

Packet Sniffers

Utilities known as *sniffers* capture data from the network into a buffer or a file. After the data is captured, you can display the contents one frame or datagram at a time. Packet sniffers are useful for analyzing subtle network excessing traffic. You can also use sniffers to find the source of corrupt packets that may have come from a malfunctioning device. You can trace an ethernet frame by its physical address. You can analyze header information from any protocol level (see Hours 3, "The Network Access Layer," 4, and 6) to look for clues.

Figure 13.7 shows the sequence of 10 datagrams that was initiated by entering a `ping` command. The top window shows the 10 datagrams starting with an ARP request and an ARP reply followed by four ICMP request/reply pairs. The middle window decodes the ICMP header, and in the bottom frame you can see the 32 bytes of data in the datagram. The data includes the complete alphabet followed by the letters `abcdef`, for a total of 32 bytes of data.

13

FIGURE **13.7**

A view of traffic cap-
tured by Microsoft's
Network Monitor util-
ity following a ping
command.

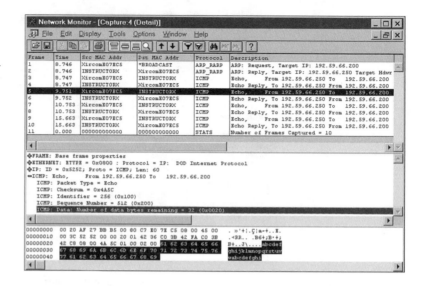

Using Connectivity Utilities to Troubleshoot Problems

By trying various applications that use TCP or UDP that operate at different levels of the protocol stack, you can often zero in on which component in the stack is causing a problem.

As was mentioned when discussing the ping utility, there is a definite order that you should follow when troubleshooting network problems. Networking problems can be extremely varied, but they are usually caused by some application such as a Web browser being incapable of displaying Web pages. In troubleshooting, you typically start with simple basic commands. If these work as expected, you then continue to build on what you know to be working by using commands that require progressively more network functionality. To troubleshoot a network problem, follow these steps:

1. Start with ipconfig (or winipcfg) to ensure you know the current IP address, subnet mask, and default gateway parameters.

2. Move on to the ping command and follow the sequence of ping commands described earlier. If the ping commands work as expected, you have gained some confidence in the two lower layers, including the network adapter and the network cabling.

3. Use an application such as a Web browser to access a Web server. If this works, you know that TCP and the sockets interface work; if it doesn't work, try another application that uses TCP and sockets, such as the FTP client. If this doesn't work either, you probably want to concentrate on TCP or sockets as a source of the problem.

Summary

The utilities presented in this hour give you a number of tools for identifying the state of TCP/IP communication on your network and troubleshooting breakdowns of that communication. Each utility displays only a small amount of information about the activity on your network. However, when the results of these utilities are combined in a useful manner, they can provide a more complete picture of the operation of TCP/IP on your computer.

Q&A

Q Which utility displays a path taken by datagrams?

A Traceroute

Q Which utility type is used to examine the contents of datagrams?

A A network sniffer

Q Which utility displays statistics for TCP/IP protocols?

A Netstat

Q Which utility displays statistics for NetBIOS-based networks?

A Nbtstat

Q Which utility allows you to test your connection to a specific IP address?

A Ping

Q Which utility displays the hostname of your computer?

A Hostname

13

Workshop

Perform the following commands and view the responses on your computer:

`ipconfig /all`, `winipcfg`, and `ifconfig -a` (Not all TCP/IP stacks implement these.)

`ping 127.0.0.1`

`ping w.x.y.z`   Replace `w.x.y.z` with the IP address of your computer.

`ping w.x.y.z`   Replace `w.x.y.z` with the IP address of another local computer.

`ping w.x.y.z`   Replace `w.x.y.z` with the IP address of your default gateway.

`ping w.x.y.z`   Replace `w.x.y.z` with the IP address of a remote computer.

`ping localhost`

`ping http://www.whitehouse.gov`   If you are connected to the Internet and have a DNS server.

`hostname`

`ping <hostname>`   Replace `<hostname>` with the your actual hostname.

`arp -a` or `arp -g`   One or both might work. Wait a few minutes then repeat.

`netstat -s`

`nbtstat -n`   Not all TCP/IP stacks implement nbtstat.

Key Terms

Review the following list of key terms:

arp—A utility that configures and displays the contents of the Address Resolution Protocol (ARP) table.

hostname—A utility that outputs the hostname of the local host.

ipconfig—A Unix/Linux utility that displays TCP/IP configuration information.

nbtstat—A utility that provides statistics and other diagnostic information on NetBIOS over TCP/IP.

netstat—A utility that provides statistics and other diagnostic information on TCP/IP protocols.

network sniffer—A class of diagnostic applications or hardware devices that can capture and display the contents of datagrams.

ping—A diagnostic utility used to check connectivity with another host.

route—A utility that configures and displays the contents of a routing table.

traceroute—A utility that displays the router path a packet takes from its source to its destination.

tracert—The Microsoft equivalent of the traceroute utility.

13

Hour **14**

File Transfer and Access Utilities

One of the greatest things about TCP/IP is that it provides a very flexible environment in which systems of many different types can communicate. Regardless of what hardware or operating systems are in use, two hosts on a TCP/IP network can talk to one another if they use the same protocols. Usually these hosts need access to special utilities as well.

File access and transfer is usually one of the biggest uses of any network. TCP/IP contains a couple of protocols that are used specifically for file access and transfer. Most operating systems also provide built-in utilities designed to take advantage of these protocols. This hour discusses the File Transfer Protocol (FTP), Trivial File Transfer Protocol (TFTP), and the Remote Copy (rcp) command. I also explain the network file system (NFS).

At the completion of this hour you will be able to

- Explain the purpose and use of FTP
- Initiate an FTP session and use ftp commands to traverse remote directory structures, transfer files to or from the remote system, and create or remove directories
- Explain the purpose and use of TFTP
- Construct a command to transfer a file using TFTP
- Explain the purpose and use of the rpc command
- Explain the purpose and use of NFS

File Transfer Protocol (FTP)

The File Transfer Protocol (FTP) is a widely used utility that enables a user to transfer files between two computers on a TCP/IP network, regardless of the type of computers or operating systems in use. The user runs an FTP client program on one computer, and the other computer runs an FTP server program such as ftpd (FTP daemon) on a Unix box, or an FTP service on other platforms. Many FTP client programs are command-line based, but graphical versions are available as well. FTP is used primarily to transfer files, although it can perform other functions such as creating directories, removing directories, and listing files.

NEW TERM In the Unix world, a *daemon* is a process that runs in the background and performs a service when that service is requested. A daemon is called a *service* in the Windows world.

FTP uses the TCP protocol and therefore operates through a reliable, connection-oriented session between the client and server computers. The standard FTP daemon (on the server) listens on TCP port 21 for a request from a client. When a client sends a request, a TCP connection is initiated (see Hour 6, "The Transport Layer"). The remote user is then authenticated by the FTP server, and a session begins. A classic text-based FTP session requires the remote user to interact with the server through a command-line interface. Typical commands start and stop the FTP session, navigate through the remote directory structure, and upload or download files. Newer GUI-based FTP clients offer a graphic interface (rather than a command interface) for navigating directories and moving files.

FTP is also widely used on the World Wide Web, and the FTP protocol has been integrated into most Web browsers. Sometimes when you're downloading a file through a Web browser, you may notice the URL in the address box begins with ftp://.

On most computers you start a text-based FTP session by entering `ftp` followed by the hostname or IP address of the FTP server. FTP then prompts you for a user ID and a password, which are used by the FTP server to validate you as an authorized user and determine your rights. For example, the user account you log on with might be assigned read-only access, or it might be configured for both read and write operations. Many FTP servers are available for public use and allow you to log on with a user ID called `anonymous`. When the `anonymous` account is used as the user ID, you can enter virtually any password. However, it is customary to enter your e-mail account name as the password. When FTP servers are not intended for general public use, the servers are configured to not allow `anonymous` access. In that case, you must enter a user ID and password to gain access. The user ID and password are typically set up and provided by the FTP server administrator.

Many FTP client implementations allow you to enter either Unix-based commands or DOS-based commands. The actual commands available depend on the client software being used. When you transfer files using FTP, you must specify to FTP the type of file that you are about to transfer; the most common choices are binary and ASCII. Choose ASCII when the type of file you want to transfer is a simple text file. Choose binary when the type of file you want to transfer is either a program file, a word processing document, or a graphics file. The default file transfer mode is ASCII.

Be aware that many FTP servers reside on Unix boxes. Because Unix is case sensitive—that is, it distinguishes between uppercase and lowercase letters—you must match the case exactly when entering filenames. The current directory on the local computer from which you start an FTP session is the default location where files are transferred to or from.

The following is a list of commonly used FTP commands and explanations of the commands. When Unix commands and DOS commands perform the same function, both are introduced at the same point in the list.

- `ftp`   The `ftp` command is used to start the FTP client program. You can enter `ftp` by itself or you can follow it with an IP address or domain name. In Figure 14.1, an FTP session to `rs.internic.net` was started by typing `ftp rs.internic.net`. As you can see, a lot of information was returned.

  The first line tells you that you are connected. All of the lines between and including those preceded by `220` are a customized logon message presented to all users. The next line asks for a user ID; here it is entered as `anonymous`. The line preceded by `331` is a customized system message requesting your e-mail address as a password. A number always precedes a system message. As you can see by the final line, the password is not displayed when typed.

14

FIGURE 14.1

Starting an FTP session.

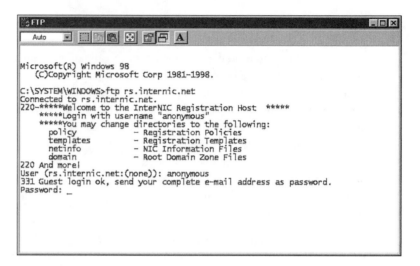

```
FTP                                                              _ □ ✕
 Auto      ▼  □ ▣ ▣ ▣  ▣▣  A

Microsoft(R) Windows 98
   (C)Copyright Microsoft Corp 1981-1998.

C:\SYSTEM\WINDOWS>ftp rs.internic.net
Connected to rs.internic.net.
220-*****Welcome to the InterNIC Registration Host  *****
     *****Login with username "anonymous"
     *****You may change directories to the following:
        policy             - Registration Policies
        templates          - Registration Templates
        netinfo            - NIC Information Files
        domain             - Root Domain Zone Files
220 And more!
User (rs.internic.net:(none)): anonymous
331 Guest login ok, send your complete e-mail address as password.
Password: _
```

- user   The user command is used to change the user ID and password information of the current session. You will be prompted to enter a new user ID and password, exactly as when you use the ftp command. This command is effectively the same as quitting FTP and starting again as a new user.

- help   The help command displays the ftp commands that are available on your FTP client.

- ls or dir   The Unix ls or ls -l command or the DOS dir command is used to list the contents of a directory. The response from these commands lists the file-names and directory names contained within the current working directory on the FTP server. The result of the ls command is shown in Figure 14.2. Between the two system messages (the lines preceded by 150 and 226) is the actual directory listing, which contains all of the files and subdirectories within the current working directory. The ls -l command is similar to the ls command but lists additional details such as read and write permissions and file creation dates.

- pwd   The pwd command is used to print the name of the current working directory. This is the directory on the remote server, not the directory on your local computer.

- cd   The cd command is used to change the current working directory on the FTP server.

- mkdir   The Unix mkdir command is used to create a directory on the FTP server inside the current working directory. This command is typically not allowable during an anonymous FTP session.

FIGURE 14.2

The ls *command.*

```
FTP                                                                    _ 8 X
Auto    ▼  □  🖻  🖿  🖾  🖬  🖨  A
150 Opening ASCII mode data connection for file list.
NIC-support
archives
billing
domain
home
internic
netinfo
netprog
nsf
policy
presentations
pub
scout
templates
usr
bin
etc
dev
ls-ltR
rfc
template
226 Transfer complete.
ftp: 168 bytes received in 0.05Seconds 3.36Kbytes/sec.
ftp>
```

- rmdir   The Unix rmdir command is used to remove a directory on the FTP server from the current working directory. This command is typically not allowable during an anonymous FTP session.

- binary   The binary command is used to switch the FTP client to binary transfer mode from the default ASCII transfer mode. Binary mode is useful when transferring binary files, such as programs and graphics, using the get, put, mget, and mput commands.

- ascii   The ascii command is used to switch the FTP client to ASCII transfer mode from binary mode. ASCII is the default transfer mode and is used when transferring text files.

- type   The type command displays the current mode (ASCII or binary) for file transfer.

- status   The status command displays information about the various settings on the FTP client. Such settings include the mode (binary or ASCII) the client is set to and whether the client is set to display verbose system messages.

- get   The get command is used to retrieve a file from an FTP server to an FTP client. Using the get command followed by a single filename will copy that file from the FTP server to the working directory on the FTP client. If the get command is followed by two filenames, the second name is used to designate the name of the new file created on the client. If you omit the second filename, FTP will usually prompt you for it.

- mget   The mget command is similar to the get command except that it lets you retrieve multiple files.

14

- put   Use the put command to transfer a file from the FTP client to the FTP
  server. Using the put command followed by a single filename will copy the file
  from the FTP client to the FTP server. If the put command is followed by two file-
  names, the second name is used to designate the name of the new file created on
  the server. If you omit the second filename, FTP will usually prompt you for it.

- mput   The mput command is similar to the put command except that it enables
  you to transfer multiple files with one command.

- open   The open command allows you to establish a new session with an FTP
  server. This is essentially a shortcut to quitting FTP and starting it again. The open
  command can be used to open a session with an entirely different FTP server or to
  reopen a session with the current server.

- close   The close command is used to end the current session with an FTP server.
  The FTP client program remains open, and you can start a new session with the
  server by using the open command.

- bye or quit   These commands close the current FTP session and terminate the
  FTP client.

Although the preceding list does not list every ftp command, it gives you an idea of
those used most often during an FTP session. To learn more about the FTP protocol, see
RFC 959.

Trivial File Transfer Protocol (TFTP)

The Trivial File Transfer Protocol (TFTP) is used to transfer files between the TFTP
client and a TFTP server, a computer running the tftpd TFTP daemon. This protocol
uses UDP as a transport and, unlike FTP, does not require a user to log on in order to
transfer files. Because TFTP does not require a user logon, it is often considered a security hole, especially if the TFTP server permits writing.

The TFTP protocol was designed to be small so that both it and the UDP protocol could
be implemented on a PROM (Programmable Read Only Memory) chip. The TFTP protocol is limited (hence the name trivial) when compared to the FTP protocol. The TFTP
protocol can only read and write files; it cannot list the contents of directories, create or
remove directories, or allow a user to log on as the FTP protocol allows. The TFTP protocol is primarily used in conjunction with the RARP and BOOTP protocols to boot
diskless workstations and, in some cases, to upload new system code or patches to
routers or other network devices. The TFTP protocol can transfer files using either an
ASCII format known as netascii or a binary format known as octet; a third format known
as mail is no longer used.

When a user enters a `tftp` statement on a command line, it initiates a connection to the server and performs the file transfer. At the completion of the file transfer, the session is closed and terminated. The syntax of the TFTP statement is as follows:

```
TFTP [-i] host [get | put] <source filename> [<destination filename>]
```

To learn more about the TFTP protocol, see RFC 1350.

Remote Copy (RCP)

The `rcp` command provides an alternative to `ftp`; it allows users to copy files over the network. The `rcp` command is the remote version of the Unix `cp` (copy) command. When using the `rcp` command, you do not need to supply a user ID or password; this might be considered a security hole. However, a level of security is provided by the fact that the name of your computer must reside in either of two server-based files named `rhosts` and `hosts.equiv`. The `rcp` command allows a user to copy files between a local computer and the host server or between two remote computers. The syntax for the `rcp` command is

```
rcp [hostname1]:filename1 [hostname2]:filename2
```

- *hostname1*   Optionally indicates the hostname or Fully Qualified Domain Name (FQDN) of the source computer. Use this hostname if the source file is located on a remote computer. See Hour 11, "Name Resolution," for more on hostnames and FQDNs.
- *filename1*   Indicates the path and filename of the source file.
- *hostname2*   Optionally indicates the hostname or FQDN of the destination computer. Use this hostname if the destination file is located on a remote computer.
- *filename2*   Indicates the path and filename of the destination file.

The following are three examples using the `rcp` command.

This example copies a file from the remote Unix computer to the local host:

```
rcp server3.corporate.earthquakes.txt earthquakes.txt
```

This example copies a file from the local host to a remote computer:

```
rcp earthquakes.txt server3.corporate.earthquakes.txt
```

You can also use `rcp` to copy a file from one remote host to another remote host. See Hour 15, "Remote Access Utilities," for more on `rcp` and other remote access options.

14

Network File System (NFS)

The network file system (NFS) was originally developed by Sun but is now supported on Unix, Linux, and many other systems. NFS allows users to access (read, write, create, and delete) directories and files located on a remote computer as if those directories and files were located on the local computer. Because NFS is designed to provide a transparent interface between local file systems and remote file systems, and because it is implemented within the operating system of both computers, it does not require any changes to application programs. Programs are capable of accessing both local files and remote files and directories via NFS without any recompilation or other changes. To the user, all files and directories appear and operate as if they existed only on the local file system.

The original implementation of NFS used the UDP protocol for its transport and was intended for use on a LAN. However, later revisions allow use of the TCP protocol; the additional reliability of TCP over UDP allows for expanded capabilities of NFS, which can now operate in a WAN.

NFS is designed to be independent of operating systems, transport protocols, and physical network architecture. This allows an NFS client to interoperate with any NFS server. This independence is achieved by using Remote Procedure Calls (RPCs) between the client and server computers. RPC is a process that enables a program running on one computer to make calls on code segments inside a program running on another computer. It has been around for many years and is supported on many operating systems. In the case of NFS, the operating system on the client issues an RPC to the operating system on the server. Because RPCs reside at a higher level on the protocol stack than the transport protocols, it can work with either TCP or UDP and of course lower-level implementations such as ethernet and token ring.

Before remote files and directories can be used on the NFS system, they must first go through a process known as *mounting*. After they are mounted, the remote files and directories appear and operate as if they were located on the local file system.

For additional information on the NFS protocol, see RFC 1094, which addresses implementation of NFS version 2. Also see RFC 1813 for updates relative to NFS version 3. NFS implementations vary with the operating system. See the vendor documentation for more on how to configure NFS for your system.

Summary

A number of TCP/IP-based utilities allow the user to transfer files to or from a remote computer or to access files located on the remote computer as if they were local. Of these, the FTP protocol is the most commonly used. It allows a user to connect to a remote system anonymously or to connect using a specific user ID and password.

With the proper permissions, the user can use ftp commands to copy files, create or remove directories, and traverse the directory structure on the remote computer.

The TFTP protocol provides basic file-transfer capability using the UDP protocol. It does not require a user login and is rarely used directly by ordinary users. The TFTP protocol is used primarily to boot diskless workstations or upload code to network devices.

The RCP protocol provides an alternative to the FTP protocol and allows the user to copy files between a between two computers. (You'll learn more about RCP in Hour 15.)

NFS allows a user to access a portion of a remote file system as if it were local. In fact, the user might be unaware that some of the files are actually located on a remote computer.

Q&A

Q What is the default representation (transfer type) for FTP?

A ASCII

Q What ftp command displays your current working directory on the remote FTP server?

A pwd (print working directory)

Q What FTP commands typically are not allowed when a user is connected using the anonymous account?

A The anonymous account is usually configured for read-only access. Commands that write to a file or change the directory structure on the FTP server are not allowed. These commands include put, mkdir, rmdir, mput, and mget.

Q Can you list the files in the directory using TFTP?

A No. TFTP can only transfer files. You can't use TFTP to view the remote directory.

Q What advantage does RCP have over FTP?

A Easier syntax; also, a login is not required in order to copy files.

Q What is the main functional difference between FTP and NFS?

A FTP is used to copy files from one computer to another, whereas NFS is used to provide access to files as if they were part of the local file system.

Workshop

14

In this workshop you connect to an FTP server, view directory listings, traverse the directory structure, and copy files to your computer. To perform this exercise, you must have an FTP client running on your computer. Windows NT/2000 and most Unix/Linux systems have built-in FTP support.

The following procedure worked at the time this book was written, but
things change on the Internet without notice, so it might not work forever.

1. Gain access to the Internet either by dialing in to your ISP or by accessing a live
   Internet connection.
2. Start an FTP session and log in to `rs.internic.net`. In other words, enter `ftp`
   `rs.internic.net`. Enter the username `anonymous`. Enter your complete e-mail
   address as your password.
3. Enter the `ls` or `ls -l` command. Compare the ways the two commands display the
   names of files and directories.
4. Enter `cd usr` to change the current directory to the `/usr` directory.
5. Use the `pwd` command to display the path to your current working directory.
6. Use the command `cd ..` to change your current working directory back to the parent directory.
7. Use the `type` command to display the default representation format.
8. Use the `status` command to display the current status of your FTP client.
9. Use the `help` command to see the other commands that are available with your
   FTP client software.
10. Use the `close` command to terminate the session with `rs.internic.net`.
11. Use the `bye` command to terminate the session with `rs.internic.net` and also the
    current FTP session.

Key Terms

Review the following list of key terms:

File Transfer Protocol (FTP)—A client/server utility and protocol used to transfer files
between two computers. In addition to transferring files, the FTP utility can create and
remove directories and display the contents of directories.

Network File System (NFS)—NFS allows the user on an NFS client computer to access
files located on a remote NFS server computer transparently.

Remote Copy (RCP)—This Unix-based utility allows you to copy files between computers using syntax that is similar to the Unix `cp` command. It provides a simple syntax to
copy files and does not require the user to log in prior to initiating the file copy process.

Trivial File Transfer Protocol (TFTP)—A client/server utility and protocol used to
transfer files between two computers.

HOUR 15

Remote Access Utilities

Networks are for sharing resources remotely, so almost anything you do on a network could fall within the definition of remote access. Still, by tradition, a few TCP/IP utilities are classified as remote access utilities. These remote access utilities grew up around Unix, but many have been ported to other operating systems. The purpose of these utilities is to give a remote user some of the capabilities a local user might have. In this hour, you'll learn about the popular Telnet application, and you'll learn about the Berkeley r* utilities—a collection of utilities designed to support remote access.

At the completion of this hour, you'll be able to

- Explain the purpose of Telnet
- List some of the Berkeley r* utilities
- Describe trusted access security

Telnet

Telnet is a set of components that provide terminal-like access to a remote computer. A Telnet session requires a Telnet client that will serve as the remote terminal and a Telnet server, which receives the connection request and allows the connection. This relationship is depicted in Figure 15.1. On Unix systems, the `telnetd` daemon acts as the server. (In the Unix world, *daemons* are programs that execute in the background and perform services when needed.)

FIGURE 15.1

A Telnet server and client.

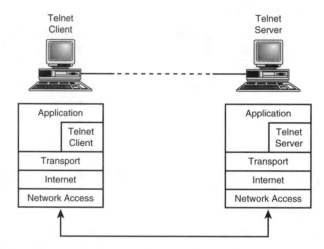

Telnet is also a protocol—a system of rules defining the interactions between Telnet servers and clients. The Telnet protocol is defined in a series of RFCs. Because Telnet is based on a well-defined open protocol, it can be and has been implemented on a wide range of hardware and software systems. The basic purpose of Telnet is to provide a means by which keyboard commands typed by a remote user can cross the network and become input for a different computer. Screen output related to the session then crosses the network from that different computer (the server) to the client system (see Figure 15.2). The effect is that the remote user can interact with the server as if he were logged in locally.

On Unix systems, the `telnet` command is entered at the command prompt, as follows:

`telnet hostname`

where *hostname* is the name of the computer to which you'd like to connect. (You can also enter an IP address instead of a hostname.) The preceding command launches the Telnet application. When Telnet is running, the commands you enter are executed on the remote computer. Telnet also provides some special commands that you can use during a Telnet session, as follows:

FIGURE 15.2
Network input and output with Telnet.

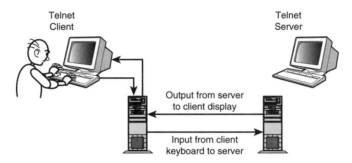

Telnet
Client

Telnet
Server

Output from server
to client display

Input from client
keyboard to server

15

- `close`   Use this command to close the connection.
- `display`   Use this command to display connection settings, such as the port or terminal emulation.
- `environ`   Use this command to set environment variables. Environment variables are used by the operating system to provide machine-specific or user-specific information.
- `logout`   Use this command to log out the remote user and close the connection.
- `mode`   Use this command to toggle between ASCII or binary file transfer mode (see Hour 14, "File Transfer and Access Utilities," for an explanation of file transfer mode).
- `open`   Use this command to connect to a remote computer.
- `quit`   Use this command to exit Telnet.
- `send`   Use this command to send special Telnet protocol sequences to the remote computer, such as an abort sequence, a break sequence, or an end-of-file sequence.
- `set`   Use this command to set connection settings.
- `unset`   Use this command to unset connection parameters.
- `?`   Use this command to print Help information.

On graphics-based platforms such as Microsoft Windows, a Telnet application might have its own icon and run in a window, but the underlying commands and processes are the same as with a text-based system. Consult your vendor documentation.

Telnet is an extremely useful and important tool on internal Unix networks. A system administrator can use Telnet to perform routine administration on remote computers. An admin can work from a single desktop computer and access a server across the network to restart a process, delete a file, create a new directory, or check system statistics. The recent emphasis on security has placed some restrictions on the free use of Telnet.

The problem is that Telnet gives network intruders what they want more than anything—direct access to a terminal session on a remote server. The Telnet standard supports password authentication, but passwords typically are transported as clear text. You almost never see Telnet deployed on the open Internet and, on internal networks where security is important, Telnet is usually deployed with some restrictions on who uses it and what they can do with it.

Berkeley Remote Utilities

The Berkeley Systems Design (BSD) Unix implementation, known as BSD Unix, was a major step in Unix's development. Many innovations that began with BSD Unix are now standard on other Unix systems and have been incorporated into other operating systems in the world of TCP/IP and the Internet.

One of the innovations of BSD Unix was a small set of command-line utilities designed to provide remote access to Unix systems. This set of utilities became known as the Berkeley r* utilities, because the name of each utility begins with an *R* for *remote*. The Berkeley r* utilities are still available on Unix systems, and versions of most of the r* utilities are distributed with OpenVMS, Linux, Windows NT, Windows 2000, and other operating systems. However, even though TCP/IP is becoming more popular and more universal, these TCP/IP utilities have received comparatively less attention.

Some of the Berkeley r* utilities are as follows:

- **Rlogin**   This utility allows users to log in remotely.
- **Rcp**   This utility provides remote file transfer.
- **Rsh**   This utility executes a remote command through the rshd daemon.
- **Rexec**   This utility executes a remote command through the rexecd daemon.
- **Ruptime**   This utility displays system information on uptime and the number of connected users.
- **Rwho**   This utility displays information on users who are currently connected.

The r* utilities were designed in an earlier and simpler time for TCP/IP networking. The creators of these utilities expected that only trusted users would access these utilities. Today, many admins reject the whole concept of a "trusted" user. The r* utilities are generally considered too risky for today's open and interconnected networks and, even on an internal network, you must be very careful about how and when to use these utilities. The r* utilities do have a rudimentary security system that, if implemented properly, offers a measure of protection in very restricted and trusted environments.

In recent years, more secure versions of some of the r* utilities have been developed to meet the need for security in today's Internet environment. Ssh, for example, is a secure remote shell application that replaces rsh and rlogin. Ssh uses encryption for secure authentication over hostile networks. You'll learn more about encryption and other security measures in Hour 20, "TCP/IP Security."

The r* utilities use a concept called *trusted access*. Trusted access allows one computer to trust another computer's authentication. In Figure 15.3, if Computer A designates Computer B as a *trusted host*, users who log in to Computer B can use the r* utilities to access Computer A without supplying a password. Computer A can also designate specific users who will be *trusted users*. Trusted hosts and users are identified in the /etc/hosts.equiv file of the remote machine to which the user is attempting to gain access. The .rhosts file in each user's home directory can also be used to grant trusted access to the user's account.

Because the /etc/hosts.equiv file and the .rhosts file grant access to system resources, they are a major target for network intruders. See Hour 19, "What Hackers Do," for more on network attacks. The vulnerability of the hosts.equiv file and the .rhosts file is one reason why the r* utilities are no longer considered secure.

FIGURE 15.3
Unix trusted access.

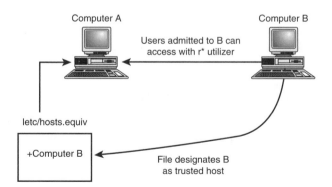

The following sections discuss some of the Berkeley r* utilities.

Rlogin

Rlogin is a remote login utility. You can use rlogin to connect with a Unix host that is running the server daemon `rlogind` (d stands for daemon). Rlogin serves the same purpose as Telnet, but rlogin is considerably less versatile. Rlogin is designed specifically to provide access to Unix systems, whereas Telnet, which is covered under a TCP/IP standard, can have a broader application. Also, rlogin does not provide some of the configuration negotiation features available with Telnet.

A significant feature of rlogin is that, because it uses the r* utilities security model, it supports remote login without a password. No-password access is a property of all r* utilities, but some users consider a passwordless terminal session a little more unsettling than some of the other functions achievable through the r* utilities. Nevertheless, the r* utilities' security model does limit access to trusted users.

> It is important to keep in mind that network operating systems such as NetWare and Windows NT/2000 also provide methods for passwordless access to network resources after the user has achieved some form of initial authentication. Many of the benefits of the r* utilities can now be achieved through other, more secure methods.

The syntax for the `rlogin` command is as follows:

`rlogin hostname`

where *hostname* is the hostname of the computer to which you'd like to gain access. If no username is specified, the username defaults to the user's username on the local computer. Otherwise, you can specify a username as follows:

`rlogin hostname -l username`

where *username* is the username you want to use for the login.

The server daemon `rlogind`, which must be running on the server machine, then checks `host.equiv` and `.rhosts` files to verify host and user information. If this authentication is successful, the remote session begins.

Rcp

Rcp provides remote file access to Unix systems. Rcp is not as versatile or as widely used as FTP, but it is still sometimes used for file transfer in the Unix world. See Hour 14 for more on rcp.

Rsh

Rsh lets you execute a single command on a remote computer without logging in to the remote computer. Rsh is short for *remote shell*. (A *shell* is a command interface to the operating system.) The rshd daemon, running on the remote computer, accepts the rsh command, verifies the username and hostname information, and executes the command. Rsh is useful when you want to enter one command and don't need or want to establish a terminal session with the remote computer.

The format for the rsh command is

```
rsh -l username hostname command
```

where *hostname* is the hostname of the remote computer, *username* is the name to use when accessing the remote computer, and *command* is the command you would like to execute.

The username (preceded by the -l) is optional. If you do not include a username, it will default to the name on the local host as follows:

```
rsh hostname command
```

Rexec

Rexec is like rsh in that it instructs the remote computer to execute a command. Rexec uses the rexecd daemon.

The syntax for the rexec command is as follows:

```
rexec hostname -l username command
```

where *hostname* is the name of the host, *username* is the user account name on the remote computer, and *command* is the command you want to execute. If you omit *-l username,* the username will default to the username on the local computer.

Ruptime

Ruptime displays a summary of how many users are logged in to each computer on the network. Ruptime also lists how long each computer has been up—hence the name *r-up-time*—and displays some additional system information.

To generate a ruptime report, you need only enter

```
ruptime
```

Both ruptime and rwho (see the next section) use the rwhod daemon. Actually, each computer on the network has an rwhod daemon that broadcasts regular reports of user activity. Each `rwhod` daemon receives and stores the reports from other `rwhod` daemons for a network-wide view of user activity.

Rwho

Rwho reports on all users who are currently logged on to network computers. Rwho lists usernames, the computer each user is logged in to, the time of login, and the time elapsed since login.

The syntax of the `rwho` command is simply

```
rwho
```

The default report excludes users whose terminals have been inactive more than an hour. For a report on all users, use the `-a` option:

```
rwho -a
```

Rwho, like ruptime, uses the `rshod` daemon.

Remote Access and the Web

A new wave of remote access options has recently developed around the Internet. Remote access applications such as Netopia's Timbuktu and Symantec pcAnywhere provide the remote user with the ability to view and control the desktop of the target computer. Microsoft now provides many of these features through the NetMeeting application.

The infinitely scriptable Linux also adds a new dimension to the concept of remote access. A Web page on a Linux or Unix computer (or any other popular Web server, for that matter) can reference a script that performs a task on the local network. A remote user can then access the Web page via the Internet (or an intranet) and initiate the task through a Web browser. This technique, of course, is no more secure than the communication link between the browser and the server. If security is an issue, it is usually better to do this only on protected networks or through some secure communications channel. See Hour 20 for more on securing TCP/IP using techniques such as Secure Sockets Layer (SSL). See Hour 17, "HTTP, HTML, and the World Wide Web," for more on HTML and the World Wide Web.

Summary

This hour covered some of the TCP/IP remote access utilities that have evolved around TCP/IP. You learned about Telnet and the r* utilities. You can use these utilities to execute commands and access information on a remote computer.

Q&A

Q Is Telnet a server application, a client application, or a protocol?

A The term Telnet could refer to either the server or the client Telnet application, or it could refer to the Telnet protocol.

Q Which file should you use if you want to designate a host as a trusted host?

A Use the /etc/hosts.equiv file or the rhosts file in a user's home directory to designate a trusted host.

Q What utility would tell me if the user Ethelred is currently logged in to the network?

A The rwho utility displays information on current users.

Key Terms

Review the following list of key terms:

rcp—A remote file transfer utility.

rexec—A remote command-execution utility.

rlogin—A remote login utility.

rsh—A remote command-execution utility.

ruptime—A utility that displays system information on uptime and the number of connected users.

rwho—A utility that displays information on currently connected users.

Telnet—A remote terminal utility.

trusted access—A weak security system in which a system administrator designates remote hosts and users who are trusted to access the local system.

PART V
TCP/IP and the Internet

Hour

Hour **16**

The Internet: A Closer Look

The ever-expanding Internet is the world's biggest example of a TCP/IP network. This hour gives a brief look at the Internet's structure. You'll also learn about some important Internet services. This discussion of the Internet continues in the next two hours, which discuss the World Wide Web (Hour 17, "HTTP, HTML, and the World Wide Web") and e-mail (Hour 18, "E-Mail").

At the end of this hour, you'll be able to

- Briefly describe the structure of the Internet
- Describe important Internet services such as the World Wide Web, e-mail, newsgroups, and chat

How the Internet Looks

You'll have to look hard to find a description of what the Internet really is. Most descriptions of the Internet, unfortunately, favor simplicity over detail, and the reader is left with little more than the vague impression that the Internet is "a highway for data."

In fact, the details of Internet topology are so complex that few professional network administrators can tell you precisely what happens to the data that leaves their lines. Nor is it necessary for them to know. The stability and versatility of TCP/IP make it possible for a datagram to enter the cloud of the Internet and emerge without oversight in exactly the right place on the other side of the Earth. Where does the datagram go when it enters that cloud?

Today's Internet is too big for the structure depicted in Figure 10.5, in which a single backbone serves an orderly constellation of autonomous networks. Today's Internet consists of multiple backbone networks, many of them managed by private corporations such as Sprint or MCI WorldCom.

> It should come as no surprise that long distance phone companies such as Sprint and MCI WorldCom are major players in the Internet topology. The presence of these long distance carriers underscores the fact that the Internet, like the phone system, is built from lots and lots and lots of cable strung over vast distances.

These backbone networks intersect at large switching facilities called *Network Access Points* (*NAPs*). WorldCom's MAE East (in the Washington, D.C., area) and MAE West (in the San Jose, California, area) are two of the busiest and most important NAPs in the United States. The MAE East and MAE West sites are considered national connection points for major ISPs. A second tier of regional NAP sites are in locations such as Chicago, Dallas, Houston, and New York.

ISPs attach to the Internet through a NAP. NAP sites such as WorldCom's MAE sites do not provide routing services. Instead, the individual ISPs supply and maintain their own routers within a secure space made available at the NAP facility.

The ISP leases what is called a Point of Presence (POP) connection (see Figure 16.1). ISPs that connect to big NAP sites are usually major Internet vendors. Some of these ISPs may be wholesalers who lease bandwidth to smaller ISPs. The smaller ISPs may lease the lines to even smaller ISPs or to corporations.

FIGURE 16.1

An ISP leases a Point of Presence (POP) on the Internet.

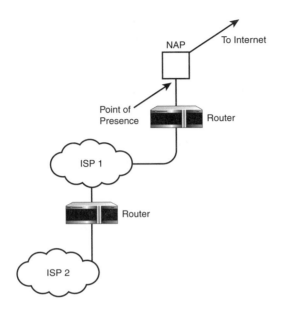

16

What Happens on the Internet

What is the point of this whole lavish labyrinth of technology? A far greater number of readers would have asked that question a few years ago. Almost anyone able to buy this book probably has some idea of what the Internet is and what it is for. Still, a short summary of the principal activities is a useful beginning for the study of the Internet landscape that begins in this hour and continues in Hours 17 and 18.

The Internet really is a big TCP/IP network, and if you're not worried about security or time delays, you can use the Internet for almost anything you can do on a routed corporate LAN.

> Of course, the security considerations are substantial. You definitely *should not* use the Internet for anything you could do on a routed corporate LAN, but you could if you wanted to.

It is important to remember that all computers participating in a networking activity (on the Internet or on any other network) have one thing in common: They are running software that was designed for the activity in which they are engaged. Networking doesn't just happen. It requires protocol software (such as the TCP/IP software described in Hours 2–7), and it also requires applications at each end of the connection that are specifically designed to communicate with each other. As shown in Figure 16.2, most computers on the Internet can be classified as either *clients* (computers that request services) or *servers* (computers that provide services). A client application on the client computer was written specifically to interact with the server application on the server computer. The server application was written to listen for requests from the client and to respond to the requests. Most of the major Internet activities fit closely with this paradigm. The principal activities include the following:

- the World Wide Web
- E-mail
- FTP
- Newsgroups
- Chat groups

FIGURE 16.2

On the Internet, a computer typically acts as a client or a server.

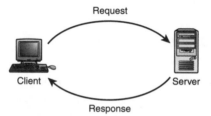

The World Wide Web, for example, is really a combination of Web clients (Web browsers) that are able to request, receive, and present data supplied in a predetermined format and Web servers, which listen for requests and transmit the Web data requested by the client.

The following sections take a closer look at the World Wide Web, e-mail, newsgroups, and chat. See Hour 14, "File Transfer and Access Utilities," for more on FTP. It is important to keep in mind, however, that the possibilities for Internet services are endless. Computers can now use the Internet for anything from a classroom to an operating room. In every case, a connection is successful because a client application and a server application know exactly what to expect from each other.

See Hour 17 for more about the World Wide Web and Hour 18 for more about e-mail.

The World Wide Web

It is no secret that the past four years have witnessed an explosion in the development of the phenomenon known as the World Wide Web. Millions of organizations now make documents available through Web sites. Some younger users think that the Web *is* the Internet.

The Web is not really a place or a thing. It is more like a method for communication. As you'll learn in the next hour, a Web server is a server that communicates using Hypertext Transfer Protocol (HTTP). When a client application that can communicate using HTTP (a Web browser) connects to the Web server, it receives a burst of data that is assembled by the browser into the image of a Web page.

16

Web browsers are constantly growing more sophisticated, adding still more features to the rich set of Web activities. The browser is evolving into something like a universal user interface for network applications, and many believe that in a few years average users will be able to conduct all of their digital business without ever having to leave the browser window.

Hour 17 provides a detailed description of the Web and how it works.

> Remember that the Internet is a big TCP/IP network connecting computers all over the world. The Web is a collection of Internet resources that use the HTTP protocol.

E-Mail

E-mail (short for electronic mail) was the first truly revolutionary innovation to emerge from the Internet culture, and it may yet prove to be the most enduring. The user writes a letter using an e-mail client application and sends that letter over the Internet to another user, who may be on the other side of the world.

As you'll learn in Hour 18, each user on an e-mail system has a mailbox on a mail server computer. The *mailbox* is a file or directory where messages collect until the user wants to read them. When the user checks for mail, the messages are downloaded to the user's home computer.

See Hour 18 for more on e-mail.

Newsgroups

Another rich source of information on the Internet is through Internet news servers. Unlike Web servers, which typically do not allow the user to add or alter Web content, news servers enable remote users to post messages. News servers provide what are called newsgroups. Each newsgroup is targeted at a specific topic, interest, or concern. A client application called a newsreader connects to the news server. The newsreader lets the user view the list of available newsgroups and subscribe to newsgroups in which the user has an interest. After a user has subscribed to a newsgroup, she can display messages posted by others or post new messages to the newsgroup.

Some newsgroups are moderated to ensure that inappropriate messages are not available. However, other newsgroups are not moderated.

A newsreader requires some initial setup before you can view news messages. First the newsreader must download the names of available newsgroups. Then the user can select the newsgroup(s) that she is interested in joining. Finally, news messages are downloaded from the selected newsgroup(s) for viewing, as shown in Figure 16.3.

FIGURE 16.3

View the content of individual news messages.

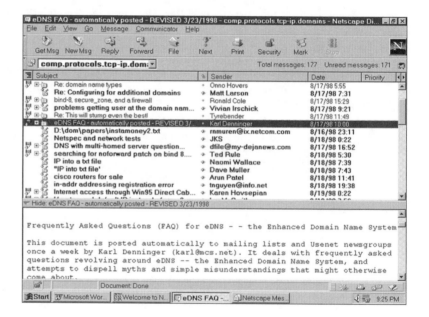

Chat

Internet chat is an interactive text-based conversation. Users converse by writing interactive messages to each other. These messages appear on the screen in a continuous transcript.

Chat groups (sometimes called *chat rooms*) are commonly organized around a shared interest. For instance, you might find a chat room for Solaris admins or medieval musicologists. Recently, online magazines have begun to use the chat format for real-time interviews with celebrities. Chat groups differ from newsgroups in that chat is interactive. If you post a message with a newsgroup, you might have to come back later to get a response. If you enter the message in a chat room, you may get a response immediately, but that response can only be from someone else who happens to be visiting the chat room at the time.

Summary

This hour offered a brief look at how the modern Internet is constructed. You learned about Network Access Points (NAPs) and Internet Point of Presence (POP) connections. This hour also described some of the services available on the Internet, including the World Wide Web, e-mail, newsgroups, and chat. Another important Internet service (FTP) was discussed in Hour 14.

Q&A

Q My company wants to become an Internet service provider (ISP). We have attempted to establish a Point of Presence (POP) connection with a nearby NAP, but no places are available. How can we get connected?

A You can lease bandwidth from a wholesale ISP.

Q My company wants to create a service for customers to post questions about our products. Every week, a technical expert will post responses to the customers' questions so the answers will be available for all customers. What Internet service should we use?

A Use an Internet newsgroup.

Q My company wants to advertise our products for users on the Internet. We want full graphics capability so that we can show pictures from our catalog. We also want users to be able to download catalogs and other product information. What Internet service should we use?

A Use the World Wide Web.

Q I manage the Web site for a famous rock star. We have posted several intimate pictures of the star, but his fans still tend to think of him as remote. How can I use the tools of the Web to bring the rock star closer to his audience?

A One idea would be to host a weekly chat room so that visitors could converse directly with the rock star in real time.

Key Terms

Review the following list of key terms:

chat—A text-based interactive discussion.

e-mail—An electronic message sent from one user to another on a network or the Internet.

Network Access Point (NAP)—A facility that connects Internet backbone networks.

newsgroup—An online bulletin board where users with a common interest can post messages and receive responses.

newsreader—A client application that participates in a newsgroup.

Point of Presence (POP)—An attachment point to the Internet leased by an ISP.

World Wide Web—A client/server process that uses the Hypertext Transfer Protocol (HTTP).

Hour 17

HTTP, HTML, and the World Wide Web

At the completion of this hour you will be able to

- Show how the World Wide Web works
- Describe URLs and formulate your own URLs
- Build a basic Web page using text and HTML tags
- Discuss the HTTP protocol and describe how it works
- List the benefits of server-end and client-end scripting

What Is the World Wide Web?

As you learned in Hour 16, "The Internet: A Closer Look," the view of the Web page that you see through the window of your Web browser is the result of a conversation between the browser and a Web server computer. The language used for that conversation is called Hypertext Transfer Protocol (HTTP). The data that is delivered from the server to the client is a finely crafted jumble of text, images, addresses, and formatting codes rendered to a unified document through an amazing versatile formatting language called Hypertext Markup Language (HTML).

HTML is conceptually similar to a word processing format. In fact, the best way to begin a discussion of HTML is to consider how word processing documents evolved. Experts have always recognized the need to store and transmit information written in a human language (such as English or Russian or French). Strategies quickly evolved for efficiently storing and displaying alphanumeric characters. In the United States, the ASCII standard coded each letter and number (and many punctuation signs) into a single bit pattern. ASCII text files were used throughout the computing world for configuration files, online help documents, and electronic mail messages. Text files are still an important feature on Unix/Linux operating systems. At some point, the rapidly evolving computer technology began to merge with the rapidly evolving word processing technology. For professional printed documents, vendors needed a way to introduce formatting into the text file. Was it possible to make a heading appear in boldface, change a margin, or change to a different font? The vendors developed numerous systems (many of them proprietary) for coding formatting information into a text document. Some of these systems used ASCII-based codes. Others used different digital markers to denote formatting information.

 Of course, these formatting code systems work only if the application that writes the document and the application that reads the document agree on what each code means.

These word processing systems became increasingly sophisticated. Some developed the capability to reference another file, such as a figure, that would then appear in the text when the document was displayed.

The creators of HTML wanted to develop a universal, vendor-neutral system for encoding format information. They wanted to include not just typesetting codes but also pictures and layout information. And they added another innovation that was to become a powerful and important feature of the new format: the hypertext link.

A link is a segment of text, or even just a region of the screen, that causes the browser to open a new page or move to a different part of the page. Links let the reader view the online information in small doses. The reader can choose whether or not to link to another page for additional information. HTML documents can be assembled into unified systems of pages and links (see Figure 17.1). A visitor can find her way through the data depending on how she traverses the links. And the Web developer has almost unlimited ability to define where a link will lead. The link can lead to another HTML document in the same directory, a document in a different directory, or even a document on a different computer. The link might lead to a totally different Web site on another computer across the world.

FIGURE 17.1

A Web site is a unified system of pages and links.

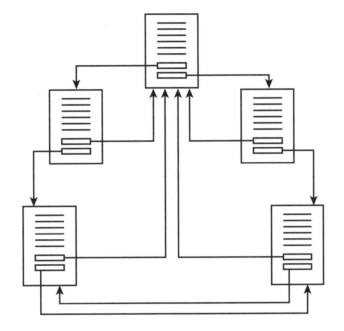

Within the HTML code, the link takes the form of a special address called a uniform resource locator (URL). The form of URL most associated with the Web is

`http://www.dobro.com`

The URL specifies the protocol to use to access a resource and the DNS name of the Web server. This example is readily identified by anyone who has ever worked with a Web browser. It is also common to see a path and filename appended to the URL:

`http:/www.dobro.com/techniques/repair/fix.html`

The URL can actually transmit a number of additional parameters. You sometimes see a long, complex URL with additional parameters in the address box of the browser window after you access a site through one of the Internet search engines. You'll learn more about the general form of URLs in the next section.

You may have noticed that the URL for a typical Web site (such as www.whitehouse.gov) includes only a DNS domain name and doesn't seem to make reference to a filename. If the filename is not specified, the browser automatically opens a default filename for the site.

A Web browser navigates by URLs. You access a Web page by entering the URL of the page in the address box of the browser window (see Figure 17.2). When you click on a link, the browser opens the Web page specified in the link's URL.

FIGURE 17.2

Enter the URL in the address box of the browser window.

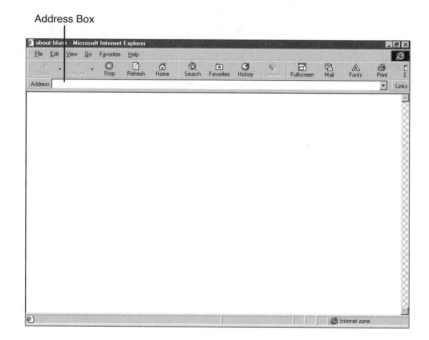

To summarize this brief introduction, an HTML document contains some combination of

- Text
- Graphics
- Text formatting codes (font and layout information)
- References to secondary files such as graphics files
- Links to other HTML documents or to other locations in the current document

To visit a Web site, the user enters the URL of the Web site into the Web browser window. The browser initiates a connection to the Web server specified in the URL. The server sends the HTML data across the network to the Web browser. The Web browser assembles the HTML data into the view of the Web page that appears in the browser window. The following sections discuss this process in greater detail. Of course, the process has recently gotten complicated by new features such as scripting and Dynamic HTML. You'll learn about these new features also.

A Closer Look at URLs

URLs are so common now that they appear with little or no explanation on TV commercials and bubble gum wrappers. But the home page URLs you hear in the media are only a small subset of the many options available with this versatile form. The URL is defined in RFC 1738.

Not all URLs refer to HTTP. In fact, the URL form was devised as a universal method for several different Internet protocols. The protocol portion of the URL is referred to as the *scheme*. The scheme identifies a protocol and therefore tells the computer how to interpret the rest of the URL. The general format for a URL is described in RFC 1738 as

`<scheme>:<scheme-specific-part>`

Table 17.1 shows some of the scheme options defined in RFC 1738. Other schemes are also possible. In fact, some new schemes have been added in later RFCs.

TABLE 17.1 URL Schemes

Scheme	Description
ftp	File Transfer Protocol
http	Hypertext Transfer Protocol
gopher	The Gopher protocol
mailto	Electronic mail
news	Usenet news
nntp	Usenet news with NNTP access
telnet	Interactive session (see Hour 15)
wais	Wide area information servers
file	Host-specific filenames

As the `<protocol-specific-part>` term in the general form of the URL demonstrates, the structure of the URL may differ, depending on the URL's scheme. The computer first reads the scheme, and the scheme tells the computer how to interpret the rest of the URL. Since this hour focuses on HTTP, this section will focus primarily on the HTTP form of the URL. But it is worth noting that you'll also encounter other schemes as you browse the Web. The `ftp` scheme is another common variant. Most modern Web browsers are capable of recognizing alternative schemes such as `ftp` and responding to the URL accordingly.

The general form for an HTTP URL is

```
http://<host>[:<port>]/<path>[;<parameters>][?<search>]
```

`<host>` is the DNS name of the server (for example, `www.dobro.com`), and `<path>` is the path to the HTML document or other resource. The other options are less common and are less familiar to the average user. Those options include

- `<port>`—The port number of the daemon or service to which the browser is connecting. (See Hour 6, "The Transport Layer," for more on port numbers.) The port number reserved for HTTP servers is TCP port 80. If the port number is omitted, port 80 is assumed.

- `<parameters>`—Optional parameters supplied by the client. The user almost never has to enter parameters in order to access a Web site. However, parameters are sometimes passed to the server through scripts.

- `<search>`—Lets the client send a query string to the user. The user almost never enters a query into a URL by hand. Watch the URL box of your Web browser when you enter a search through one of the Internet search engines. You may see a query sting transmitted to the search server through the URL.

Complex URLs containing ports, parameters, and queries are sometimes used to reconfigure the Web server itself. The Web server must possess the necessary extensions and scripts to process the configuration request.

If a connection has already been established, it is not necessary to use the entire URL to identify a resource. HTTP and RFC 1738 permit the use of a relative URL. The relative URL gives the URL as referenced from the current page or from a default `<BASE>` location defined in the document. For example, if you are already on the home page specified with the URL `http://www.dobro.com`, the relative URL to the file

```
http:/www.dobro.com/techniques/repair/fix.html
```

is `techniques/repair/fix.html`.

The relative URL might seem like a confusing way to save a few bits and keystrokes, but it offers benefits in building and deploying Web sites. As shown in Figure 17.3, if the

Webmaster uses relative URLs for the internal links within a Web site, the complete directory structure for the site can be copied to a different server without disrupting the integrity of the links.

FIGURE 17.3
Relative URLs make a
Web site portable.

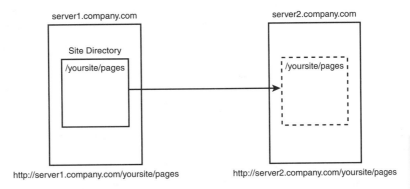

Understanding HTML

HTML is the payload that is transmitted through the processes of HTTP. As you learned earlier in this hour, an HTML document includes text, formatting codes, references to other files, and links. When you inspect the contents of a basic HTML document using a text processing application such as Windows Notepad or Unix's vi, you'll find that the document is actually an ordinary text file. The file contains any text that will appear with the page, and it also includes a number of special HTML codes called *tags*. Tags are instructions to the browser. They do not appear as written on the Web page, but they affect the way the data appears and the way the page behaves. The HTML tags supply all the formatting, file references, and links associated with a Web page. Some important HTML tags are shown in Table 17.2.

TABLE 17.2   Some Important HTML Tags

Tag	Description
\<HTML>	Marks beginning and end of HTML content in the file.
\<HEAD>	Marks the beginning and end of the header section.
\<BODY>	Marks the beginning and end of the body section, which describes the text that will appear in the browser window.
\<H1> \<H2> \<H3> \<H4> \<H5> \<H6>	Marks the beginning and end of a heading. Each heading tag represents a different heading level. H1 is the highest level.
\<B>	Marks the beginning and end of a section of bold text.
\<U>	Marks the beginning and end of a section of underlined text.

17

TABLE 17.2   continued

Tag	Description
<I>	Marks the beginning and end of a section of italicized text.
<FONT>	Marks the beginning and end of a section with special font characteristics. See Table 17.3 for some of the available font attributes.
<A>	Marks the beginning and end of a hypertext link. The link destination URL appears inside the first <A> tag as a value for the HREF attribute (as described later in this section).
<IMG>	Specifies an image file that should appear in the text. The file URL appears in the tag as a value for the SRC attribute. (You'll learn more about attributes later in this section.)

Of course, there is much more to HTML than a single table can convey. Many tags apply to a block of text. If so, the tag appears at the beginning and the end of the block. The tag at the end of the block includes the slash character (/) to signify that it is an end tag. In other words, the callout for an H1 heading would be tagged as follows:

```
<H1>Dewey Defeats Truman</H1>
```

An HTML document is supposed to begin with a <!DOCTYPE> declaration. The !DOCTYPE defines the version of HTML used for the document. For HTML 4.0, the !DOCTYPE command is

```
<!DOCTYPE HTML PUBLIC "-//W3C/DTD HTML 4.0//EN">
```

(Web pages that use special browser extensions may specify a different document type.)

Most browsers don't require the !DOCTYPE statement, and many HTML tutorials don't even discuss the !DOCTYPE.

Following the !DOCTYPE statement is the <HTML> tag. The rest of the document is enclosed between the <HTML> tag and a corresponding </HTML> tag at the end of the file. Within the beginning and ending <HTML> tags, the document is divided into the following two sections:

- The head (enclosed between the <HEAD> and </HEAD> tags) contains information about the document. The information in the head does not appear on the Web page, although the <TITLE> tag specifies a title that will appear in the title bar of the browser window. The <TITLE> is a required element. Other elements of the <HEAD> section are optional, such as the <STYLE> tag for information on document styles. See an HTML text for more on <STYLE>.

- The body (enclosed between the <BODY> and </BODY> tags is the text that actually appears on the Web page and any HTML tags related to that text.

A very simple HTML document is as follows:

```
<!DOCTYPE HTML PUBLIC "-//W3C/DTD HTML 4.0//EN">
<HTML>
<HEAD>
<TITLE> Ooh This is Easy </TITLE>
</HEAD>
<BODY>
Easy!
</BODY>
<HTML>
```

If you save the preceding HTML to a text file and then open the file with a Web browser, Easy! will appear in the browser window. The title bar will include the title Ooh This is Easy (see Figure 17.4).

FIGURE 17.4

A very easy Web page example.

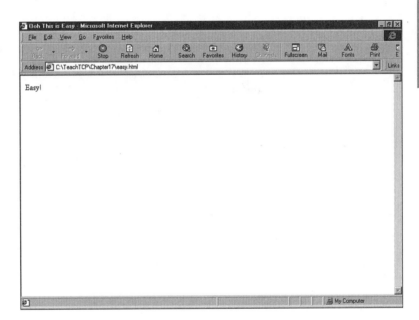

You can spice up the page with additional text and formatting in the body section. The following example adds the <H1> and <H2> tags for headings, the <P> tag for a paragraph, the <B> tag for bold, the <I> tag for italics, and the <FONT> tag for font information. Note that the <FONT> tag includes an attribute. Attributes are parameters enclosed within the tag that provide additional information. See Table 17.3 for other font attributes.

```
<!DOCTYPE HTML PUBLIC "-//W3C/DTD HTML 4.0//EN">
<HTML>
<HEAD>
<TITLE> Ooh This is Easy </TITLE>
```

```
</HEAD>
<BODY>
<H1>The Easy and Hard of HTML</H1>
<P><U>Webster's Dictionary</U> defines HTML as <I>"a small snail found
originally in the Archipelago of Parakeets." I borrow from this theme in
my consideration of HTML.</P><H2>HTML is Easy</H2>
<P>HTML is easy to learn and use because everyone reacts to it
energetically. You can walk into a bar and start speaking HTML, and the
man beside you will <B>happily</B> tell you his many accomplishments.</P>
<H2>HTML is Hard</H2>
<P>HTML is hard because the options are bewildering. You never know when
to use <FONT SIZE=1>small text</FONT> and when to use <FONT SIZE=7>big
 text</FONT>.</P>
</BODY>
</HTML>
```

The preceding example appears in the browser as shown in Figure 17.5.

FIGURE 17.5

Expanding the easy example.

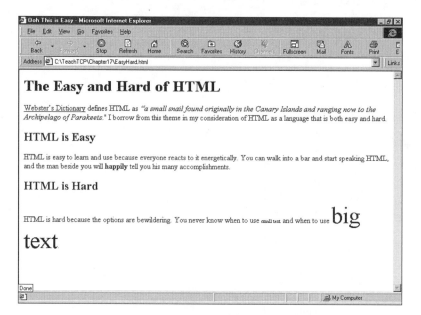

TABLE 17.3   HTML <FONT> Tag Attributes

Attribute	Description
SIZE	Relative font size setting. Values vary from 1 to 7: <FONT SIZE=7>.
LANG	Language code denoting the language in which the text is written.
FACE	Typeface setting: <FONT FACE="Arial">.
COLOR	Color of the text: <FONT COLOR="RED">.

As you learned earlier in this hour, the hypertext link is a very important element of Web design. A link is a reference to another document or another part of the current document. If the user clicks on the highlighted text of the link, the browser immediately opens the document referenced in the link. The effect is that the user appears to lilt through an endless garden of colorful and informative content.

It is occasionally worth remembering that the term *browser* originally referred to a giraffe or a large dinosaur eating leaves out of the trees.

A link appears in the HTML file as a tag. The simplest form of a link uses the <A> tag with the URL of the link destination given as a value for the HREF attribute. For instance, in the preceding example, if you would like the words "Archipelago of Parakeets" to appear as hypertext with a link to a Web site that tells about the archipelago, enclose the words within <A> tags as follows:

```
originally in the <A HREF=http://ArchipelagoParakeets.com> Archipelago of
Parakeets</A>. I borrow from this theme
```

The versatile HTML format includes many additional options that cannot be included in this brief introduction. You can place a hotspot link inside a picture. You can create your own style sheets with special tags for preformatted paragraph styles. You can structure the Web page with tables, columns, forms, and frames. Or you can add radio buttons, checkboxes, and pull-down menus. In the early days of HTML, designers coded all the HTML directly into their documents using text editors (as described in the preceding examples). Professional Web designers now work with special Web development applications, such as Dreamweaver or FrontPage, that hide the details of HTML and let the designer view the page as it will appear to the user.

Static, preformed HTML documents like those described in this section are still widely used, but many Web sites today use Dynamic HTML techniques to generate the Web content at the time of the request. You'll learn more about Dynamic HTML later in this hour.

Understanding HTTP

As you learned earlier, Web servers and browsers communicate using the Hypertext Transfer Protocol (HTTP). The current version of HTTP (HTTP 1.1) is described in RFC 2616. The purpose of HTTP is to support the transfer of HTML documents. HTTP is an application-level protocol. The HTTP client and server applications use the reliable TCP transport protocol to establish a connection.

HTTP has the following duties:

- To establish a connection between the browser (the client) and the server
- To negotiate settings and establish parameters for the session
- To provide for the orderly transfer of HTML content
- To close the connection with the server

Although the nature of Web communication has become extremely complex, most of that complexity relates to how the server builds the HTML content and what the browser does with the content it receives. The actual process of transferring the content through HTML is relatively uncluttered.

When you enter a URL into the browser window, the browser first checks the scheme of the URL to determine the protocol. (As you learned earlier in this hour, Web browsers support other protocols besides HTTP.) If the browser determines that the URL refers to a resource on an HTTP site, it extracts the DNS name from the URL and initiates the name resolution process. The client computer sends the DNS lookup request to a name server and receives the server's IP address. The browser then uses the server's IP address to initiate a TCP connection with the server. (See Hour 6 for more on TCP.)

In older versions of HTTP (before version 1.1), the client and server opened a new TCP connection for each item transferred. Recent versions of HTTP allow the client and server to maintain a persistent connection.

Once the TCP connection is established, the browser uses the HTTP GET command to request the Web page from the server. The GET command contains the URL of the resource the browser is requesting and the version of HTTP the browser wants to use for the transaction. The browser can send the relative URL with the GET request (rather than the full URL) because the connection with the server has already been established:

```
GET /watergate/tapes/transcript HTTP/1.1
```

The server receives the request and returns the requested document. Along with the document is a header containing several settings. The parameters specified in the header take the form:

```
keyword:value
```

Table 17.4 lists some of the HTTP header fields. All fields are optional, and any field that is not understood by the browser is ignored.

TABLE 17.4   Examples of HTTP Header Fields

Field	Value Must Be	Description
Content-Length	integer	Size of the content object in octets •
Content-Encoding	x-compress x-gzip	Value representing the type of encoding associated with the message
Date	standard date format defined in RFC 850	Date in Greenwich mean time when the object was created
Last-modified date	standard date format defined in RFC 850	Date in Greenwich mean time when the object was last modified
Content-Language	language code per ISO 3316	The language in which the object was written

As you can see from Table 17.4, some of the header fields are purely informational. Other header fields may contain information necessary to parse and process the incoming HTML document.

| The header field format used with HTML is borrowed from the e-mail header format specified in RFC 822. |

The Content-Length field is particularly important on today's Internet. In the earlier HTTP version 1.0, each request/response cycle required a new TCP connection. The client opened a connection and initiated a request. The server fulfilled the request and then closed the connection. In that situation, the client knew when the server had stopped sending data because the server closed the TCP connection. Unfortunately, this process required the increased overhead necessary for continually opening and closing connections. More recent versions of HTTP (HTTP 1.1 and later) allow the client and server to maintain the connection for longer than a single transmission. In that case, the client needs some way of knowing when a single response is finished. The Content-Length fields specifies the length of the HTML object associated with the response. If the server doesn't know the length of the object it is sending—a situation increasingly common with the appearance of Dynamic HTML—the server sends the header field Connection:close to notify the browser that the server will specify the end of the data by closing the connection.

HTTP also supports a negotiation phase in which the server and browser agree to common settings for certain format and preference options.

Advanced HTML Techniques

The Web grew up around the vision of the HTML file as a simple, static text file served uniformly to all requests, but this vision has gotten complicated in recent years by advances in Web technology. Web sites now commonly generate Web content at the time of the client's request. These Dynamic HTML techniques allow the content to adapt to the specific preferences and requests of the user. Dynamic HTML also simplifies the task of Web design (once you get past the programmatic hurdles) because the Web server can serve up unlimited combinations of output through a single template.

At the same time, another vision is now playing out in the Web world: client-side programming. In this vision, programmatic instructions are passed to the client along with the HTML data, and these instructions execute on the client computer while the user views the Web page.

You'll learn more about these server-side and client-side HTML techniques in the following sections.

Server-Side HTML Techniques

You may have noticed in the earlier discussion of HTML code that there is nothing difficult or complex about pasting HTML tags into a text file. In fact, it is a fairly simple matter to get a computer program or script to assemble HTML content. This dynamic approach enables a Web site to interact with the user. The server can formulate the Web page in response to user input. Server-side scripting also lets the server accept input from the client and process that input behind the scenes. A common server-side scripting scenario is show in Figure 17.6. The process is as follows:

1. The user browses to a page that includes a form for purchasing a product or entering visitor information.

2. The server generates the form based on user choices and transmits the form to the browser.

3. The user enters the necessary information into the form, and the browser transmits the form back to the server. (Note that the HTML form feature reverses the usual process. The browser sends content to the server at the server's request.)

4. The server accepts the data from the browser and uses a programming interface to pass the data to programs that process the user information. If the user is purchasing a product, these behind-the-scenes programs may check credit card information or send a shipment order to the mail room. If the user is adding her name to a mailing list or joining a restricted online site, a program may add the user information to a database.

FIGURE 17.6

A server-side scripting scenario.

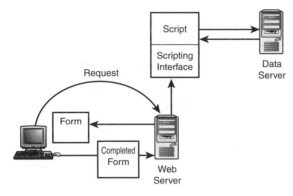

One of the more popular methods for interfacing a program or script with a Web page is through the common gateway interface (CGI). CGI was developed to accept form-based input from a Web user, process that input, and then generate output in the form of HTML. CGI scripts are commonly written in the Perl language, but CGI is compatible with other languages, including C.

Once the control passes through the CGI interface to the program, the program can take on any of the tasks typically accomplished through software. You can use a CGI script to process an order, respond to a query, or assemble a custom view of the Web page.

CGI is only one of several methods for integrating server-end processing with a Web page. Other methods include the following:

- **NSAPI** Netscape Server Application Programming Interface, a programming interface designed for the Netscape Web server product.
- **ISAPI** Internet Server Application Programming Interface, a programming interface designed for Microsoft's Web server product.
- **Active Server Pages** A server-side scripting environment developed by Microsoft.
- **Allaire ColdFusion** A Web application development package for developing dynamic Web sites. ColdFusion places special emphasis on database connectivity.

As Figure 17.6 shows, one of the most important uses for this server-end processing capability is so that the Web server can interact with a database system. Through this feature, the Web page can serve as a transaction processor and remote query interface. Some Web server applications have begun to include built-in database interface features. The huge commercial Web sites are almost always integrated with equally huge and well-designed database systems.

Another emerging use for server-end processing technology is as a network configuration and management tool. In this scenario, a set of management utilities is launched and monitored through a Web-based interface. Some network devices, such as routers or NAT devices, have built-in mini-Web servers that enable the administrator to access the devices through a browser for configuration and maintenance. Larger Web-based management systems that monitor a whole network are also available.

The power and usefulness of the Web-based programming interface seemed nearly unlimited a few years ago. These techniques are still an integral part of today's Internet, but experts have begun to realize that these types of tools can cause security problems if they aren't implemented carefully. By their very design, these programs essentially invite the remote user (often an anonymous Web user) to execute a program on the server machine. Hostile intruders have become increasingly adept at exploiting the possibilities of these tools for gaining entry to the Web server's security system. You'll learn more about security issues in Hour 19, "What Hackers Do," and Hour 20, "TCP/IP Security."

Client-Side HTML Techniques

Client-side processing has also enhanced and transformed the Web experience. Today's browsers are capable of executing code passed directly to the client computer from the Web server. Client-side processing reduces the processor load on the server infrastructure and often reduces the total amount of information that must be transmitted over the network. Java applets (and other, similar technologies) are the basis for the bouncing balls and laughing monkeys that move about in the browser window when you access certain Web sites. These technologies also have a more serious side. Client-side scripts can be used to check the integrity of a data entry form. Microsoft's ActiveX controls provide a link to other program objects on the client computer, offering powerful possibilities for integrating Web and workstation.

A few years ago, many believed the future of computing was in a complete Java-based operating environment that would download to the client at startup. This concept seems to have cooled recently, but the idea underscores the untapped potential of client-side processing techniques.

Summary

This hour described the processes at work behind the famous Internet service known as the World Wide Web. You learned about how the Web works. You learned about URLs and received a brief introduction to HTML documents. This hour also described the HTTP protocol that facilitates the delivery of HTML content from the server to the client. Finally, you learned about server-end and client-end scripting techniques and how they enhance the capabilities of a Web site.

Q&A

Q What is the URL of a Web resource called `gaunt.html` in the `thin/MoreThin` directory associated with the server `www.railman.com`?

A `http://www.railman.com/thin/MoreThin/gaunt.html`

Q What are the major sections of an HTML document?

A The HTML content falls between the `<HTML>` `</HTML>` tags. Within these tags are the `<HEAD>` section and the `<BODY>` section. The `<HEAD>` section contains title, style, and control settings. The `<BODY>` section contains the content that will appear in the Web browser window. The specification calls for a `!DOCTYPE` statement before the first HTML tag. The `!DOCTYPE` statement is often omitted.

Q What HTML tag changes the color of text?

A To change the color of text, use the `<FONT>` tag with the `COLOR` attribute:

`<FONT COLOR="RED"> red text </FONT>`

Q What HTML tag defines a hypertext link?

A For a hypertext link, use the `<A>` tag with the `HREF` attribute:

`<A HREF=www.ElvisIsDiseased.com>I'm All Shook Up</A>`

17

Workshop

The popular browsers Internet Explorer and Netscape Navigator both have options that let the user view the HTML code used to generate a Web site. Other browsers provide similar options.

For Internet Explorer:

1. Visit your favorite Web site. Take a good look at how the site appears to the user.

2. Select the View menu from the Internet Explorer menu bar and choose Source.

3. The HTML source code that generated the Web page appears in a text editor window. The HTML for the site probably contains tags that weren't discussed in this hour. See an HTML text for additional information.

For Netscape Navigator:

1. Visit your favorite Web site. Take a good look at how the site appears to the user.

2. Select the View menu from the Netscape Navigator menu bar and choose Page Source.

3. The HTML source code that generated the Web page appears in a secondary window. The HTML for the site probably contains tags that weren't discussed in this hour. See an HTML text for additional information.

Most people think of a browser as a tool that interacts directly with a Web server, but a browser can also open a file on the local computer as a word processor or a spreadsheet application would do. You can create your own HTML page using the tags described in this hour and view that page using your Internet browser.

1. Start a text editor on your computer. On Windows systems, start the Notepad accessory (don't use WordPad!). For Unix/Linux systems, start any text editor, such as vi or Emacs.

2. Build your own HTML page using the techniques described earlier in this hour, in the section "Understanding HTML."

3. Save the HTML file you created in step 2.

4. Start your Web browser.

5. Open the HTML file you created in step 2. For Internet Explorer, choose the File menu and select Open. Enter the directory path and filename of the HTML document. In Netscape Navigator, choose the File menu and select Open Page. Enter the directory path and filename and click Open in Navigator.

6. See if the page turned out as you expected. Experiment with editing the HTML and viewing the changes in the browser. (Don't forget to refresh the browser view after you make a change to the HTML document. In Netscape, click the Reload button. In IE, click the Refresh button.)

Key Terms

Review the following list of key terms:

body—The section of the HTML document that contains the text that will actually appear in the browser window. The body section is enclosed between the <BODY> and </BODY> tags.

browser—An HTTP client application. Most modern browsers can also process other protocols, such as FTP.

CGI (common gateway interface)—A programming interface that lets a designer integrate scripts and programs with a Web page.

head—The beginning section of an HTML document containing the title of the document and other optional parameters. The head section is enclosed between the <HEAD> and </HEAD> tags.

HTML (Hypertext Markup Language)—A markup language used for building Web pages. HTML consists of text and special codes describing formatting, links, and graphics.

HTTP (Hypertext Transfer Protocol)—The protocol used to transmit HTML content between the server and client.

hypertext link—A highlighted portion of a Web page. When the user clicks on the link, the browser goes to an alternative document or location specified as a URL in the link definition.

scheme—The protocol portion of a URL.

tag—An HTML instruction.

uniform resource locator (URL)—A character string in a standard format describing a resource and a protocol to use for accessing that resource. URLs are used to identify resources on the World Wide Web.

17

Hour **18**

E-Mail

You don't have to be a computer professional to notice that e-mail is becoming an extremely common feature of the modern world. Both professional and personal relationships now depend on e-mail for fast, reliable communication across great distances. This hour introduces some important e-mail concepts and shows how electronic mail services operate on a TCP/IP network.

At the completion of this hour you will be able to

- Describe the parts of an e-mail message
- Discuss the e-mail delivery process
- Describe how an SMTP transmission works
- Discuss the mail retrieval protocols POP3 and IMAP4
- Describe the role of an e-mail reader

What Is E-Mail?

An e-mail message is an electronic letter composed on one computer and transmitted across a network to another computer (which may be nearby or may be on the other side of the world). E-mail developed early in the history of networking. Almost as soon as computers were linked into networks, computer engineers began to wonder if humans as well as machines could communicate across those same network links.

The current Internet e-mail system dates back to ARPAnet days. Most of the Internet's e-mail infrastructure is derived from a pair of documents published in 1982: RFC 821 (Simple Mail Transfer Protocol) and RFC 822 (Standard for the Format of ARPA Internet Text Messages). Other proposed e-mail formats have developed since then (such as the X.400 system, as well as several proprietary formats), but the simplicity and versatility of SMTP-based electronic mail have made it the dominant form and the *de facto* standard for the Internet.

Electronic mail was invented in the days of the text-based user interface, and the original purpose of e-mail was to transmit text. The e-mail message format is designed to transmit text efficiently. The original e-mail specifications did not include provisions for sending binary files. One of the primary reasons for the efficiency of e-mail is that ASCII text is light and simple to transmit. But emphasis on ASCII text ultimately proved limiting. In the 1990s, the e-mail format was extended to include binary attachments. An attachment can be any type of file, as long as it doesn't exceed the maximum size allowed for the e-mail application. As you'll learn in this hour, these attachments are typically encoded in Multipurpose Internet Mail Extensions (MIME) format. Users today commonly attach graphics files, spreadsheets, or word processing files to their e-mail messages.

How E-Mail Looks

Your e-mail reader applications assemble a message into the format necessary for Internet transmission. If your network uses a different protocol system (or a different e-mail system), the message may pass through one or more e-mail gateways that convert the message into the Internet-ready format described in this hour. An e-mail sent over the Internet consists of two parts:

- The header
- The body

Like the body of the message, the header is transmitted as ASCII-based text. The header consists of a series of keyword field names followed by one or more comma-separated values. Most of the mail header fields are familiar to anyone who has worked with e-mail. Some of the important header fields are given in Table 18.1.

TABLE 18.1   Some Important Mail Header Fields

Header Field	Description
To:	E-mail address(es) of mail recipient(s).
From:	E-mail address of sender.
Date:	Date and time the message was sent.
Subject:	A brief description of the message subject.
Cc:	E-mail addresses of other users who will receive a copy of the message.
Bcc:	E-mail addresses of users who will receive a blind copy of the message. A *blind copy* is a copy of the message that the other recipients don't know about. Any e-mail address listed in the Bcc field will not appear in the header received by the other recipients.
Reply-To:	E-mail address that will receive replies to this message. If this field is not given, replies will go to the address referenced in the From: field.

Following the header is a blank line, and following the blank line is the body of the message (the actual text of the electronic letter).

Users often want to send more than just text with an e-mail message. A number of methods have emerged for transmitting binary files through e-mail. Most of these strategies use some utility to convert the binary bits into some ASCII equivalent. The resulting file looks like ASCII text—in fact, it is ASCII text—but you can't read it because it is just a jumble of letters representing the original binary code. The BinHex utility (originally developed for the Macintosh) and the Uuencode utility (originally developed for Unix) use this method. You or your e-mail reader must have the necessary decoding utility to convert the file back to its binary form.

A more general and universal solution for sending binary files through e-mail has emerged through the Multipurpose Internet Mail Extensions (MIME) format. MIME is a general format for extending the capabilities of Internet e-mail. A MIME-enabled e-mail application encodes the message into MIME format before transmission. When the message is downloaded to the recipient, a MIME-enabled e-mail application on the recipient's computer decodes the message and restores it to its original form.

MIME brings several innovations to Internet mail, including

- Expanded character sets. MIME is not limited to the standard 128-character ASCII set. This means you can use it to transmit special characters and characters that aren't present in American English.
- Unlimited line length and message length.
- Standard encoding for attachments.
- Provisions for integrating images, sound, links, and formatted text with the message.

18

Most e-mail reader applications support MIME. MIME format is described in several RFCs, including RFCs 1521, 1522, 1563, and 1590.

How E-Mail Works

Like other Internet services, e-mail is built around a client/server process. However, the e-mail process is a bit more complicated. To put it briefly, the computers at both ends of the e-mail transaction act as clients, and the message is passed across the network by servers in between. The e-mail delivery process is shown in Figure 18.1. A client sends a message to an e-mail server. The server reads the address of the intended recipient and forwards the message to another e-mail server associated with the destination address. The message is stored on the destination e-mail server in a mailbox. (A *mailbox* is similar to a folder or queue of incoming mail messages.) The user to whom the message is addressed occasionally logs on to the e-mail server to check for mail messages. If incoming messages are waiting in the user's mailbox, the messages are downloaded to the user's computer. The user can then read, store, delete, forward, or reply to the e-mail message.

FIGURE 18.1

The e-mail delivery process.

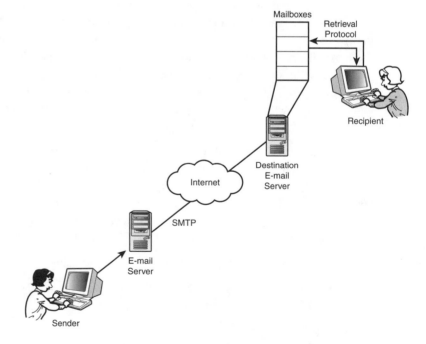

As you'll learn later in this hour, a client application called an *e-mail reader* tends to the details of sending outgoing mail and logging on to the server to download incoming mail. Most users interact with the e-mail process through the interface of an e-mail reader. The process of sending a message and forwarding it between servers is managed by an e-mail protocol called Simple Mail Transfer Protocol (SMTP).

The e-mail address gives the addressing information the server needs to forward the message. RFC 822 spells out the format of the ever more popular Internet e-mail address format:

```
user@server
```

or (for example)

```
BillyBob@Klondike.net
SallyH@montecello.com
cravenprof@harvard.edu
```

In this standard format, the text after the @ symbol is the name of the destination e-mail server. The text before the @ symbol is the name of the recipient's Imailbox on the e-mail server.

> In reality, the text after the @ symbol usually represents the domain name of the default e-mail server on the recipient domain.

18

The format of the e-mail address underscores an important observation about e-mail on the Internet: The destination of an e-mail message is not the recipient's computer but the recipient's mailbox on the e-mail server. The final step of transferring waiting e-mail messages from the e-mail server to the computer of the recipient is really a separate process. You'll learn later in Ithis hour that this final step is managed through a mail retrieval protocol such as Post Office Protocol (POP) or Internet Message Access Protocol (IMAP).

Some networks use a hierarchy of e-mail servers for more efficient delivery. In this scenario (see Figure 18.2), a local e-mail server forwards messages to a relay e-mail server. The relay e-mail server then sends the mail to another relay server on the destination network, and this relay server sends the message to a local server associated with the recipient.

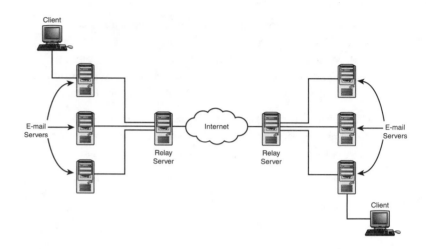

FIGURE 18.2
Relay servers often add efficiency to the process of delivering mail.

Simple Mail Transfer Protocol (SMTP)

Simple Mail Transfer Protocol (SMTP) is the protocol that e-mail servers use to forward messages across a TCP/IP network. The client computer that initiates an e-mail message also uses SMTP to send that message to a local server for delivery.

A user never has to speak SMTP. The SMTP communication process goes on behind the scenes. However, it is occasionally important to know a little about SMTP in order to interpret error messages for undelivered mail. Also, programs and scripts sometimes access SMTP directly to send e-mail warnings and alerts to network personnel.

Like other TCP/IP application services, SMTP communicates with the network through the TCP/IP protocol stack. The duties of the e-mail application are kept simple because the application can count on the connection and verification services of the TCP/IP protocol software. SMTP communication occurs through a TCP connection to port 25 on the SMTP server. The dialog between the client and server consists of standard 4-character commands (and data) from the client interspersed with 3-digit response codes from the server. Table 18.2 shows some SMTP client commands. The corresponding server response codes are shown in Table 18.3.

TABLE 18.2   SMTP Client Commands

Command	Description
HELO	Hello. (Client requests a connection with the server.)
MAIL FROM:	Precedes e-mail address of sending user.
RCPT TO:	Precedes e-mail address of receiving user.
DATA	Announces an intention to start transmitting the contents of the message.

TABLE 18.2   continued

Command	Description
NOOP	Asks the server to send an OK reply.
QUIT	Asks the server to send an OK reply and terminate the session.
RESET	Aborts the mail transaction.

TABLE 18.3   Some SMTP Server Response Codes

Code	Description
220	\<domain> service ready.
221	\<domain> service closing transmission channel.
250	Requested action completed successfully.
251	User is not local. Message will be forwarded to \<path>.
354	Start sending data. End data with the string \<CRLF>.\<CRLF> (which signifies a period on a line by itself).
450	Action was not taken because mailbox is busy.
500	Syntax error: command not recognized.
501	Syntax error: problem with parameters or arguments.
550	Action was not taken because mailbox was not found.
551	User is not local. Try sending the message to \<path>.
554	Transaction failed.

18

The process is roughly as follows. As mentioned earlier in this hour, this process is used to send a message from the initiating client to the local e-mail server and also to forward the message from the local server to the destination server or to another server on the relay path:

1. The sending computer issues a HELO command to the server. The name of the sender is included as an argument.
2. The server sends back the 250 response code.
3. The sender issues the MAIL FROM: command. The e-mail address of the user who sent the message is included as an argument.
4. The server sends back the 250 response code.
5. The sender issues the RCPT TO: command. The e-mail address of the message recipient is included as an argument.

6. If the server can accept mail for the recipient, the server sends back the 250 response code. Otherwise, the server sends back a code indicating the problem (such as the 550 code, which indicates that the user's mailbox wasn't found).

7. The sender issues the DATA command, indicating that it is ready to start sending the contents of the e-mail message.

8. The server issues the 354 response code, instructing the sender to start transmitting the message contents.

9. The sender sends the message data and ends with a period (.) on a line by itself.

10. The server sends back the 250 response code, indicating that the mail was received.

11. The sender issues the QUIT command, indicating that the transmission is over and the session should be closed.

12. The server sends the 221 code, indicating that the transmission channel will be closed.

The network uses this SMTP communication process to pass the e-mail message to the user's mailbox on the destination e-mail server. The message then waits in the user's mailbox until the user logs in and downloads any waiting mail. This final download is a separate process that requires a different protocol. You'll learn more about mail retrieval protocols in the following sections.

Retrieving the Mail

The SMTP delivery process described in the preceding section is not designed to deliver mail to a user but only to deliver mail to the user's mailbox. The user must then access the mailbox and download the mail. This additional step may complicate the process, but it offers the following advantages:

- The server will continue to receive mail for the user even when the user's computer is not on the network.
- The e-mail delivery system is independent of the recipient's computer or location.

The latter advantage is a feature with which many e-mail users are well acquainted. This feature enables the user to check his e-mail from multiple locations. Theoretically, any computer with access to the Internet and an e-mail reader application can be configured to check the user's mailbox for messages. You can check your mail from home, from an office, or from a hotel room. This process of accessing the mailbox and downloading messages requires a mail retrieval protocol. In the following sections, you'll learn about Post Office Protocol (POP) and Internet Message Access Protocol (IMAP).

In reality, network security structures such as firewalls sometimes prevent the user from checking e-mail from any random spot on the Internet.

The e-mail server that holds user mailboxes typically must support both the SMTP service (for receiving incoming messages) and a mail retrieval protocol service (for giving users access to the mailbox). This process is depicted in Figure 18.3. This interaction requires coordination and compatibility between the SMTP service and the mail retrieval service so that data doesn't become lost or corrupt when the services access the same mailbox simultaneously.

FIGURE 18.3

The SMTP service application and the mail retrieval service application must coordinate access to the mailbox.

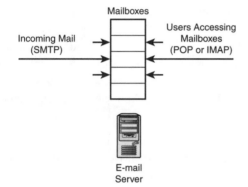

POP3

Post Office Protocol version 3 (POP3) is a widely used message retrieval protocol. If you are using Internet e-mail now, the chances are good that you are using a POP3-compliant e-mail client.

POP3 is described in RFC 1939. The client initiates a TCP connection to the POP3 server application on the e-mail server. The POP3 server listens for connections on TCP port 110. Once the connection has been established, the client application must send username and password information to the e-mail server. If the login credentials are accepted, the user can access the mailbox to download or delete messages.

Like the SMTP client, the POP3 client uses a series of 4-character commands for communicating with the server. The server responds with a very small number of alphabetic responses, such as +OK (indicating that the command was executed) and -ERR (indicating that the command resulted in an error). The responses may also include additional arguments or parameters. Each message in the mailbox is referenced by a message number. The client sends a RETR (retrieve) command to the server to download a message. The DELE command deletes a message from the server.

The messages sent between the POP3 client and server are invisible to the user. These commands are issued by the e-mail reader application as a response to the user's activities within the e-mail reader user interface.

One disadvantage of POP3 is the limited number of functions that can take place at the server. The user can only list the messages in the mailbox, delete messages, and download messages. Any manipulation of the message contents must occur on the client side. This limitation can cause delays and increase network traffic as messages are downloaded from the server to the client. The newer and more sophisticated IMAP protocol was developed to address some of these shortcomings.

IMAP4

Internet Message Access Protocol version 4 (IMAP4) is a message retrieval protocol that is similar to POP3. IMAP4, however, offers several new features that aren't available with POP3. With IMAP4, you can browse server-based folders and move, delete, and view messages without first copying the messages to your local computer. IMAP4 also allows you to save certain settings such as client window appearance or search messages on the server for a specified search string. You can also create, remove, and rename mailboxes on the server computer.

Most recent e-mail readers support both POP3 and IMAP4. Although POP3 currently has a wider user base, the many advantages of IMAP ensure that e-mail installations will continue converting to the IMAP4 protocol.

E-Mail Readers

An e-mail reader is a client application that runs on a user's workstation and communicates with an e-mail server. As you learned earlier in this hour, the local workstation does not form a direct connection with the recipient of an e-mail message. Instead, the workstation sends the message to an e-mail server using an e-mail reader. The server sends the message on to the e-mail server assigned to the recipient. The user who will receive the message checks his mailbox on the e-mail server, and the message is downloaded to the user's workstation. The first step and the last step in this process (sending the message to the original server and downloading the message from the receiving server) are typically performed by an e-mail reader application.

The e-mail reader serves three functions:

- Sends outgoing messages to an outgoing e-mail server using SMTP.
- Collects incoming e-mail messages from an e-mail server using POP3 or IMAP.
- Serves as a user interface for reading, managing, and composing mail messages.

The e-mail reader must be capable of serving as both an SMTP client and a mail retrieval (POP or IMAP) client.

The e-mail protocols discussed earlier in this hour provide a clear roadmap for electronic mail communication and, for that reason, e-mail readers are all similar. The details of how to configure an e-mail reader may vary but, if you are familiar with the processes described in this hour, it usually isn't difficult to figure out how to get it working. Like other network client applications, an e-mail reader communicates with the network through the protocol stack. The computer with the e-mail reader must have a working TCP/IP implementation, and it must be configured so that the e-mail application can reach the network through TCP/IP.

E-mail has been around since long before the glory days of the Internet, and many proprietary networking systems have similar messaging features. You can also send and receive e-mail on networks that use other protocols, such as IPX./SPX or SNA. However, you must have TCP/IP to send and receive e-mail on a TCP/IP network such as the Internet.

18

Once you have established that your computer is functioning properly as a client on a TCP/IP network, you'll need a obtain a few additional parameters from an official of your network in order to configure an e-mail reader on your system. If you are a home user, obtain this information through your ISP. If you are a corporate user, obtain this information from your network administrator.

You'll need to know the following:

- The fully qualified domain name of the e-mail server to use for outgoing mail. This server often receives the hostname SMTP followed by the domain name (for example, SMTP.rosbud.org).
- The fully qualified hostname of the POP or IMAP server.
- The username and password of an e-mail user account on the POP or IMAP server.

The task of configuring an e-mail reader is largely a matter of obtaining these parameters and entering them into the e-mail reader application. The next few sections discuss some popular e-mail readers.

Some networks may also require additional settings, such as authentication parameter settings.

Pine

Pine is an e-mail system that was developed by the University of Washington. It allows a user to compose and read e-mail using a simple terminal interface. You can use Pine to compose and read e-mail messages, maintain address books, create and manage folders, add attachments to e-mail messages, perform spell-check functions, reply to messages, and forward messages to others.

In recent years, Pine has been overshadowed by many newer GUI-based e-mail readers. However, Pine (and other character-based systems such as Elm) is still preferred by many Unix or Linux users who prefer or require a text-based user interface.

Pine is built into many Unix and Linux systems. If your system includes Pine, just type **pine** at the command prompt. To configure parameters such as the SMTP server, access the Setup menu (usually by typing **s**).

Eudora

Eudora is a popular and stable e-mail reader from QUALCOMM Inc. Because Eudora is independent of the major software vendors such as Microsoft and Netscape, you can use it without taking a side in the battle of the Titans. More importantly, third-party products such as Eudora are often much simpler than huge integrated products such as Outlook and Netscape. The automated, object-oriented functions of Outlook can actually cause security problems if they aren't properly implemented. And even in the best case, large, integrated application suites sometimes offer more complexity than users want. Eudora built a large consumer base a few years ago, before e-mail became a built-in feature on Windows computers, but even now, third-party e-mail readers such as Eudora are preferred by many users.

The Eudora Light main window is shown in Figure 18.4. You can organize received e-mail messages into folders. In Figure 18.4, folders are shown in the tree on the left. Click on a folder to view a list of messages saved in the folder. Double-click on an entry in the message list to read the message. The various buttons in the toolbar let you send, receive, reply to a message, or compose a new message.

To enter configuration parameters such as the SMTP server and the POP server, select the Tools menu and choose Options. The Options dialog box offers several configuration options (see Figure 18.5).

FIGURE 18.4

The Eudora Light main window.

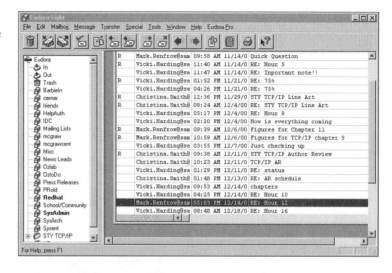

FIGURE 18.5

Configuring e-mail options in Eudora Light.

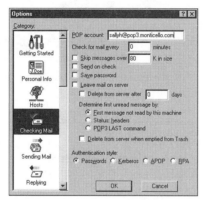

18

Integrated E-Mail Applications

Integrated Internet applications such as Netscape Communicator and Internet Explorer include e-mail readers. The Microsoft e-mail reader Outlook Express is included on many Windows systems, and an enhanced version is included with the Microsoft Office suite. Integrated e-mail applications such as Outlook Express are similar to other e-mail readers except that they support a higher degree of integrated processing. The e-mail reader can interact directly with other components, responding to scripts or borrowing features from a spreadsheet or word processing application.

In the case of the Microsoft products, the e-mail reader treats an incoming attachment as an object and, depending on the instructions within the attachment, may pass control to some other application within the integrated suite. This amazing automation feature is very convenient if used appropriately, but it has also spawned a whole new generation of macro viruses delivered through e-mail attachments. A typical macro virus might access the user's address book to learn new e-mail addresses, then automatically e-mail itself to the other users in the address book (see Figure 18.6).

FIGURE 18.6

An e-mail virus.

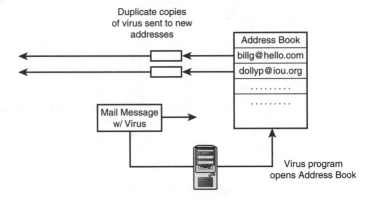

The birth of the e-mail virus illustrates a constant struggle in the computer industry between the opposing needs for security and convenience. Integrated e-mail readers such as Outlook Express offer powerful advantages, but all of that power requires an added measure of attention from the user.

It isn't as though the user has no defense against e-mail viruses. It is possible to turn off some of the automated features in Windows. A good anti-virus application may also be able to detect known viruses as they arrive. Consult your vendor documentation.

Web-Based E-Mail

The recent rise of the World Wide Web has created a whole new category of e-mail designed around HTML. These Web-based e-mail servers do not require an e-mail reader. The user simply visits the Web site with an Internet browser and accesses the e-mail through a Web interface. The user's e-mail is therefore accessible from any computer that can reach the Internet. Portals such as Yahoo! and Hotmail offer Web-based e-mail services. These services are often free—or almost free—because the provider makes enough money on advertising to support the whole infrastructure.

Web-based e-mail is versatile and easy to use. The option is a good choice for non-technical home users who are accustomed to the Web and don't want to have to configure and troubleshoot an e-mail application. Some corporations now use Web-based e-mail in certain situations because their firewalls permit HTTP traffic and prevent SMTP. Web-based e-mail may seem insecure at a glance, and it probably is. Anyone on the Internet knows how to reach the Yahoo! site and can probably figure out how to reach the Yahoo! mail site. But it is important to remember that traditional e-mail isn't that secure either, unless you take steps to secure it. Anyone who has your username and password can probably check your mail. The major Web-based e-mail sites provide secure logon and other safeguards. If you're considering a small, local, Web-based e-mail service, it is a good idea to find out about security for the system.

Summary

If you have an Internet account, you probably have experience with sending and receiving e-mail. This hour described what happens to an e-mail message after it leaves your computer. You looked behind the scenes at the e-mail delivery process. You learned about SMTP and the mail retrieval protocols POP3 and IMAP4. This hour also discussed the role of the e-mail reader application.

Q&A

18

Q I can send messages but I can't connect to my mail server to download new messages. What should I check?

A Your e-mail reader application uses SMTP to send messages and a mail retrieval protocol (probably POP or IMAP) to check the server for incoming messages. You might have a problem with the transmission of your mail retrieval protocol. Many networks use different servers for incoming and outgoing messages. Your POP or IMAP server might be down. Look for a configuration dialog box in your e-mail reader application that gives the name of your POP or IMAP server. Try to ping the server and see if it responds.

Q I'm working onsite at a military institution that uses text-based Unix terminals for electronic communication. What e-mail reader should I use?

A Several text-based e-mail readers exist in the Unix world. This hour discussed Pine. Elm is another popular Unix mail application.

Q A Turkish accounting firm ordered 14 computers from my company. They insist that the e-mail applications included with the computers support MIME. Why are they so adamant?

A E-mail was originally designed to support the ASCII character set, a collection of characters developed for users who write in English. Many characters used in other languages are not present in the ASCII set. MIME extends the character set to include other non-ASCII characters.

Workshop

If you have an Internet account, open the e-mail reader you use for sending and viewing e-mail. Try to figure out where the SMTP server (for outgoing mail) and the POP or IMAP server (for incoming mail) are configured.

If you're feeling really adventurous, ask a close friend if you can configure an e-mail reader on the friend's computer to check your e-mail account. Some e-mail readers support multiple e-mail accounts. Or, you may be able to configure a built-in e-mail reader that your friend isn't currently using.

> You may find that you can check your mail from your friend's ISP network but you can't send outgoing mail from your friend's network to the SMTP server on your own ISP's network. Many ISPs do not allow external e-mail messages to bounce off their SMTP servers.
>
> If you try this exercise, it is also important to remember that, although reading e-mail is independent of the task of establishing an Internet connection, most e-mail readers offer the option of automatically establishing a connection when you check your mail. You'll need to make sure you're connected to the Internet when you try this experiment.

Key Terms

Review the following list of key terms:

e-mail body—The section of an e-mail message that includes the text of the message.

e-mail header—The preliminary section of an e-mail message, consisting of informational fields and associated values.

e-mail reader—A client e-mail application that is responsible for sending mail, retrieving mail, and managing the user interface through which the user interacts with the mail system.

e-mail virus—A software virus propagated as an attachment to an e-mail message.

Internet Message Access Protocol (IMAP)—An enhanced mail retrieval protocol that provides several features not available with POP. For instance, you can access mail messages without first downloading the messages from the server.

mailbox—A location on an e-mail server where incoming messages are stored for a user.

multipurpose Internet mail extensions (MIME)—An e-mail format that extends the capabilities of Internet mail.

Pine—A terminal-based e-mail reader program that runs on a Unix computer.

Post Office Protocol (POP)—A popular mail retrieval protocol used on the Internet. POP enables the user to log on to an e-mail server and download or delete waiting messages.

Simple Mail Transfer Protocol (SMTP)—A protocol used for sending mail on TCP/IP networks.

18

HOUR 19

What Hackers Do

When the experts started designing networks, they had no idea that legions of unauthorized users would spend thousands of hours trying to get inside. This hour describes some of the methods used for Internet attacks.

At the completion of this hour, you'll be able to

- Describe how hackers obtain passwords
- Describe how intruders access systems using buffer overflow, script tricks, session hijacking, and e-mail worms
- Discuss methods for establishing permanent control of a system
- Describe denial of service attacks

What Is a Hacker?

The word *hacker* has come to refer to a computer user who trespasses on computer systems for fun or profit. The growth of the Internet has created unlimited opportunity for these intruders to steal secrets, tinker with Web sites, abscond with credit card information, or just generally make mischief.

Computer hackers have also spawned a whole new mythology. They are celebrated for their skill and daring. Some ascribe lofty artistic and political motives to these bandwidth banditos. But the professionals who install and maintain computer networks are not impressed with computer hackers.

This hour explores some of the techniques hackers use to gain control of computer systems. As you study these techniques, you'll notice that many of the concepts are built around fundamental properties of TCP/IP that you learned about in earlier hours. The next hour explores some of the security techniques used to keep intruders off the network.

The Internet literature is full of vague psycho-profiles of who the hacker is and what the hacker thinks. Much of this information is based on anecdotes and speculation. However, there is general agreement that computer attackers tend to fall within the following broad categories:

- **Adolescent amateurs**   These are kids who are really just playing around. The so-called *script kiddies* often have only a rudimentary knowledge of computer systems and primarily just apply intrusion scripts and techniques available on the Internet.

- **Recreational hackers**   This category of adult intruders encompasses a broad range of motivations. Most are in it purely for the intellectual challenge. Some want to make a statement against a particular industry or organization, and others are disgruntled former employees.

- **Professionals**   This relatively small but very dangerous group consists of experienced experts who know a lot about computers. They are very hard to trace because they know all the tricks. In fact, they invented some of the tricks. These intruders are in the game strictly for the financial reward, but they wouldn't have gotten where they are if they didn't love what they do.

It is impossible to describe all the various scams and tricks used by intruders to gain access to computer systems. This hour is intended only as an introduction to some important techniques. As you read through the techniques described in this hour, remember the most important rule of computer security: If you think you've secured your network, think again. Someone out there is spending a lot of time and effort trying to find a new way in.

To many, a *hacker* is simply a high-end user who is obsessed with and devoted to working with computers—whether or not that user has any malicious intent. Many of these high-end users are proud to call themselves hackers and object to the use of the word *hacker* for Internet burglars and vandals. These users prefer to use the word *cracker* for cyber-vandals. Unfortunately, one cannot easily restrain a word from finding its definition. The term *hacker* is now widely applied to computer intruders, and the verb *to hack* is commonly used for Internet attacks. We can sympathize with high-end good guys who want a label that is more romantic than *power user*, but unfortunately they'll have to share the term. Waylon Jennings, after all, calls himself an outlaw but has never robbed a bank.

What Do Hackers Want?

As the preceding section mentioned, hackers approach their craft from a number of motivations. Their goals may differ, but they all have the goal of gaining power and control of a computer network. Many of their intermediate steps are therefore the same.

The computer attack and infiltration process is organized around the following steps:

1. Get access to the system
2. Get privileges
3. Get comfortable
4. Get ready for the next attack

These steps are discussed in upcoming sections. It is worth noting that, for coordinated and well-organized attacks on computer networks, a separate reconnaissance phase often precedes these steps. You'll learn some of these reconnaissance techniques in the section "Attacking a Network," later in this hour.

Getting Passwords

The classic way to gain access to a computer system is to find out the password and log in. An intruder who gains interactive entry to a system can employ other techniques to build system privileges. Therefore, finding a password—any password—is often the first step in cracking a network. Methods for getting passwords range from very high-tech (password-cracking dictionary scripts and de-encryption programs) to extremely low-tech (digging around in trash cans and peeking in users' desk drawers). Some common password attack methods include

- Looking outside the box
- Trojan horses
- Guessing
- Intercepting

The following sections discuss these methods for clandestinely obtaining users' passwords.

Looking Outside the Box

No matter how secure your system is, your network won't be safe unless users protect their passwords. A major source of password compromise is the inattentiveness of users. The earliest hackers often obtained passwords by looking for clues in discarded computer printouts. Since that time, operating system vendors thankfully have become more sophisticated about protecting password information. However, a significant percentage of password-compromise cases still results from offline detection. Users tell their passwords to other users or write down their passwords in some easily accessible place. The physical security of a workplace often is far less rigid than network security. Janitorial staff, disgruntled co-workers, or even unauthorized outsiders are often free to slip into the office unsupervised and look for password clues. When a worker quits or is dismissed, the worker's account is deactivated, but what about other user accounts belonging to users who have shared their passwords with the former employee?

Some experienced hackers are skilled at getting users to reveal their passwords or getting network admins to tell them passwords. They'll call the help desk, act a little lost, and say, "Uhh, I forgot my password." This sounds silly, but it saves the intruder a lot of effort, and it is often the first thing he tries. Every organization should clearly instruct computer professionals not to reveal password information to any user without taking precautions to ensure the request is legitimate.

As you'll learn later in this hour, the ultimate goal of the intruder is to achieve administrative-level privileges. Every password should be protected, since any access can often lead to administrative access, but it is especially important to protect administrative accounts from compromise. The administrative username is another line of defense against intrusion that should also be protected. Most computer systems come with a well-documented and well-known default administrative account. An intruder who is familiar with the operating system has a head start in gaining administrative privileges if he knows the username of the administrative account. Experts therefore recommend changing the username of the administrative account.

Trojan Horses

A common tool of computer intruders is the so-called "Trojan horse." In general, a Trojan horse is a computer program that purports to do one thing but actually takes other unseen and malicious actions behind the scenes. One early form of the Trojan horse was a fake login screen. The screen looks just like the login screen used for the system, but when the user attempts to log in, the username and password are captured and stored in some secret location accessible to the intruder (see Figure 19.1).

FIGURE 19.1

Stealing passwords with a Trojan horse login program.

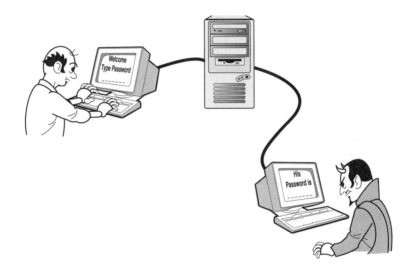

As you might guess, this technique for stealing passwords is designed for a public set-ting such as a computer lab in which multiple users may use a common set of terminals or workstations. In recent years, operating systems have gotten better at preventing or detecting this form of password capture. Microsoft claims that Windows NT and Windows 2000 are immune from this form of password-capture attack because the secu-rity subsystem suspends all background processes. However, "immune" is a bold word in the field of network security. Many Trojan horses exploit subtleties in the actual oper-ating system code, and a great many attack methods have been developed that don't appear possible from documentation of the OS vendor.

Unix systems are still vulnerable to this form of password-capture attack. In the book *Hacking Exposed* (by Joel Scambray, Stuart McClure, and George Kurtz—Osborne), the authors state that, once an intruder has obtained root access to a Unix system, he can "Trojanize" almost any Unix command, including the Unix login command. Password-capturing Trojan horse programs are often uploaded to a compromised system to catch new passwords and expand the hacker's hold on the network.

19

Not all Trojan horses capture passwords, and not all password Trojans are as blatant as the example described in this section. Many other types of Trojan horse programs are available on the Internet. Some take the form of games or false system utilities. Many of these Trojan horse programs are distributed as freeware or shareware over the Internet. The best defense against this kind of attack is to be careful what you download. Free software is often worth every penny you pay for it. Or, to paraphrase the princess Cassandra, who prophesized the arrival of a particularly virulent Trojan horse at the gates of her city in 800 B.C., "Beware of geeks bearing gifts."

Guessing

Some passwords are so simple or poorly formed that they can easily be guessed by the intruder. You would be surprised how many users use a password that is the same as their username. Some users use a street name, a maiden name, or the name of a child for a password, and some use easily guessable character combinations, such as 123456, abcde, or zzzzzz.

An intruder who knows a little about the user can often guess bad passwords the user might choose. In fact, the intruder doesn't even have to guess anymore, because tools now exist that automate the process of guessing passwords. These tools simply start trying to log in to a given user account by guessing common bad passwords. The attack tools guess through a list of obvious character combinations. Some tools even use a dictionary to guess every possible word or name in the language. This might require thousands of attempts, but computers can guess very quickly.

Unix systems are particularly vulnerable to these so-called *brute force* attacks. Brute force attacks can be used not only for the initial login but also for new shells and password-protected services. Several tools exist for logging unsuccessful login attempts and alerting network personnel when an attack is taking place.

Windows systems are also susceptible to brute force attacks, although the Windows password policy feature makes it easy to disable the system after a predetermined number of unsuccessful login attempts.

The best defense against password-guessing attacks is to force the users to use good passwords. See the section "What to Do About Password Attacks," later in this hour, for more on good password policy.

Intercepting

Packet sniffers and other tools that monitor network traffic can easily capture passwords transmitted over the network in clear text (unencrypted) form. Many classic TCP/IP utilities such as Telnet and the r* utilities (see Hour 15, "Remote Access Utilities") or SNMP (see Hour 21, "Network Management Protocols") were designed to transmit passwords in clear text form. Some later versions of these utilities offer password encryption or operate through secure channels (see Hour 20, "TCP/IP Security"). In their basic form, however, the clear text password security of these applications makes them hopelessly ill-suited for an open and hostile environment such as the Internet.

> Even in a closed environment such as a corporate network, clear text passwords are not really safe. Some experts estimate that one corporate employee in a hundred is actively engaged in trying to thwart network security. One percent is a small fraction, but when you consider a network with 1000 users, that one percent amounts to 10 users who would love to get their hands on someone else's clear text password.

Several methods exist for encrypting passwords. These password-encryption methods are much better than the clear text option, but password encryption still has some limitations. Tools such as the L0phtcrack utility capture encrypted NT logons and decode them offline through brute force techniques.

Recent developments in encrypted channel technologies, such as SSL and IPSec (see Hour 20) raise the bar considerably higher for intruders who want to eavesdrop on TCP/IP to obtain sensitive information such as passwords.

19

What to Do About Password Attacks

The best defense against password attacks is eternal vigilance. Networks have employed a number of strategies for reducing the incidence of password compromise. A few of the more obvious guidelines are

1. Provide a good, clear password policy for the users in your organization. Warn them about the danger of telling their password to other users, writing their password down on paper, or even storing their password in a file.

2. Configure all computer systems to support mandatory password policies. Force users to change their passwords at some regular interval. Set a minimum length for passwords (usually 6–8 characters). Don't let a user use the name of his dog or the name of his child as a password. In fact, passwords should not consist of any standard word, phrase, or name. All passwords should contain a combination of

letters and numbers and at least one non-alphanumeric character that is not the first or last character. To prevent password-guessing attacks, make sure the computer is configured to disable the account after a predefined number of failed logon attempts.

3. Make sure that passwords are never transmitted over public lines in clear text form. If possible, it is better not to transmit clear text passwords on your internal network either, especially on large networks.

Some systems have methods for controlling the number of passwords that each user must remember. Microsoft networks feature a passwords cache and a unified network logon through the domain security system. Unix systems offer Kerberos authentication (see Hour 20). These methods are very useful for controlling password proliferation in some environments. The downside of these unified logon methods is that, once an intruder gets one password, he has unlocked access to all the user's resources.

See Hour 20 for more on protecting passwords through encryption.

Other Access Techniques

Password access isn't the only way to gain entry to a system. The following sections discuss some other common access techniques, including

- Buffer overflow
- Script tricks
- Session hijacking
- E-mail worms

Buffer Overflow

When a computer receives data over a network connection (or for that matter, even when it receives data from a keyboard), the computer must reserve enough memory space to receive the complete data set. This reception space is called a *buffer*. Network computer applications must provide a buffer to receive input. If user input overflows the buffer, strange things happen. If the input is not properly managed, the data that overflows the buffer can become resident in the CPU's execution area, which means that commands sent to the computer through a buffer overflow can actually be executed. The commands execute with the privileges of the application that received the data.

To avoid buffer overflow problems, applications must provide a means for receiving and checking the size of the data before inserting the data into an application buffer. The solutions are largely a matter of good programming practice. Poorly designed applications are especially susceptible to buffer overflow attacks.

Some very popular and famous network applications have buffer overflow vulnerabilities. Many of these exploits are well known around the Internet, so intruders know exactly how and where to launch an attack. The Unix-based e-mail server Sendmail is a common target for buffer overflow attacks. When a vendor discovers a possible buffer overflow vulnerability, the vendor often releases a patch that fixes the problem. However, new buffer overflow possibilities are discovered daily.

Part of the solution to buffer overflow is good programming. The other part of the solution is to limit the scope of privileges available to the remote user who is attempting to exploit a buffer overflow. If possible, don't let network applications run with root or administrative privileges. For applications that require a high privilege level in order to function, tools such as chroot can create a limited security environment that prevents the intruder from gaining access to the system.

Script Tricks

As you learned in Hour 17, "HTTP, HTML, and the World Wide Web," common gateway interface (CGI) is an application interface used for integrating scripts with Web sites. CGI was greeted with much fanfare a few years ago, and CGI scripts are used widely on the Web. However, experts have discovered that CGI scripts (especially poorly written CGI scripts) are often vulnerable to attack.

In some cases, scripts that receive input from the user can be tricked into executing commands or providing output that the scripts were never intended to provide. The most susceptible CGI scripts are scripts that

- Start a subshell for interactive input.
- Do not check input carefully.
- Allow unrestricted use of *metacharacters*, characters that represent patterns. (The most familiar metacharacter is the asterisk (*), which represents all strings or all strings matching the rest of the search pattern.)

Input is often sent to CGI scripts through a URL query. If the CGI program does not contain the necessary safeguards, an intruder can phrase a query that will cause the CGI script to open a shell or output a critical system file.

Session Hijacking

Session hijacking is an advanced technique that exploits a vulnerability in the TCP protocol. As you learned in Hour 6, "The Transport Layer," the TCP protocol establishes a session between network hosts. Session hijacking calls for the intruder to eavesdrop on a TCP session and insert packets into the stream that appear to be part of the TCP session.

19

The intruder can use this technique to slip commands into the security context of the original session. One common use of session hijacking is to get the system to reveal or change a password.

Of course, a hacker does not manually compose spoofed TCP segments on-the-fly. Session hijacking requires special tools. One famous tool used for session hijacking is a freeware application called Juggernaut.

E-Mail Worms

Hour 18, "E-Mail," describes how hackers use malicious e-mail attachments to infiltrate a system. Certain e-mail clients (most notably Microsoft's Outlook clients) treat an e-mail attachment as an object and execute that object when you click on the icon. The Windows operating environment includes components that make it easy for applications to interact with other applications and execute commands related to the operating system itself.

The e-mail worm arrives in the user's mailbox. When the user opens the attachment, instructions encoded with the attachment operate behind the scenes to open a pathway for an intruder. For example, the worm might make a change to Registry settings that will enable the intruder to achieve or expand system access.

Getting Comfortable

Once the intruder has successfully gained access to a single system, he begins settling in and getting comfortable. One of the first tasks is to obtain additional system privileges. Most really serious hacking requires a high level of access to the system. Intruders employ a number of strategies for increasing their access privileges. One method is to search around for files with password information. Even an encrypted password file can be downloaded to a safe location and attacked through a brute force dictionary attack. A hacker can use Trojan horses or buffer overflow techniques to trick the system into giving him additional privileges.

The Holy Grail of the hacker is always administrative or root access to the system. A user with root access can execute any command or view any file. When you have root access, you can essentially do whatever you want to do with the system.

Once the intruder has gained root access, one of the first tasks is to upload what is called a *root kit*. A root kit is a set of tools used for establishing a more permanent foothold on the system. Some of the tools are used to compromise new systems and new accounts. Other tools are designed to hide the hacker's presence on the systems. These tools may include doctored versions of standard network utilities such as netstat or applications that remove the trail of the intruder from system log files. Some root kits used with Unix or Linux systems may actually enable the intruder to alter the kernel itself to include new clandestine features.

The intruder then sets out to establish one or more back doors to the system—secret ways of getting in to the system that are difficult for a network administrator to detect. The point of a back door is to enable the intruder to avoid the logging and monitoring processes that surround everyday interactive access. A back door may consist of a hidden account or hidden privileges associated with an account that should have only limited access. In some cases, the back door path may include services such as Telnet mapped to unusual port numbers where the local administrator would not expect to find them.

Another goal of this "getting comfortable" phase may be to accomplish any dastardly business the hacker has in mind for the network. This may consist of stealing files or credit information. As you'll learn in the next section, the hacker's goal might be simply to upload tools for the next attack.

Getting Ready for the Next Attack

A careful intruder never likes to leave a trail to his own network. The preferred method is to launch an attack from a system that has already been compromised. Some hackers operate through a chain of several remote systems. This strategy makes it almost impossible to determine where the hacker is actually located.

Once a hacker has established a foothold, he may upload tools to assist with infiltrating other systems on the network. He also might use the compromised system to attack other computers elsewhere on the Internet. Intruders are constantly engaged in building their webs of connections.

The recent popularity of denial of service (DOS) attacks creates yet another role for the compromised system. You'll learn more about denial of service attacks in a later section.

19

Attacking a Network

A network attack is often an elaborate and methodical operation. A hacker sometimes spends days or weeks scouting and mapping the system so he'll know exactly how the network is organized. The reconnaissance process typically consists of the following:

- **Gathering information** A full-scale network attack begins with a broad sweep to determine as much information as possible about the company. This process is sometimes called *footprinting*. Some of this information can be collected over the

Web: company locations, e-mail addresses, and affiliations, as well as links to other Web sites. The intruder attempts to obtain any and all domain names used by the company. The domain names are then used to query DNS servers for company IP addresses.

- **Scanning**   As you learned in Hour 6, application services are accessible from the network through a TCP or UDP port address. The scanning phase tells the intruder which services are running on each host and which ports the services are using. Several tools are available for assisting with the scanning process. One of the most common port scanning tools is nmap.

- **Probing**   In the final phase of the reconnaissance process, the intruder looks deeper into the network. At this stage, he must have obtained some form of network privilege. By now he is actually logging on to systems and poking around in configuration files. He looks for specific resources such as devices and file resources and searches for information on user and group security.

By the time the reconnaissance is complete, the intruder will have a detailed map of the network and a clear indication of any vulnerabilities. He will then employ some of the other strategies discussed in this hour to expand system privileges, establish back doors, and engage in his chosen mischief.

Denial of Service Attacks

The latest craze in Internet intrusion is denial of service (DOS) attacks. A denial of service attack is almost impossible to stop once it starts, because it does not require the attacker to have any particular privileges on the system. The point of a denial of service attack is to tie up the system with so many requests that system resources are all consumed and performance degrades. High-profile denial of service attacks have been launched against Web sites of the U.S. government and those associated with major Internet search engines.

The most dangerous denial of service attack is the so-called distributed denial of service attack. The hacker in a distributed denial of service attack uses several remote computers to direct other remote computers into launching a coordinated attack. Sometimes hundreds or even thousands of computers can participate on an attack against a single IP address.

Denial of service attacks often use standard TCP/IP connectivity utilities. The famous Smurf attack, for instance, uses the ping utility (see Hour 13, "Connectivity Utilities") to unleash a flood of ping responses on the victim (see Figure 19.2). The attacker sends a ping request to an entire network through directed broadcast. The source address of the ping is doctored to make it appear that the request is coming from the victim's IP address. All the computers on the network then simultaneously respond to the ping. The effect of the Smurf attack is that the original ping from the attacker is multiplied into many ping on the amplification network. If the attacker initiates the process on several networks at once, the result is a huge flood of ping responses tying up the victim's system.

FIGURE 19.2

A denial of service attack.

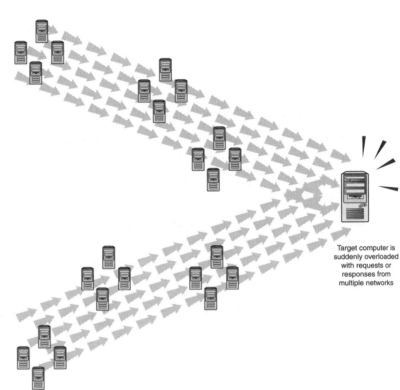

Target computer is suddenly overloaded with requests or responses from multiple networks

19

Summary

This hour described various methods that Internet intruders use for gaining access to a network. You learned about password collection, buffer overflow, session hijacking, and tricks with CGI scripts. You also learned about root kits, back doors, and denial of service attacks.

Key Terms

Review the following list of key terms:

back door—A hidden pathway for gaining entry to a computer system.

buffer overflow—An attack method that lets the attacker deliver malicious commands to a system by overrunning an application buffer.

denial of service attack—An attack design to cripple the victim's system by consuming system resources.

e-mail worm—A malicious script or program transmitted through an e-mail message.

hacker—A user who trespasses on computer systems for fun or profit. To some, a hacker is any high-end user who is obsessed with and devoted to working with computers.

root access—The highest level of access to a computer system. root access offers nearly unlimited control of the system.

root kit—A set of tools used by an intruder to expand and disguise his control of a system.

script kiddie—A young, usually adolescent hacker who works mostly with ready-made scripts and tools available on the Internet.

session hijacking—An attack method that lets the attacker insert malicious packets into an existing TCP session.

Trojan horse—A program that purports to do one thing but actually takes other unseen and malicious actions behind the scenes.

PART VI
Advanced Topics

Hour

HOUR 20

TCP/IP Security

As you learned in the last hour, unauthorized users will go to great effort just to sneak onto other people's networks. The experts have been getting better at hiding TCP/IP communication so intruders can't learn secrets on the network. In this hour, you'll learn some of the important methods for securing TCP/IP.

At the completion of this hour, you'll be able to

- Define the terms encryption algorithm and encryption key
- Discuss symmetric and asymmetric encryption
- Describe digital signatures and digital certificates
- Describe the TCP/IP security protocol systems SSL and IPSec
- Describe the Kerberos authentication process

Encryption

It is very easy to intercept and read an unprotected packet of data traveling over a public network. In some cases, that data might contain user or password information. In other cases, the data may contain other sensitive information you don't want anyone else to see, such as credit card numbers or company secrets. The fact is that even if the data isn't particularly secret, many users are justifiably uncomfortable with the prospect of eavesdroppers listening in on their electronic communication.

The security methods discussed later in this hour are designed to make the network more secret. Many of these methods use a concept known as encryption. *Encryption* is the process of systematically altering data to make it unreadable to unauthorized users. Data is *encrypted* by the sender. The data then travels over the network in coded, unreadable form. The receiving computer then *decrypts* the data in order to read it.

In fact, encryption does not require a computer at all. Encryption methods have been around for centuries. As long as people have written secret messages, they have looked for codes or tricks to keep those messages secret. In the computer age, however, encryption has gotten much more sophisticated because of the ease with which computers can manipulate huge, messy numbers. Most computer encryption algorithms result from the manipulation of large prime numbers. The algorithms themselves are intensely mathematical, and I do not exaggerate to say that most of the experts who create and deploy encryption algorithms have graduate degrees in computer science or mathematics.

Encryption is an important foundation of almost all TCP/IP security. The following sections discuss some important encryption concepts. As you read the rest of this hour, it is important to keep in mind that the security infrastructure actually has multiple goals, and security methods must address multiple needs. The beginning of this section discussed the goal of confidentiality (keeping data secret). The security system must also address such needs as

- **Authentication**   Making sure that the data really comes from the source to which it is attributed.
- **Integrity**   Making sure that data has not been tampered with in transit.

Encryption techniques are used to help ensure authentication and integrity as well as confidentiality.

Algorithms and Keys

As you learned in the previous section, encryption is a process for rendering data unreadable to everything and everyone who doesn't have the secret for unlocking the encryption code. For encryption to work, the two communicating entities must have the following:

- A process for making the data unreadable (encryption). This process will be used by the entity that transmits the data.

- A process for restoring the unreadable data to its original, readable form (decryption). This process will be used by the entity that receives the data.

When programmers first began to write encryption software, they realized they must contend with the following problems:

- If every computer used the exact same process for encrypting and decrypting data, the program would not be acceptably secure because any eavesdropper could just obtain a copy of the program and start decrypting messages.

- If every computer used a totally different and unrelated process for encrypting and decrypting data, every computer would need a totally different and unrelated program. Each pair of computers that wanted to communicate would need separate software. This would be highly expensive and impossible to manage on large, diverse networks.

Intractable as these problems may seem, the large minds who develop encryption techniques quickly saw a solution. The solution is that the process for encrypting or decrypting the data must be divided into a standard, reproducible part (which is always the same) and a unique part (which forces a secret relationship between the communicating parties).

The standard part of the encryption process is called the *encryption algorithm*. The encryption algorithm is essentially a set of mathematical steps used to transform the data into its unreadable form. The unique and secret part of the process is called the *key*. The science of encryption is extremely complex, but for purposes of discussion, you can think of the key as a large number that is used within the algorithm as a variable. The result of the encryption process depends on the value of the key. Therefore, as long as the value of the key is kept secret, unauthorized users will not be able to read the data even if they have the necessary decryption software.

The strangeness and obscurity of good encryption algorithms cannot be overstated. However, the following example illustrates the key and algorithm concepts.

A man does not want his mother to know how much he pays for furniture. He knows his mother is mathematically inclined, and he does not want to risk using a simple factor or multiplier to obscure the true value for fear that she will uncover the pattern. He has arranged with his lover that, if his mother is visiting and asks the cost, he will divide the real cost by a new, spontaneous number, multiply the result by two, and then add 10 dollars. In other words, the man arranges to use the following algorithm:

$$\frac{(\text{real cost})}{n} \times 2 + \$10 = \text{reported cost}$$

20

The new, spontaneous number (n) is the key. This same algorithm can be used every time the mother visits. The mother will have no way of determining a pattern for obscuring the real cost of the item as long as she does not know the key used in the calculation.

If the man comes home with a chair or table and sees his mother in the yard, he secretly signals a number to his lover (see Figure 20.1). When his mother asks the cost of the piece, he processes the algorithm and uses the number he signaled to his lover as the key. For instance, if the key is 3 and the chair cost is $600, he would report

$$\frac{\$600 \times 2}{3} + \$10 = \$410$$

The lover, who is aware of the shared secret, knows that she must process the algorithm in reverse to obtain the true cost:

$$\frac{(\$410 - \$10)}{2} \times 3 = \$600$$

FIGURE 20.1

An extremely primitive algorithm for disguising communication.

This simple example does not reveal the real complexity of computer encryption methods. It is also important to remember that the goal of changing a value is not exactly the same as the goal of making data unreadable. However, in the binary world of computers, this distinction is less pronounced than it might seem. This example is intended only as an illustration of the important difference between an algorithm and a key.

Symmetric (Conventional) Encryption

Symmetric encryption is sometimes called *conventional encryption* because it preceded the development of newer, asymmetric techniques. Symmetric encryption is still the most common form, although public-key asymmetric encryption (discussed later in this hour) has recently received considerable attention.

Symmetric encryption is called symmetric because the decryption process is exactly the reverse of the encryption process. Figure 20.2 describes a symmetric encryption/decryption process. The steps are as follows:

1. A secret key is made known to both the sending and receiving computers.
2. The sending computer encrypts the data using a prearranged encryption algorithm and the secret key.
3. The encrypted (unreadable) text is delivered to the destination computer.
4. The receiving computer uses a decryption algorithm that is exactly the reverse of the encryption algorithm in step 2 (along with the secret key) to decrypt the data.

FIGURE 20.2

The symmetric encryption process.

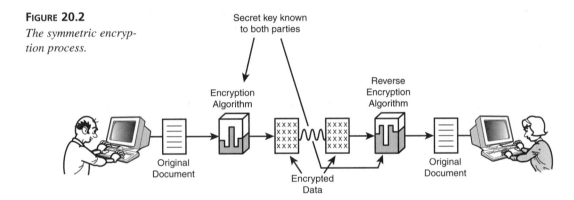

The furniture man and his lover (see the example in the preceding section) use a symmetric algorithm to hide the true value of the chair. The receiver works backward through the original algorithm, using the same secret key originally used to encrypt the data.

20

You might be wondering how one could ever have an encryption method that *doesn't* use the original key with the reversed algorithm to decrypt the data. This question is understandable, considering that, after centuries of encryption dating back to the Greeks and Romans, no one thought about doing it any other way until the 1970s. You'll learn more about asymmetric encryption later in this hour.

Symmetric encryption can be extremely secure if it is performed carefully. The most important considerations for the security of any encryption scheme (symmetric or asymmetric) are as follows:

- The strength of the encryption algorithm
- The strength of the key(s)
- The secrecy of the key(s)

Breaking through an encryption algorithm that uses a 128-bit key may seem completely impossible, but it can happen if the algorithm and key are not sufficiently secure. Still, the easiest way to steal encrypted data usually is to steal the key. The software must provide some secure means for delivering the key to the receiving computer. Various key delivery systems exist, and you'll learn about some of these systems later in this hour. In the case of symmetric encryption, the secret key is the whole secret. If you capture the key, you have everything. Most systems therefore call for a periodic renewal of the key. The unique key used by a pair of communicating computers might be re-created with every session or after a given time interval. Key renewal increases the number of keys crossing the network, which compounds the need for effective key protection.

Several common encryption algorithms make use of symmetric encryption. The most famous symmetric algorithm may be the Data Encryption Standard (DES). DES is used with several common encryption techniques, including Kerberos 4.0. DES uses a 56-bit key, which many experts say is too short. In fact, the DES algorithm was actually cracked through brute-force techniques in a test lab in 1998. Other symmetric encryption algorithms include the 128-bit key IDEA algorithm. The Blowfish symmetric algorithm typically uses a 128-bit key, although key length may vary to up to 448 bits.

The Kerberos authentication system (described later in this hour) provides a good example of the kind of procedures necessary to protect the keys in symmetric encryption.

In general, the key distribution methods techniques include

- Using a trusted authentication server to distribute keys to the computers that want to communicate (the method used by Kerberos).
- Having one of the communicating hosts send a new key encrypted inside an old key. (This approach is sometimes effective, but the problem of sending the first key must still be addressed somehow.)

Another method that could be added to this list is the option of physically delivering the key offline, on a floppy disk or some other transportable medium.

Asymmetric (Public Key) Encryption

An alternative encryption method that has emerged over the last 25 years provides an answer to some of the key distribution problems implicit with symmetric encryption. Asymmetric encryption is called *asymmetric* because the key used to encrypt the data is different from the key used to decrypt the data. Instead, the algorithms are designed so that, if one key is used to encrypt the data, another key can be used to decrypt it. This process is shown in Figure 20.3.

FIGURE 20.3

The asymmetric encryption process.

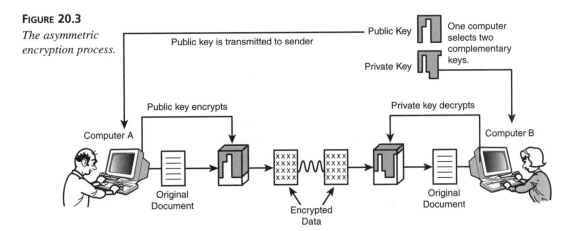

Asymmetric encryption is commonly associated with an encryption method known as public key encryption. In public key encryption, one of the two keys (called the *private key*) is held securely on a single computer. The other key (the *public key*) is made available to computers that want to send data to the holder of the private key. This process is depicted in Figure 20.3. The steps are as follows:

1. Computer A attempts to establish a connection with Computer B.

2. The encryption software on Computer B generates a private key and a public key. The private key is shared with no one. The public key is made available to Computer A.

3. Computer A encrypts the data with the public key received from Computer B and transmits the data. The public key from Computer B is stored on Computer A for future reference.

4. Computer B receives the data and decrypts it using the private key.

20

An important aspect of public key methods is that the encryption performed through the public key is a one-way function. The public key can be used to encrypt the data, but only the private key can decrypt the data once it is encrypted. An eavesdropper who intercepts the public key will still not be able to read messages encrypted using the public key.

> It can be argued that, although an eavesdropper who intercepts the public key cannot read data sent from Computer A, the eavesdropper can still pretend to be Computer A by encrypting new data and sending it on to Computer B. Thus, although public key encryption provides confidentiality, it does not necessarily provide authenticity. However, several methods exist for enclosing authentication information within the encrypted data, so that when the data is decrypted, Computer B will have some assurance that the data actually came from Computer A. See the sections "Digital Signatures" and "Digital Certificates," later in this hour.

Public key encryption methods are commonly used for protected Internet transactions. You'll learn later in this hour about public key certificates, which are used for TCP/IP security protocols such as Secure Sockets Layer (SSL) and IP Security (IPSec).

Digital Signatures

It is sometimes important to ensure the authenticity of a message even if you don't care whether the content of the message is confidential. For instance, a stock broker might receive an e-mail message that says

```
Sell 20 shares of my Microsoft stock.
-Bennie
```

Selling 20 shares might be an entirely routine event for this investor. The investor and the broker might not care if the transaction is totally immune from eavesdropping. However, they might consider it extremely important to ensure that this sell notice came from Bennie and not from someone pretending to be Bennie.

A digital signature is a method for ensuring that the data came from the source to which it is attributed and that the data has not been altered along its delivery path.

A digital signature is a block of encrypted data included with a message. The block of encrypted data is sometimes called an *authenticator*. A digital signature typically uses the public key encryption process in reverse (see Figure 20.4):

1. Computer B wants to send a document to Computer A that bears a digital signature. Computer B creates a small segment of data with information necessary to verify the contents of the document. In other words, some mathematical calculation

is performed on the bits in the document to derive a value. The authenticator may also contain other information useful for verifying the authenticity of the message, such as a time stamp value or other parameters that will associate the authenticator with the message to which it is attached.

2. Computer B encrypts the authenticator using a private key. (Note that this is backward from the public key encryption process described in the preceding section. In the preceding section, the private key decrypts the data.) The authenticator is then affixed to the document, and the document is sent to Computer A.

3. Computer A receives the data and decrypts the authenticator using Computer B's public key. The information inside the authenticator lets Computer A verify that the data has not been altered in transit. The very fact that the data could be decrypted using Computer B's public key proves that the data was encrypted using Computer B's private key, which ensures that the data came from Computer B.

FIGURE 20.4

The digital signature process.

Receiving computer
checks authentication
data w/ document

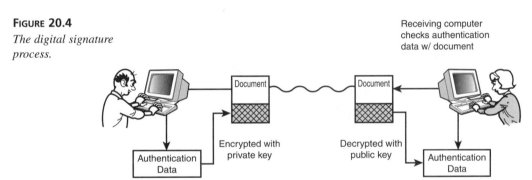

The digital signature thus ensures that the data was not altered and that it came from its presumptive source. As a rudimentary security measure, the entire message could be encrypted with Computer B's private key rather than just the authenticator. However, encrypting with a private key and decrypting with a public key does not really offer confidentiality, since the public key, which is used for decryption, is sent over the Internet and therefore may not be secret. An eavesdropper who has the public key can decrypt the encrypted authenticator. However, the eavesdropper will not be able to encrypt a new authenticator and therefore cannot pretend to be Computer B.

Digital Certificates

The grand design of making the public key available to anyone who requests it is an interesting solution, but it still has some limitations. The fact is, an attacker can still make mischief with the public key. The attacker may be able to decrypt digital signatures (see the preceding section) or even read passwords encrypted with the user's private key.

20

It is safer to provide some kind of security system for ensuring who gets access to a public key.

One answer to this problem is what is called a digital certificate. A digital certificate is essentially an encrypted copy of the public key. The certificate process is shown in Figure 20.5. This process requires a third-party *certificate server* that has a secure relationship with both the parties that want to communicate. The certificate server is also called a certificate authority (CA).

FIGURE 20.5

Authentication using digital certificates.

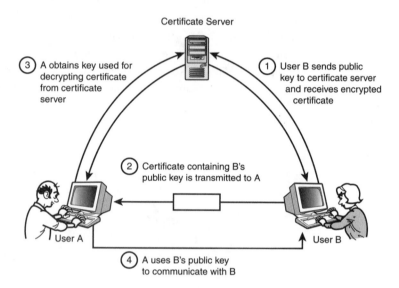

Several companies provide certificate services for the Internet. One major certificate authority is VeriSign Corp. Some large organizations provide their own certificate services. The certificate process varies among the various vendors. A rough schematic description of the process is as follows:

1. User B sends a copy of his public key to the certificate server through a secure communication.

2. The certificate server encrypts User B's public key (along with other user parameters) using a different key. This newly encrypted package is called the certificate. Included with the certificate is the digital signature of the certificate server.

3. The certificate server returns the certificate to User B.

4. User A needs to obtain User B's public key. Computer A asks Computer B for a copy of User B's certificate.

5. Computer A obtains a copy of the key used to encrypt the certificate through a secure communication with the certificate server.

6. Computer A decrypts the certificate using the key obtained from the certificate server and extracts User B's public key. Computer A also checks the digital signature of the certificate server (see step 2) to ensure that the certificate is authentic.

The best known standard for the certification process is the X.509 standard, which is described in several RFCs. X.509 version 3 is described in RFC 2459.

The digital certificate process is designed to serve a community of users. As you might guess, the security of the process depends on the safe distribution of any keys necessary for communicating with the certificate server. This may seem like simply transferring the problem. (You guarantee safe communication with the remote host by presupposing safe communication with the certificate server.) However, the fact that the protected communication channel is limited to a single certificate server (as opposed to any possible host within the community) makes it much more feasible to impose the overhead of additional safeguards necessary for ensuring a secure exchange.

The certificate process described earlier in this hour conveniently assumes the certificate server assigned to Computer A is the same server that provides certificates for User B. The certificate process may actually require a number of certificate servers spread across a large network. In that case, the process may require a series of communications and certificate exchanges with other certificate servers in order to reach the server that provided the User B certificate. As RFC 2459 states, "In general, a chain of multiple certificates may be needed, comprising a certificate of the public key owner (the end entity) signed by one CA, and zero or more additional certificates of CAs signed by other CAs. Such chains, called *certification paths*, are required because a public key user is only initialized with a limited number of assured CA public keys." Luckily, like most of the details related to encryption, this process is built into the software and doesn't require direct oversight from the user.

The X.509 certificate process is used in some of the TCP/IP security protocols discussed later in this hour, such as Secure Sockets Layer (SSL) and IP Security (IPSec).

Securing TCP/IP

In recent years, vendors have been busy extending and expanding their TCP/IP implementations to incorporate the security and encryption techniques discussed earlier in this hour. The following sections describe how encryption techniques are integrated into two Internet security protocol systems:

- SSL
- IPSec

20

Other public security protocols are also in development, and some security software vendors have developed their own systems. The following sections are intended to give you an idea of the kind of solutions necessary to incorporate the promise of encryption into the business of a real network. Following the discussions of these Internet security protocol systems is a short section on PGP, a common and very practical application used for encrypting files and e-mail messages.

SSL

Secure Sockets Layer (SSL) is a collection of TCP/IP security protocols introduced by Netscape that is now on the path for ratification as an Internet standard. The purpose of SSL is to provide a layer of security between the sockets at the Transport layer (see Hour 6, "The Transport Layer") and the application accessing the network through the sockets. Figure 20.6 shows the position of SSL in the TCP/IP protocol stack. The idea is that, when SSL is active, network services such as FTP and HTTP are protected from attack by the secure SSL protocols.

FIGURE 20.6

The TCP/IP stack with SSL.

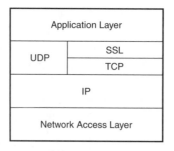

A closer look at the SSL layer reveals two sublayers (see Figure 20.7). The SSL Record Protocol is a standard base for accessing TCP. Above the Record Protocol is as a group of SSL-related protocols that perform specific services:

- **SSL Handshake Protocol**   The base protocol used to access TCP
- **SSL Change Cipher Spec Protocol**   Supports changes to encryption suite settings
- **SSL Alert Protocol**   Sends alerts

SSL-enabled services, such as HTTP, operate directly through the SSL Record Protocol. Once the connection is established, the SSL Record Protocol provides the encryption and verification necessary to ensure the confidentiality and integrity of the session.

As with other protocol security techniques, the trick is to verify the identity of the participants and securely exchange the keys that will be used for encrypting and decrypting transmissions. SSL uses public key encryption and provides support for digital certificates (described earlier in this hour).

FIGURE 20.7
SSL sublayers.

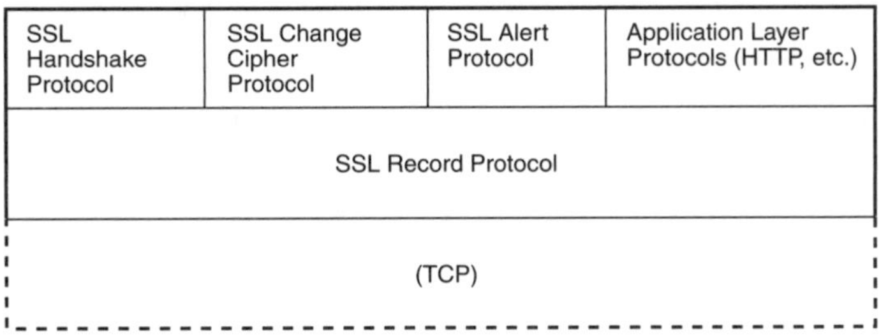

SSL Handshake Protocol	SSL Change Cipher Protocol	SSL Alert Protocol	Application Layer Protocols (HTTP, etc.)
SSL Record Protocol			
(TCP)			

The SSL Handshake Protocol establishes the connection and negotiates any connection settings (including encryption settings).

SSL is used on many Web sites to establish a secure connection for the exchange of financial information and other sensitive data. Most mainstream browsers are capable of establishing SSL connections with little or no input from the user. One problem with SSL is that, because SSL operates above the Transport layer, the applications using the connection must be SSL-aware. The next section describes an alternative TCP/IP security system (IP Security) that operates at a lower layer and therefore hides the details of the security system from the application.

IPSec

IP Security (IPSec) is an alternative security protocol system used on TCP/IP networks. IPSec operates inside the TCP/IP protocol stack, beneath the Transport layer. Because the security system is implemented beneath the Transport layer, the applications operating above the Transport layer do not have to have knowledge of the security system. IPSec is designed to provide support for confidentiality, access control, authentication, and data integrity. IPSec also protects against replay attacks, in which a packet is extracted from the data stream and reused later by the attacker.

IPSec, which is essentially a set of extensions to the IP protocol, is described in several RFCs, including RFCs 2401, 2402, 2406, and 2408. The RFCs describe IP security extensions for both IP version 4 (see Hour 4, "The Internet Layer") and IP version 6 (see Hour 22, "The New Internet").

IPSec provides the benefit of encryption-based security to any network application, regardless of whether the application is security-aware. However, the protocol stacks of both computers must support IPSec. Because the security is invisible to high-level applications, IPSec is ideal for providing security for network devices such as routers and firewalls. IPSec can operate in either of two modes:

- Transport mode provides encryption for the payload of an IP packet. The payload is then enclosed in a normal IP packet for delivery.

- Tunnel mode encrypts an entire IP packet. The encrypted packet is then included as the payload in another outer packet.

Tunnel mode is used to build a secure communication tunnel in which all details of the network are hidden. An eavesdropper cannot even read the header to obtain the source IP address. IPSec tunnel mode is often used for virtual private network (VPN) products, which are intended to create a totally private communication tunnel across a public network.

IPSec uses a number of encryption algorithms and key distribution techniques. Data is encrypted using conventional encryption algorithms such as DES, RC5, or Blowfish. Authentication and key distribution may employ public key techniques.

Pretty Good Privacy (PGP)

Pretty Good Privacy (PGP) is a popular open source confidentiality and authentication application. PGP is often used for encrypting files and e-mail messages. PGP, which was written by Phil Zimmerman, is available as freeware on the Internet. Commercial versions are also available.

PGP compresses, encrypts, and signs files and messages. Authentication is through public key techniques. A symmetric session key is then provided for encrypting the file or message using conventional algorithms such as IDEA or CAST-128.

Unlike most of the security techniques discussed in this hour, PGP and similar security applications operate at the application level and therefore do not involve the protocol stack. You do not need a specially adapted TCP/IP stack in order to use PGP.

Kerberos

Kerberos is a network-based authentication and access control system designed to support secure access over hostile networks. Kerberos was developed at MIT as part of the Athena project. The Kerberos system was originally intended for Unix-based systems, but it has since been ported to other environments. Microsoft provides a version of Kerberos for Windows 2000 networks.

As you have probably figured out by now, the short answer to the question of secure communication on hostile networks is encryption. The long answer is providing a means for protecting the security of the encryption keys. Kerberos offers a methodical process for distributing keys to the communicating hosts and verifying the credentials of a client requesting access to a service.

The Kerberos system uses a server called the Key Distribution Center (KDC) to manage the key distribution process. The Kerberos authentication process results from a relationship of three entities:

- **The client**   A computer requesting access to a server
- **The server**   A computer offering a service on the network
- **The KDC**   A computer designated to provide keys for network communication

The Kerberos authentication process is shown in Figure 20.8. Note that this process presupposes that the KDC already has a shared secret key it can use to communicate with the client and a shared secret key it can use to communicate with the server. These keys are used to encrypt a new session key, which the client and server will use to communicate with each other. The separate keys used by the KDC to encrypt data for the client and server are called *long-term keys*. The long-term key is typically derived from a secret shared by the KDC and the other computer. Commonly, the client long-term key is derived from a hash of the user's logon password, which is known to both the client and the KDC.

Figure 20.8

The Kerberos authentication process.

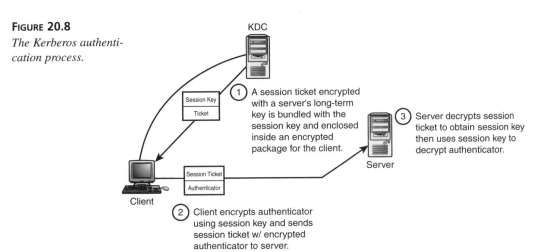

The process is as follows. As you read through this process, keep in mind that Kerberos uses conventional (symmetric) encryption rather than public key (asymmetric) encryption. In other words, the same key is used at both ends of each exchange:

1. The client wants to access a service on Server A. The client sends the KDC a request for access to the service on Server A. (In some cases, the client has already undergone an authentication process and received a separate session key for encrypting communication with the ticket granting service on the KDC.)

2. The KDC performs the following steps:

   a. The KDC generates a session key that will be used to encrypt communication between the client and Server A.

   b. The KDC creates a session ticket. The session ticket includes a copy of the session key generated in step 2a. The ticket also contains time stamp information and information about the client that is requesting access, such as client security settings.

   c. The KDC encrypts the session ticket using Server A's long-term key.

   d. The KDC bundles the encrypted session ticket, a copy of the session key, and other response parameters for the client and encrypts the whole package using the client's key. The response is then sent to the client.

3. The client receives the response from the KDC and decrypts it. The client obtains the session key necessary for communicating with Server A. Also included in the package is the session ticket, which is encrypted with the server's long-term key. The client cannot read the session ticket, but it knows it must send the ticket to the server in order to be authenticated. The client creates an authenticator (a string of authentication parameters) and encrypts it with the session key.

4. The client sends Server A an access request. The request includes the session ticket (encrypted with the server's long-term key) and the authenticator (encrypted with the session key). The authenticator includes the user's name, network address, time stamp information, and so forth.

5. Server A receives the request. Server A uses its long-term key to decrypt the session ticket (see step 2c). Server A extracts the session key from the session ticket and uses the session key to decrypt the authenticator. Server A verifies that the information in the authenticator matches the information included in the session ticket. If so, access to the service is granted.

6. As an optional final step, if the client wants to verify the credentials of Server A, Server A encrypts an authenticator with the session key and returns this authenticator to the client.

The Kerberos system is gradually becoming more popular as a means of providing a unified logon system for a network. Kerberos 4 used DES encryption, which, as this hour has already noted, is considered insecure by many encryption experts. Kerberos 5 (described in RFC 1510) supports other encryption types.

If you've ever read a description of Kerberos, you probably know the standard description of where Kerberos got its name. In Greek mythology, Kerberos (also called Cerberus) is a three-headed hound that guards the gates of the underworld. The story now is that the three heads are the three elements of the Kerberos authentication process (the client, the server, and the KDC). The original intent for the name, however, is a little murkier. In his book *Network Security Essentials* (Prentice Hall), William Stallings points out that the Kerberos system was originally intended to guard the gates of the network with the three heads of authentication, accounting, and audit, but the latter two heads (accounting and audit) were never implemented. The security community apparently found it easier to realign the metaphor than to rename the protocol for an equivalent one-headed canine, such as Lassie or Buck the Alaskan sledge dog.

Summary

This hour described some common techniques for securing TCP/IP communication. You learned about symmetric and asymmetric encryption, digital signatures, and digital certificates. You also learned about the TCP/IP security protocol systems SSL and IPSec. The hour concluded with a discussion of Kerberos authentication.

Q&A

Q Bob encrypted a file and copied it to a floppy disk. He also placed his key on the floppy to decrypt the file. Does Bob's encryption program use symmetric or asymmetric encryption?

A Bob's encryption program uses symmetric encryption. You can tell because he plans to use the same key to decrypt the file that he used to encrypt it. Does it seem strange to you that Bob included the key on the floppy along with the encrypted file? This is a very bad idea. What is the point of encrypting the file if you are going to transport the key along with it? Anyone who finds the file will also find the key.

Q Why doesn't SSL work with UDP?

A As you learned in Hour 6, UDP is a Transport layer protocol like TCP that also provides ports and sockets for accessing the network. However, SSL must operate through a connection, and UDP is a connectionless protocol. Therefore, SSL is designed to work only with TCP.

20

Q **Ellen must figure out a way to make several legacy network applications work on a Windows 2000 computer. She has been instructed to provide confidentiality for communication using these ancient apps. Should she use SSL or IPSec?**

A SSL operates above the Transport layer, so an application that uses SSL must be able to be aware of the SSL interface. IPSec, on the other hand, operates lower in the stack. The application doesn't have to know about IPSec. From the sound of this scenario, it appears that Ellen may be better off trying IPSec.

Q **What happens if an intruder tricks a Kerberos client into sending a session ticket to the wrong server?**

A Nothing (we hope). The session ticket is encrypted with the server's long-term key. As long as the intruder does not have access to the server's long-term key, he will not be able to crack the ticket. If the intruder has somehow discovered the server's long-term key, he could decrypt the ticket, extract the session key, and then possibly impersonate the server.

Key Terms

Review the following list of key terms:

asymmetric encryption—Encryption that uses different keys for encryption and decryption.

certificate authority (CA)—A central authority that oversees the certificate creation and delivery process.

digital certificate—An encrypted data structure used to distribute a public key.

digital signature—An encrypted string used to verify the identity of the sender and the integrity of the data.

encryption—The process of systematically altering data to make it unreadable to unauthorized users.

encryption algorithm—A mathematical formula or procedure used to encrypt data.

encryption key—A value (usually kept secret) used with the encryption algorithm to encrypt or decrypt data.

IPSec (IP Security)—A security protocol system consisting of extensions to the IP protocol.

KDC (Key Distribution Center)—A server that manages the key distribution process on Kerberos networks.

Kerberos—A network authentication system designed for secure access to services over hostile networks.

Pretty Good Privacy (PGP)—A common application that provides encryption for files and e-mail messages.

private key—A key used in asymmetric encryption that is kept secret and not distributed on the network.

public key—A key used in asymmetric encryption that is distributed over the network.

SSL (Secure Sockets Layer)—A security protocol system originally developed by Netscape that operates above the TCP protocol.

symmetric encryption—Encryption for which the encryption key and the decryption key are the same.

X.509—A standard that describes the digital certificate process and format.

20

HOUR 21

Network Management Protocols

Corporations or other organizations with large networks often employ people whose title or job description includes the words *network manager*. A network manager is a person who is responsible for ensuring that the network remains up and operational for employee or customer use. When a network is widely distributed, for instance national or international in scope, the network manager needs to be aware of abnormal events that occur on distant network segments. Special network monitoring software uses network management protocols to monitor and notify the network manager automatically when unusual events occur. In addition to reporting unusual events, network management software and protocols are used to query devices such as routers, hubs, and servers that are located at distant network locations. These queries could determine, for instance, whether all the ports are operational or what the average and peak datagrams processed per second values happen to be.

This hour covers the different ways to monitor a network, including the use of and differences between Simple Network Management Protocol (SNMP) and Remote Monitoring (RMON).

At the completion of this hour you will be able to

- Explain why network monitoring is essential in large networks
- Describe the software elements involved with network monitoring
- Discuss how SNMP exchanges information between a network monitoring agent and the network monitor
- Explain what a Management Information Base (MIB) is and how it is used
- Explain what RMON is and how it differs from SNMP
- Describe the functions you can perform using a network management console

Simple Network Management Protocol (SNMP)

The process of network management concerns the exchange of information about devices on the network. The network management software used by the network manager at a central location is known as a *network monitor*. The network monitor (also called a Network Management Station, or NMS) receives and displays information about the state of the network. You can configure the network monitor to notify a network manager when unusual events occur. A network monitoring agent is a program running on a network device that sends information to the network monitor. Devices such as routers, hubs, bridges, gateways, and computers can use network monitoring agents. (When used with RMON, which is discussed later in this hour, this software is called a *network monitor probe*.) Often these two pieces of software are simply referred to by the terms *monitor* and *agent* (or *probe*).

The monitor and the agent communicate with each other by using the Simple Network Management Protocol (SNMP). The SNMP protocol uses UDP ports 161 and 162. Because SNMP uses UDP for communication, a session is not established before the transmission of data (that is, there is no three-way handshake, as used with TCP). This means that a logon using a user ID and password is not performed prior to transmission of data. This can be considered a security hole because the software that is receiving a datagram has no way to verify the identity of the software that sent the datagram.

SNMP does provide a simple form of security by using what is known as a *community*. During installation of the monitor and agent software, the installer enters one or more community names. The network management software is then configured to accept datagrams from or send datagrams to only specific communities. In addition to the community names, the network software can be configured to allow the receipt of datagrams only from specific IP addresses. Agents are configured with the IP addresses of network monitors to which they can send unsolicited messages.

The SNMP Address Space

The SNMP process is predicated on both the monitor and agent software being capable of exchanging information regarding specific addressable locations within a data structure known as the Management Information Base (MIB).The MIB, shown in Figure 21.1, allows the monitor and agent to exchange information accurately and unambiguously. Both the monitor and the agent require identical MIB structures, because they must be capable of uniquely identifying a specific unit of information.

FIGURE 21.1

A small portion of the MIB.

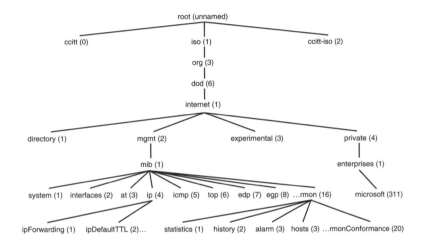

The MIB is a hierarchical address space that includes a unique address for each piece of information. In many ways, the MIB resembles DNS in that it is hierarchical, with the upper levels being administered centrally, whereas specific companies can administer their assigned location within the MIB tree. The MIB also uses dotted notation to identify each unique address within the MIB object.

> The MIB has been described in several RFCs, including RFC 1158 and RFC 1213. You'll find the official description of SNMP in RFC 1157. The latest version, SNMP v3, is described in RFC 2570 and a number of other RFCs.

The majority of the addressable locations within MIB refer to counters, which are obviously numeric. An example of a counter is `ipForwarding`, shown in Figure 21.1, or `ipInReceives` (not shown), which counts the number of inbound IP datagrams received since either the networking software was started or the counter was last reset.

21

The remainder of the locations comprise configuration information for either the networking software or for SNMP itself. This information could be in any of several forms: numeric, textual, IP addresses, and so on. An example of this configuration information is `ipDefaultTTL`; this location holds the numeric value of the TTL (Time To Live) value inserted into every IP datagram that originates on this computer.

The MIB structure is addressed by always starting at the root and progressing down through the hierarchy until you have completely identified the location that you want to read. For example, to address where `ipDefaultTTL` and `ipInReceives` are located, the SNMP monitor would send the following MIB addresses to the SNMP agent:

```
.iso.org.dod.internet.mgmt.mib.ip.ipDefaultTTL
.iso.org.dod.internet.mgmt.mib.ip.ipInReceives
```

Alternatively, these locations can also be referred to by their numerical addresses. In fact, it is this form that the network monitor uses when querying information from the agent:

```
.1.3.6.1.2.1.4.2
.1.3.6.1.2.1.4.3
```

SNMP Commands

The network monitoring agent software responds to three commands: `get`, `getnext`, and `set`. They perform the following functions:

- `get` The `get` command instructs the agent to read and return one specific unit of information from the MIB.

- `getnext` The `getnext` command instructs the agent to read and return the next sequential unit of information from the MIB. This command could be used to read a table of values, for example.

- `set` The `set` command instructs the agent to set a configurable parameter or to reset an object such as a network interface or a specific counter.

SNMP software actually works in several different ways, depending on the needs of the network administrator. Different types of SNMP behavior are described in the following list:

- A network monitor agent always operates in a query/response manner where it can receive requests from and send responses to the monitor. The agent receives either a `get` or `getnext` command and returns the information from one addressable location.

- Although optional, agents are often configured to send unsolicited messages to the network monitor when unusual events occur. These unsolicited messages are known as *trap messages* or *traps*; they occur when the agent software traps some unusual occurrence.

For example, SNMP agent software usually operates in a mode where it monitors for established thresholds to be exceeded. These thresholds are established using the set command. In the event that a threshold is exceeded, the agent traps the occurrence and then constructs and sends an unsolicited datagram to the network monitor identifying the IP address of the machine where the trap occurred, as well as which threshold was exceeded.

- Agents can also receive requests from the monitor to perform certain actions, such as to reset a specific port on a router or to set the threshold levels that are used in trapping events. Again, the set command is used for setting configurable parameters or resetting counter or interfaces.

The following example illustrates query and response commands used by SNMP. This example uses a diagnostic utility called snmputil, which allows a technician to simulate a monitor. Through the utility, a technician can issue commands to the agent. In this case, the agent is located on a computer with an IP address of 192.59.66.200, and the agent is a member of a community named public. Notice the .0 at the end of the first two commands; this is used as a suffix when reading simple variables such as counters.

```
D:\>snmputil get 192.59.66.200 public .1.3.6.1.2.1.4.2.0
Variable = ip.ipDefaultTTL.0
Value    = INTEGER - 128

D:\>snmputil getnext 192.59.66.200 public .1.3.6.1.2.1.4.2.0
Variable = ip.ipInReceives.0
Value    = Counter - 11898
```

> The default community name on many SNMP systems is public. The admin in this example should have changed the name to something else. You give an attacker a head start when you use a default name.

SNMP is useful to network administrators, but it is not perfect. Some of the shortcomings of SNMP are described in the following list:

- **Cannot see lower layers**   SNMP resides at the Application layer above UDP, so it cannot see what is happening at the lowest layers within the protocol stack, such as what is happening at the Network Access layer.

- **Requires an operational protocol stack**   A fully operational TCP/IP stack is required for an SNMP monitor and agent to communicate. If you're having network problems that prevent the stack from operating correctly, SNMP cannot help troubleshoot the problem.

21

- **Generates heavy network traffic**   The query response mechanism used by SNMP causes a great deal of network traffic. Although unsolicited traps are sent when significant events occur, in actuality network monitors generate a constant amount of network traffic as they query agents for specific information.

- **Does not provide proactive notifications**   SNMP traps notify the network monitor when an unusual event has occurred. However, SNMP traps cannot anticipate impending problems and notify the network monitor before a problem becomes serious.

- **Provides too much data and too little information**   With the literally thousands of address locations within an MIB, you can retrieve many small pieces of information. However, it requires a powerful management console to analyze these minute details and to be capable of providing useful analysis of what is occurring on a specific machine.

- **Provides view of the machine but not the network**   With SNMP and the MIB, you can see what is happening on a specific machine. However, you can't see what is occurring on the network segment.

Remote Monitoring (RMON)

Remote Monitoring (RMON) is an extension to the MIB address space and was developed to allow monitoring and maintenance of remote LANs. Unlike SNMP, which provides information retrieved from a single computer, RMON captures datagrams directly from the media and therefore can analyze the entire datagram and provide insight on the LAN as a whole.

The RMON MIB begins at address location .1.3.6.1.2.1.16 (as shown in Figure 21.1) and is currently divided into 20 groups, for example .1.3.6.1.2.1.16.1 through .1.3.6.1.2.1.16.20. RMON was developed by the IETF to address shortcomings with SNMP and to provide greater visibility of network traffic on remote LANs.

There are two versions of RMON: RMON 1 and RMON 2.

When used in conjunction with RMON, the agent software is typically referred to by the term *probe*.

- **RMON 1**   RMON 1 includes 10 groups (numbers 1 through 10) and is oriented toward monitoring ethernet and token ring LANs. All groups within RMON 1 are concerned with monitoring the bottom two layers, for example the Physical and Data Link layers of the OSI reference model (corresponding to the Network Access layer in the TCP/IP model). RMON 1 is described in RFC 1757, which updates RFC 1271, which was published in November 1991.

- **RMON 2**   RMON 2 also includes 10 groups (numbers 11 through 20). They are concerned with the upper five layers of the OSI reference model, which are the Network, Transport, Session, Presentation, and Application layers (corresponding to the Internet, Transport, and Application layers of the TCP/IP model). The specifications for RMON 2 are contained in RFCs 2021 and 2034, which were released in 1997.

> This hour mostly addresses RMON 1.

RMON addresses many of the shortcomings of SNMP, and in some cases collects useful information that SNMP is incapable of gathering. RMON 1 works by looking at the OSI Network layer (TCP/IP Internet layer). At this layer, datagrams are independent of transport protocols, so RMON 1 can examine data from TCP/IP, IPX, NetBEUI, AppleTalk, or any other upper-level protocol.

RMON 1 can examine the source and destination physical address fields of the frame to determine where the frame came from and where it is intended to be delivered on the local network. RMON 1 also can detect invalid frames, those that are too short or too long to be processed by higher-level protocols. These frames would normally be discarded or ignored by the protocol stack.

RMON software decodes and analyzes every datagram and then places entries in the appropriate MIB counters. After this process has been completed, the datagram is usually discarded. However, if there is something unusual about a datagram, such as if it is too short or too long, then the RMON could store the datagram for later examination by the network manager.

RMON information is gathered in the context of groups of statistics that correlate to different kinds of information. The RMON 1 group names are described in the following list:

- **Statistics**   The Statistics group holds statistical information in the form of a table for each network segment attached to the probe. Some of the counters within this group keep track of the number of packets, the number of broadcasts, the number of collisions, the number of undersize and oversize datagrams, and so on.

- **History**   The History group holds statistical information that is periodically compiled and stored for later retrieval.

- **Alarm**   The Alarm group works in conjunction with the Event group (described later). Periodically the Alarm group examines statistical samples from variables

21

within the probe and compares them with configured thresholds; if these thresholds are exceeded, an event is generated that can be used to notify the network manager.

- **Hosts**   The Hosts group maintains statistics for each host on the network segment; it learns about these hosts by examining the source and destination physical addresses within datagrams.

- **Host top n**   The Host Top N group is used to generate reports based on statistics for the top defined number of hosts in a particular category. For instance, a network manager might want to know which hosts appear in the most datagrams, or which hosts are sending the most oversized or undersized datagrams.

- **Matrix**   The Matrix group constructs a table that includes the source and destination physical address pairs for every datagram monitored on the network. These address pairs define conversations between two addresses.

- **Filter**   The Filter group allows the generation of a binary pattern that can be used to match, or filter, datagrams from the network.

- **Capture**   The Capture group allows datagrams selected by the Filter group to be captured for later retrieval and examination by the network manager.

- **Event**   The Event group works in conjunction with the Alarm group to generate events that notify the network manager when a threshold of a monitored object has been exceeded.

- **Token Ring**   The Token Ring group maintains collected information that is specific to token ring.

Network Management Consoles

A network management console allows the network manager to manage a large distributed network from a single location. Using a network management console, the network manager can view the current status of individual hosts that contain SNMP agents and can receive and be notified of trap messages when they arrive. In addition to these functions, a network management console can be used to reset remote equipment and monitor for congestion or down network interfaces on routers.

The network management console is typically housed on a powerful workstation computer that runs the network management software; this software is both complex and processor intensive. Usually the network management console employs a graphical interface to display status information in a format that is easy to interpret. As mentioned before, SNMP returns minute details of information; it is the network management console that takes these shreds of information, analyzes them, and produces useful information for the network manager.

Summary

In this hour you learned that the SNMP protocol is integral to providing centralized monitoring and maintenance of distant remote networks. You also learned that, by using a network management console and a central site, a network manager can be notified when abnormal events occur and can view network traffic status as reported by agents operating on routers, hubs, and servers. Also, by using the network management console, the network manager can perform functions such as resetting ports on routers or even resetting remote equipment in the event that less drastic measures don't cure a problem.

Many newer network devices include embedded RMON features. RMON provides enhanced capabilities over simple SNMP. When both RMON 1 and the newer RMON 2 groups are employed, the network manager has the capability to view what is happening at all layers within the TCP/IP stack. RMON can greatly reduce network traffic that is normally associated with SNMP and does not require a powerful network management console in order to interpret information returned by SNMP from the MIBs. However, when using RMON, a significant amount of processing occurs on the computer that is running the RMON software; much of the analysis is performed at the network segment where the datagrams are being captured.

Q&A

Q What does the acronym MIB stand for?

A Management Information Base

Q The SNMP protocol uses which transport protocol and which ports?

A UDP port 161 is used for SNMP, and port 162 is used for SNMP traps.

Q What is the name of the message that an agent can send in an unsolicited manner when an event occurs?

A A trap message

Q What layer of the TCP/IP model does RMON address?

A The Network Access layer

Q What layers of the TCP/IP model does RMON 2 address?

A The Internet, Transport, and Application layers

21

Key Terms

Review the following list of key terms:

agent—The software loaded on to a host that can read the MIB and respond to a monitor with the desired results. Agents have the capability to transmit unsolicited messages to the monitor when significant abnormal events occur.

Management Information Base (MIB)—A hierarchical address space used by monitors and agents. Specific locations within the MIB are located by using dotted notation from the top of the MIB structure down to the MIB address you want.

network management console—A workstation running network management software that is used to monitor, maintain, and configure a large distributed network.

network monitor—Another name for a network management console.

probe—Another name for an agent. The tzerm is often used in situations involving RMON.

remote monitoring (RMON)—An extension to MIB that provides enhanced capabilities over traditional SNMP functions. In order to store data in the RMON MIB, the agent or probe must include RMON software.

SNMP—Simple Network Management Protocol. A protocol used for managing resources on a TCP/IP network.

Hour **22**

The New Internet

The Internet is changing every day, and TCP/IP is changing with it. This hour examines a new standard for IP addressing that will lead TCP/IP into the next generation: IPv6.

At the completion of this hour, you'll be able to

- Explain the reason for the change to IPv6's 128-bit address format
- Describe IPv6's extension headers
- Explain how IPv6 will coexist with IPv4

IPv6

The IP addressing system described in Hour 4, "The Internet Layer," has served the Internet community for nearly a generation, and those who developed it are justifiably proud of how far TCP/IP has come. But for the past few years they've been worrying about one thing: The world is running out of addresses. This looming address crisis might seem surprising, because the 32-bit address field of the current IP format can provide over three billion possible host IDs. But it is important to remember how many of these three billion addresses are actually unusable. A network ID is typically assigned to an organization, and that organization controls the host IDs associated with its own network.

Recall from Hour 4 that IP addresses fall within address classes determined by the value of the first octet in the address field. The address classes and their associated address ranges are shown in Table 22.1. Table 22.1 also shows the number of possible networks within an address class and the number of possible hosts on each network. A Class B address can support 65,534 hosts. Many Class B organizations, however, do not have 65,534 nodes and therefore assign only a fraction of the available addresses—the rest go unused. The 127 Class A networks can support 16,777,214 addresses, many of which also go unused. It is worth noting as well that the 16,510 Class A and B networks are reportedly all taken. The Class C networks that remain face a limitation of only 254 possible addresses. (Refer to Hours 4 and 5, "Subnetting," for more on the anatomy of IP addresses.)

TABLE 22.1   Number of Networks and Addresses for IP Address Classes

Class	First Octet	Number of Networks	Possible Addresses per Network
A	0–126	127	16,777,214
B	128–191	16,383	65,534
C	192–223	2,097,151	254

> The emergence of Classless Internet Domain Routing (CIDR) has helped this problem of using Class C addresses for larger networks. You learned about CIDR in Hour 5.

Internet philosophers have known for some time that a new addressing system would be necessary, and that new system eventually found its way into the standard for IP version 6 (IPv6), which is sometimes called *IPng* for *IP next generation*. The current IPv6 specification is RFC 2460, which appeared in December 1998. (Several other preliminary RFCs set the stage for RFC 2460, and newer RFCs continue to discuss issues relating to IPv6.)

The IP address format in IPv6 calls for 128-bit addresses. Part of the reason for this larger address space is supposedly to support one billion networks. As you'll learn later in this hour, this large address size is also spacious enough to accommodate some compatibility between IPv4 addresses and IPv6 addresses.

The recent emergence of Network Address Translation (NAT) devices has reduced the threat of this looming IP-address shortage. As you learned in Hour 9, "Network Hardware," a NAT device enables a network to use a private address space and still access the Internet through a relatively smaller number of registered addresses.

Some of the goals for IPv6 are as follows:

- **Expanded addressing capabilities**   Not only does IPv6 provide more addresses, it also provides other improvements to IP addressing. For instance, IPv6 supports more hierarchical addressing levels. IPv6 also improves address auto-configuration capabilities and provides a new kind of address called an *anycast address*, which enables you to send a datagram to any one of a group of computers.

- **Simpler header format**   Some of the IPv4 header fields have been eliminated. Other fields have become optional.

- **Improved support for extensions and options**   IPv6 allows some header information to be included in optional extension headers. This increases the amount of information the header can include without wasting space in the main header. In most cases these extension headers are not processed by routers; this further streamlines the transmission process.

- **Flow labeling**   IPv6 datagrams can be marked for a specific flow level. A *flow level* is a class of datagrams that requires specialized handling methods. For instance, a real-time service might require a different flow level than an e-mail message.

- **Improved authentication and privacy**   IPv6 extensions support authentication, confidentiality, and data integrity techniques.

IPv6 has already begun to emerge into the networking world. Sun Solaris 8 includes built-in support for IPv6, and IPv6 implementations are available for Linux, BSD, and other operating systems. The following sections discuss IPv6 and some of its next-generation features.

IPv6 Header Format

The IPv6 header format is shown in Figure 22.1. Note that the basic IPv6 header is actually simpler than the corresponding IPv4 header. As was just mentioned, part of the reason for the header's simplicity is that detailed information is relegated to special extension headers that follow the main header.

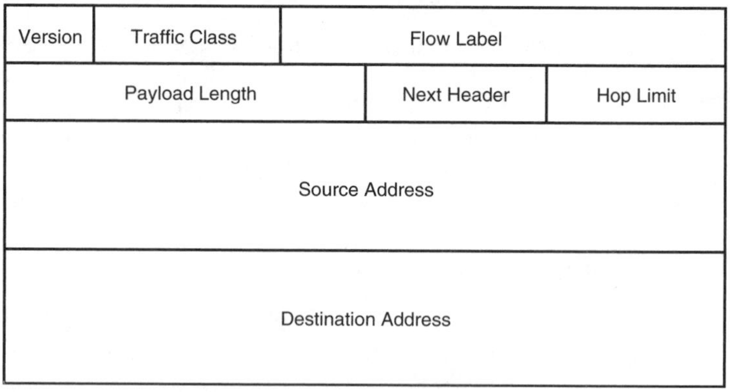

FIGURE 22.1

An IPv6 header.

Version	Traffic Class	Flow Label	
Payload Length		Next Header	Hop Limit
Source Address			
Destination Address			

The fields of the IPv6 header are as follows:

- **Version (4-bit)**   Identifies the IP version number (in this case, version 6).
- **Traffic Class (8-bit)**   Identifies the type of data enclosed in the datagram.
- **Flow Label (20-bit)**   Designates the flow level (described in the preceding section).
- **Payload Length (16-bit)**   Determines the length of the data (the portion of the datagram after the header).
- **Next Header (8-bit)**   Defines the type of header immediately following the current header. See the discussion of extension headers later in this section.
- **Hop Limit (8-bit)**   Indicates how many remaining hops are allowed for this datagram. This value is decremented by one at each hop. If the hop limit reaches zero, the datagram is discarded.
- **Source Address (128-bit)**   Identifies the IP address of the computer that sent the datagram.
- **Destination Address (128-bit)**   Identifies the IP address of the computer that receives the datagram.

As was already mentioned in this hour, IPv6 provides for bundles of optional information in separate extension headers between the main header and the data. These extension headers provide information for specific situations and at the same time allow the main header to remain small and easily manageable.

The IPv6 specification defines the following extension headers:

- Hop-by-Hop Options
- Destination Options

- Routing
- Fragment
- Authentication
- Encrypted Security Payload

Each header type is associated with an 8-bit identifier. The Next Header field in the main header or in an extension header defines the identifier of the next header in the chain (see Figure 22.2).

FIGURE 22.2
The Next Header field.

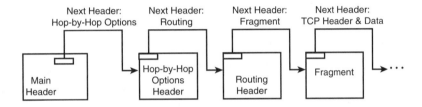

Of the extension headers described in the preceding list, only the Hop-by-Hop Options header and the Routing header are processed along the transmission path by intermediate nodes. Routers do not have to process the other extension headers; they just pass them on.

The following sections discuss each of these extension header types in greater detail.

Hop-by-Hop Options Header

The purpose of the hop-by-hop options header is to relate optional information for routers along the transmission path.

The Hop-by-Hop Options header, like the Destination Options header discussed in the next section, was included in the specification largely to provide the industry with a format and a mechanism for developing future options.

The specification includes an option type designation and some padding options for aligning the data. One option that is defined explicitly in the specification is the *jumbo payload* option, which is used to transmit a data payload longer than 65,535 bytes.

Destination Options Header

The purpose of the Destination Options header is to relate optional information to the destination node. Like the Hop-by-Hop Options header, the Destination Options header is included primarily as a framework for developing future options.

Routing Header

The Routing header is used to specify one or more routers that the datagram will route through on the way to its destination.

The Routing header format is shown in Figure 22.3.

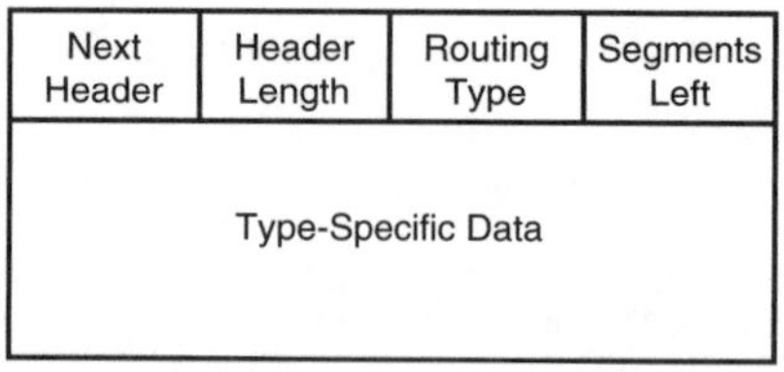

FIGURE 22.3

The Routing header.

Next Header	Header Length	Routing Type	Segments Left
Type-Specific Data			

The data fields for the Routing header are as follows:

- **Next Header**   Identifies the header type of the next header following this header.
- **Header Length (8-bit)**   Specifies the length of the header in bytes (excluding the Next Header field).
- **Routing Type (8-bit)**   Identifies the routing header type. Different routing header types are designed for specific situations.
- **Segments Left**   Indicates the number of explicitly defined router segments before the destination.
- **Type-Specific Data**   Identifies data fields for the specific routing type given in the Routing Type field.

Fragment Header

Each router along a message path has a setting for the maximum transmission unit (MTU). The MTU setting indicates the largest unit of data the router can transmit. In IPv6, the source node can discover what is called the *path MTU*—the smallest MTU setting for any device along the transmission path. The path MTU represents the largest unit of data that can be sent over the path. If the size of the datagram is larger than the path MTU, the datagram must be broken into smaller pieces so that it can be delivered across the network. The Fragment header contains information necessary for reassembling fragmented datagrams.

Authentication Header

The Authentication header provides security and authentication information. The Authentication field provides a means of determining whether a datagram was altered in transit.

Encrypted Security Payload Header

The EEncrypted Security Payload header (ESP) provides encryption and confidentiality. Using IPv6's ESP capabilities, some or all of the data being transmitted can be encrypted. Using tunnel-mode ESP, an entire IP datagram is encrypted and placed in an outer, unencrypted datagram. In Transport node ESP, authentication data and ESP header information are encrypted.

 Encryption is a technique for encoding data so that it passes over the network in an unreadable form.

IPv6 Addressing

As you'll recall from Hour 4, 32-bit IPv4 addresses are commonly expressed in dotted-decimal notation, in which each byte of the address is expressed as a decimal number of up to three digits (for example, 111.121.131.142). This string of 12 decimal digits is easier to remember than the 32 binary digits of the actual binary address, and it is possible, if you try, to even remember a dotted-decimal address. This method for humanizing a 32-bit address, however, is utterly useless for remembering a 128-bit address. A dotted-decimal equivalent of an IPv6 address looks something like this:

```
111.121.35.99.114.121.97.0.0.88.250.201.211.109.130.117
```

It's too early to predict how network administrators will accommodate these long addresses. You can certainly bet that DNS will play an important role on IPv6 networks (see Hour 11, "Name Resolution").

Engineers typically use a hexadecimal (base 16) format to express 128-bit IPv6 addresses as eight 4-digit hexadecimal values (each signifying 16 digits). Colons separate 4-digit values. This string of eight 4-digit hexadecimal numbers is easier to remember than the dotted-decimal equivalent, but it still isn't easy to remember.

As a consequence of the address assignment scheme for IPv6, it appears that all-zero bytes will be common. Eliminating leading zeros and leaving out zero strings (with a double colon to signify missing digits) should further improve memorization.

But if you traffic in 128-bit addresses every day, think about using DNS.

IPv6 with IPv4

The only way IPv6 will ever take hold, of course, is if it phases in gradually. A full-scale retooling of the Internet isn't going to happen, so engineers designed IPv6 so that it could coexist with IPv4 over a long-term transition.

The intention is that an IPv6 protocol stack will operate beside the IPv4 protocol stack in a multiprotocol configuration, just as IPv4 now coexists with IPX/SPX, NetBEUI, or other protocol stacks. The software components necessary for multiplexing IPv4 and IPv6 will then have to operate at the Network Access layer (see Figure 22.4).

FIGURE 22.4
Multiplexing IPv4 and IPv6.

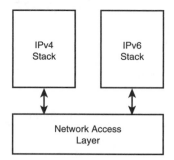

The addressing systems also provide a measure of compatibility or at least convertibility. One scheme suggests that the 32 bits of an IPv4 address could fill the lowest 32 bits of an IPv6 address. The top 96 bits could then contain a standard bit pattern.

However the various vendors decide to relate the IPv4 and IPv6 address systems, you can expect to see more on IPv6 in the coming years.

IPv6 and Quality of Service (QoS)

IPv6 addresses another challenge that has recently faced the aging IPv4 infrastructure: the need for uniform Quality of Service (QoS) levels.

In the old days, when the Internet primarily was used for e-mail and FTP-style downloads, no one thought much about prioritizing data transmission. If an e-mail message didn't arrive in two seconds, it would arrive in 2 minutes—or possibly in an hour. No one really cared about specifying or limiting the time interval in which the message could arrive. In contrast, today's Internet supports many different types of transmissions, some with very rigid delivery requirements. Internet video and television and other real-time applications cannot operate properly with long delays as packets wind their way through router buffers. Even a small delay in an Internet phone connection can have the effect of distorting the speech of the participants.

In the Internet of the future, it will be possible to prioritize IP datagrams as they wait for delivery. A datagram from an interactive video application could move to the top of the queue as it waits in a router buffer, while an e-mail datagram might pause for a momentary delay.

22

IPv6 is designed to support prioritizing through differentiated service levels. The Traffic Class and Flow Label fields of the IPv6 header provide a means for specifying the type and priority of data enclosed in the datagram (refer to Figure 22.1). Of course, new data fields in the header will not provide new functionality on the Internet until hardware vendors develop routers and other devices that recognize these new routing parameters.

> In the IPv4 world, some vendors and engineers have experimented with using the Type of Service field (refer to Figure 4.3) for differentiated service information. The IPv6 Traffic Class field is intended to support continued experimentation with differentiated service.

Summary

This hour discussed IPv6, the new version of the IP. IPv6 will eventually lead to a new form of addressing and delivery on the Internet. You also learned about some IPv6 innovations, including extension headers, jumbo payloads, and the formidable 128-bit IPv6 address.

Q&A

Q Why do many IP addresses go unused?

A An organization that is assigned an Internet address space often doesn't use all the host IDs associated with that address space.

Q What is the advantage of placing header information in an extension header instead of in the main header?

A The extension header is included only if the information in the header is necessary. Also, many extension headers are not processed by routers and therefore won't slow down router traffic.

Key Terms

Review the following list of key terms:

dotted decimal—A common format for the decimal equivalent of a 32-bit IP address (for example, 111.121.131.144).

extension header—An optional header following the main header in an IPv6 datagram. The extension header contains additional information that may not be necessary in all cases.

flow level—A designation for an IPv6 datagram specifying special handling or a special level of throughput (for example, real-time).

hop limit—The number of remaining router hops a datagram might take before it is discarded. The hop limit is specified in the IPv6 main header and then decremented at each router stop.

IPv6—A new standard for IP addressing that features 128-bit IP addresses. The intent of IPv6 designers is for IPv6 to phase in gradually over the next several years.

jumbo payload—A datagram payload with a length exceeding the conventional limit of 65,535 bytes. IPv6 enables jumbo payload datagrams to pass through the network.

payload length—The length of the data portion of an IPv6 header (excluding the header).

Hour **23**

Recent and Emerging Technologies

Anyone who has followed TCP/IP for the last 20 years will tell you that the world of networking changes rapidly. Even when you expect it to change, it still manages to slip out from under you. And many experts will tell you that the next few years will witness some of the biggest and most revolutionary changes yet, as computers and computerized gadgets grow more integrated with the routine of everyday life.

Some of these changes are the result of technological advance. Others result from economic forces and the complex interplay of marketing with personal choice. The following sections discuss some technologies emerging in the world of TCP/IP networking. At the end of this hour, you will be able to

- Describe the recent developments in network client design, including the downloadable workspace, automated updates, network computers, and terminal clients

- Discuss recent data-related technologies, such as the storage area network and LDAP

- Describe clustering and list the advantages and disadvantages of using clustering
- Discuss the wireless device architecture Bluetooth

TCP/IP in the Future

At this writing, TCP/IP can do much more than anyone guessed it would be able to do 10 years ago. You can play music and video over the Internet, access your office computer across a secure, virtually private Internet connection, and shop for rare and unusual products without ever leaving your home. But futurists, experts, and entrepreneurs aren't satisfied. The computer industry is working now to introduce new technologies that will transform the workplace and the homespace.

One of the biggest goals of the computer industry is simply to make the current systems better than they are: faster hardware, better browsers, more capable and more efficient Web sites. This challenge for better products is a central part of the economy, and it will undoubtedly continue as long as buyers have a choice. However, other forces also influence the growth and development of computer technologies:

- Bandwidth
- Security
- Simplicity
- Economy

Some of these factors were discussed in earlier hours. For instance, in Hour 22, "The New Internet," you learned how IPv6 improves the bandwidth and efficiency of the Internet. Hour 20, "TCP/IP Security," discussed several recent strategies for improving security on TCP/IP networks. This hour describes some of the initiatives that will ultimately make the computerized world simpler and more economical.

Of course, cost is a determining factor for nearly everything in our world economy. Much of the current innovation in the computer industry results from the falling cost of computer hardware. If a PC or a PC-like device costs $5,000, you probably aren't going to buy a special PC to operate your dishwasher. If a server costs $50,000, you probably won't worry about adding servers to create a cluster for your Web site. But as the cost of hardware falls and labor costs rise, a whole new gallery of solutions takes form.

The View from the Client

As you have heard many times in this book, most of what we know as networking results from the interaction of a client (a computer requesting a service) and a server (a computer supplying that service). The server is an important central feature of the network.

The server is the hub, the storehouse of services and data upon which the other computers depend. And though the server can be very busy filling requests, the activities of the server are largely predictable and passive. The client workstation is where the user sits and, ultimately, where the work gets done. The most inefficient connection in all of networking is the messy interaction of the user with a client workstation. Many believe that creating a better and more streamlined working environment for the user is the best way to reduce the cost and increase the efficiency of networking.

This viewpoint is based on the simple (and well-documented) observation that increasing the capabilities of a client computer does not always increase the efficiency of the user and, in fact, often reduces the efficiency of the user. The concept of Total Cost of Ownership (TCO) was a major buzzword a few years ago, and the principles of TCO are important to engineers and product designers. The philosophy of TCO holds that the most important consideration when weighing the cost of a workstation is not what you pay for the computer but the total cost of what you pay for the computer, the person who works on the computer, and the staff that keeps the computer operational.

According to a study by the Gartner Group, 46% of the cost of owning a corporate workstation is due to "non-billable end-user operations,"—in other words, to activities performed on the workstation that aren't directly related to the user's job. Some of these activities are related to the user troubleshooting or reconfiguring the workstation; some of this cost is related to the user operating non-productive applications or simply browsing around inside the user interface. Twenty-one percent of the cost of owning a corporate workstation goes for technical support. Much of the technical support cost is spent on activities that could easily be automated. Interestingly, as many who have worked for an IT department will quickly point out, another significant part of the total technical support cost is the expense of paying a technical support professional to fix problems caused by users configuring their own workstations.

The result of this TCO movement is the strong feeling that computers would be more efficient if they were simpler. This might mean simpler hardware with fewer components and more seamless interactivity. It might also mean simpler software that updates itself and doesn't allow (or require) the user to stray from productive activities. The ultimate goal is a more logical user environment that simplifies administration and reduces the number of choices a user must make. The following sections examine some recent initiatives related to this goal. You'll learn about

- Automated updates
- The downloadable workspace
- Client-end processing
- Network computers (NCs)
- Terminal clients

23

Automated Updates

Many commercial software packages are updated twice a year or more. One of the major costs of maintaining software is the expense of continually updating the software to keep it current. For a single user on a home PC, the price of running an update twice a year may not be significant, but picture a large corporation with 10,000 employees who all use the same word processing program. The total cost of keeping all versions of the program current is enormous.

Management programs have been available for several years to assist with the task of updating software on the network. These programs let the network administrator operate from a single console without having to walk around to every computer in the company. A common practice is to store the update software on a network server. The client computer then connects to the server through a script and executes the update over the network.

These update methods are useful, and they are more economical than having each user configure and execute the update individually. However, these methods still require effort and expense from the network administrator to set up and manage the update.

A newer, and even more painless approach, is to use Web technology to download the update directly from the application vendor (see Figure 23.1). The application automatically connects to the vendor's Web site at some predetermined interval to see if an update is available. If the current version at the Web site is newer than the version on the client computer, an update is performed automatically.

FIGURE 23.1

Automated update over the Web.

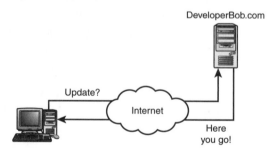

DeveloperBob.com

Update?

Internet

Here you go!

This periodic servicing may be a basic feature of the product, or it may result from a service agreement between the organization and the software vendor. Network admins can apply this same scenario to a corporate intranet setting, in which network personnel configure a local Web server to download updates to the client.

Several vendors currently provided Web-based updates for their software. This option is now available for operating systems (such as Windows 98 and Windows 2000), browsers, and several anti-virus packages, as well as other popular applications.

Downloading the Workspace

Many users are traumatized by the unfamiliar. And even if a user doesn't mind new appearances, changes to the work environment can cause inefficiency as the user adapts to new features. Also, a user's personal workspace often contains labor-saving conveniences like shortcuts, saved links, bookmarks, and the user's preferred screen settings.

Vendors and engineers have done considerable work with the concept of the roving or movable workspace (see Figure 23.2). The idea is to make the user's files and personal preference settings available on the network so that the work environment appears the same to the user no matter where the user logs in. This increases the productivity of the user because the user doesn't have to react to changes in the user interface. It is possible that this feature could ultimately change the whole concept of a user workstation. Currently, the user workstation is typically considered the personal preserve of a single user. The user sets up the workstation to reflect the user's personal preferences and responsibilities. In the world of the downloadable workspace, individual computers would truly be interchangeable. The user would receive a personalized configuration no matter where the user logged in. This might make it easier for those who use their computers only part-time to share computers. It could also reduce management costs because all workstation configurations could be the same, and all user-specific settings could be stored in one central place.

FIGURE 23.2

A downloadable work-space provides the same environment no matter where the user logs on.

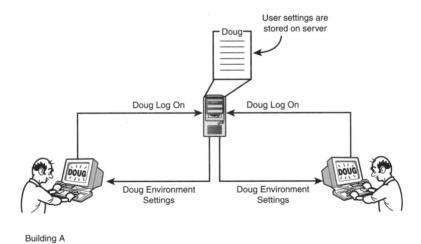

Building A

Versions of the downloadable workspace are currently available in some networking environments. The roving user profile on Windows networks is one implementation of this feature. Unix and Linux computers offer options for controlling the user environment through user configuration files. So far, the major OS vendors have not produced mainstream technologies that successfully deploy the concept of the downloadable workspace to the greater Internet. But the chat groups are full of ideas. One concept for how this technology could work on the Internet is for the user to log in to a Web site that would essentially provide a complete user interface. Another idea is for a complete Java-based work environment to download to a client at logon. You'll learn more about this idea in the next section.

Client-End Processing

Hour 17, "HTTP, HTML, and the World Wide Web" introduced some of the emerging technologies that let the client computer participate in building and interpreting the content of a Web site. Microsoft's Active Server Pages and ActiveX technologies let Web components interact with other components on the computer to increase the range of functions that can be performed over the Web. The World Wide Web Consortium (W3C) XML language—a more extensible descendent of HTML—promises to offer similar advantages in an OS-neutral format. XML is already used widely on Linux and Unix systems.

Of these client-processing technologies, Java is perhaps the most popular. Java, which was originally developed by Sun Microsystems, is a programming language designed for applications that are downloaded from the server to the client and then executed on the client. Whereas HTML specifies content that will appear on the page, Java specifies the process that the client should use for determining the content that will appear on the page.

Java, however, is much bigger than just a technique for animating Web pages. Java is used for programming embedded systems, and vendors are currently working on complete applications such as word processors and even whole operating systems written in Java (see the next section).

Network Computers

A few years ago, it seemed that the world was ready for the age of a marvelous new creation called the network computer (NC). A network computer is a computer-like device with a very fast processor and no CD, hard drive, or floppy drive. When the user logs on from the network computer (see Figure 23.3), a complete Java-based operating system downloads to the network computer. If the user starts an application, a Java-based application downloads to the network computer—possibly with some server-based processing for certain tasks. The user could save any files to a well-protected and fault-tolerant storage device on the server or elsewhere on the network. When the user turns off the network computer, the complete configuration disappears from memory. But it returns when the user logs on again. In fact, another user could log on to the same network computer and receive a completely different configuration. The new user could even receive a completely different operating system. Meanwhile, the users' files are kept safe with the ISP. All software is managed, configured, and updated from the server. And the network computer is so simple that it isn't likely to break. If it does break, you just buy a new one because it is so inexpensive. In any case, you don't have to disassemble, reassemble, or configure the network computer because there is nothing to configure.

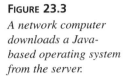

FIGURE 23.3

A network computer downloads a Java-based operating system from the server.

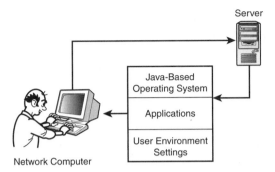

23

This amazing vision captivated market watchers when it was first proposed, but so far the revolution of the network computer hasn't happened. One reason why the network computer hasn't caught on is the fact that hardware prices have fallen so sharply. You can now buy a complete computer for what a network computer cost a few years ago. Another reason may be that, although Java development is proceeding very rapidly, we haven't yet reached the point where a complete Java-based operating system is viable for the mainstream. However, the network computer is only one of several thin-client solutions that have made their way to the market. You'll learn about another thin-client option (the terminal client) in the next section.

Terminal Clients

To an earlier generation, the terminal was an important feature of the computing environment. A terminal was nothing more than the hardware component of the user interface—a place for users to read output from the computer and enter commands interactively.

Terminals evolved around the paradigm of centralized processing. A single computer capable of supporting multiple user sessions could be attached to several terminals. All processing would take place on the central computers, but several users could work concurrently on the system.

When the personal computer (PC) arrived on the scene, most observers concluded that the era of the terminal had come to an end. Although terminals were sometimes used in certain highly specialized situations (such as to track airline flights or hospital records), the majority of businesses gradually moved away from terminal-based systems. Most terminals could only process text, not graphics), and the centralized model concentrated resources on a single processor. If the central computer was down, no one could use the system. The decentralized PC model, on the other hand, distributed processing throughout the network and limited the effect of processor failure.

In recent years, however, the terminal has been making a comeback. The reasons for this reversal are many. One important consideration is cost; a terminal client costs less than a whole computer. Apart from the hardware expense, for reasons described earlier in this hour, the increased simplicity of a terminal reduces the cost because it reduces the number of things that can go wrong. Also, the centralized management of a terminal server system increases security, improves administration, and simplifies backup and fault tolerance.

Today's terminal clients don't look much like the VT100 terminals from several years ago. Modern terminal clients typically support a graphic user interface. In many cases, the terminal client is a complete computer capable of assembling graphic images and participating in a TCP/IP network. In fact, old computers that do not have the horse-power to operate efficiently are sometimes deployed as terminal clients. In the terminal client model (see Figure 23.4), the client does not have to be capable of running the application it is using. It only has to be capable of sending instructions from the server and receiving screen update information from the application.

FIGURE 23.4

In the terminal client model, applications execute on the server.

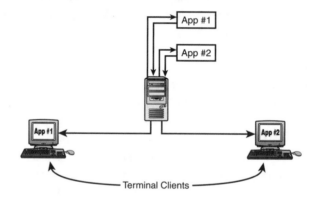

Several dedicated terminal products are now available. Products such as Wyse's Winterm provide a low-cost terminal for connecting to Microsoft's server-side Terminal Server product or third-party terminal servers, such as Citrix WinFrame. Unix systems have always been terminal ready. A new crop of X Window terminal products provide graphic terminal capability for terminal clients on Unix and Linux systems.

The View from the Server

As clients grow thinner, servers get bigger. The world of e-commerce and Web-based archives has increased the need for big, fast, and reliable servers. Servers are expected to run constantly—24 hours a day and 7 days a week. In the future, Web servers will hold medical records, bank records, library catalogs, and store catalogs. Servers will provide education and entertainment content. And servers will manage the business of sending data over the sprawling Internet. The following sections discuss some recent advances in the server industry, including

- Data technologies
- Clustering
- Server boxes

While vendors design servers to do these new things, they will also be building servers that do the old things better.

Data Technologies

In the next few years, one of the most important areas for server development will be the management of data. The industry has swerved decisively in favor of the Web-based environment, and database scenarios that once would have called for a closed, proprietary solution now must be integrated with the Web. The medical records industry, for instance, is a natural application for Web and database integration. Medical records are logically housed at a central, secure, and reliable location. A medical professional may have need to access the medical records database anytime from anywhere in the world. Several companies are currently working on solutions that provide authenticated Web users with access to a central medical records database (see Figure 23.5). This technology could ultimately lead to better, more efficient, and more timely medical care.

FIGURE 23.5

Accessing medical records over the Web.

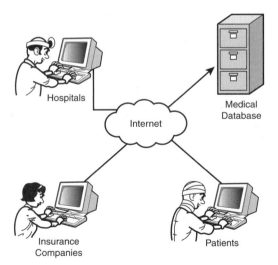

A large database requires a suitable database application (such as Oracle or MySQL), but it also requires lots of storage hardware. The data must reside in some retrievable form on a disk somewhere in the network. Hardware vendors are working on bigger, more efficient, and more reliable disk arrays for storing data, but a truly reliable system must also ensure that the path to the data remains open. In the traditional computing model, where a disk is attached to a single computer, the disk is accessible only when the computer is running. Innovations such as network file system (NFS) can make a single disk array accessible from multiple points. NFS developed within the Unix world but is now available for other networking environments. However, solutions such as NFS have management and performance limitations for high-volume and high-traffic data centers.

A new concept called a storage area network (SAN) has recently emerged. The purpose of a SAN is to make the data as independent as possible from the systems that access the data. A SAN is actually a high-speed network of independent data storage devices linked to equal and independent server nodes (see Figure 23.6). The mesh of wiring interconnecting the storage devices and server nodes of a SAN is so thick and intricate that it is referred to as *fabric*. Several vendors (including IBM, Compaq, and Nortel) currently offer SAN products. SAN solutions are extremely expensive, but this technology is extremely valuable for large, mission-critical data centers.

FIGURE 23.6

A SAN is a high-speed network of independent storage devices and server nodes.

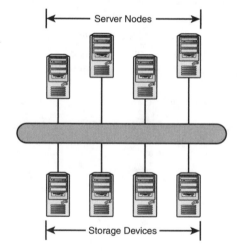

Another data-related innovation that has received considerable attention recently is the Lightweight Directory Access Protocol (LDAP). LDAP is designed for fast lookups of directory-based data over a TCP/IP network. A typical LDAP scenario is an online directory in which you enter a user's name and receive a collection of additional parameters related to the user, such as home address, phone number, e-mail address, and title.

LDAP is a natural fit for many Web-based client/server applications, and vendors such as Netscape have been quick to add LDAP support to their Web server products. Many companies have developed their own homegrown LDAP applications to manage user data or even to support unified security on a diverse internal network.

Novell NetWare has used a directory service for managing network resources since NetWare 4.0. The original NetWare directory was designed to use Directory Access Protocol (DAP)—a predecessor of LDAP—but NetWare now supports LDAP also. DAP and LDAP naming conventions are very similar.

Microsoft realized that most of the information stored on its domain controllers (information about users, resources, and the structure of the network) was easily adapted to a directory-based organization and made LDAP the centerpiece for the Windows 2000 Active Directory environment. Network information on Active Directory networks is stored, read, and referenced through LDAP. You can even configure the Windows 2000 DNS server to store name resolution information in the LDAP-based Active Directory. Results of this noble experiment are still inconclusive. In the meantime, LDAP is currently a popular tool among developers and network admins for building homegrown directories and integrating them with scripts and applications.

Clustering

Recent trends have brought more attention to the concept of using a bank of servers in parallel for a single function. The servers essentially share an identity. The client requesting the service does not know which server will perform the service. The client might not even know that the cluster exists. Requests are distributed invisibly among the members (called the *nodes*) of the cluster. A cluster is really a group of computers that appears to the outside world as a single computer. The advantages of a cluster are

- Speed—Multiple computers can perform more work in a given time than one computer.
- Processing power—Each node in the cluster participates in processing. A cluster can solve complex problems that couldn't be solved efficiently on a single computer.
- Fault tolerance—If one of the computers in the cluster crashes, the other computers will continue to operate. The service provided by the cluster will therefore continue when a computer goes down.

Server clusters are often used for critical network functions. You'll find server clusters acting as proxy servers or DNS servers. Clusters are also used for extremely complex calculations. The National Science Foundation gravity wave detector project, for instance, is expected to use a cluster of 100 Linux computers to process data from gravity wave detectors.

Several clustering products are available for Unix and Linux operating systems. The Beowulf clustering package is a popular option for Linux clusters. Microsoft provides clustering services for NT servers through the Microsoft Cluster Server product. A version of Cluster Server is included with the Advanced and Data Center versions of

Windows 2000 Server. The Microsoft clustering services do not provide the full range of parallel processing capability offered with some cluster software.

Some OS vendors (such as Sun Microsystems) are reportedly working on technology that will remove even more of the identity of individual servers within the cluster. The cluster will not be assigned to a single task but will function as a single logical server for all purposes. Java-based applications will not be loaded onto a single server but will instead be managed by the cluster itself; the cluster management software will dynamically control how and where a task is executed.

 Another variation on the clustering concept is the idea of many processors in one box. Multiprocessor systems are also becoming more popular. A multiprocessor system is a single computer with more than one processor. The processors share the workload just as they would in a cluster. A multiprocessor system is a single computer, though, with a single operating system. The operating system manages the load sharing, so the processors aren't really networked as they would be in a cluster.

Server Boxes

The principles of TCO apply to servers as well as clients. Even as some servers grow bigger and faster, others are growing smaller and simpler. Some of the roles once performed by servers are now being assigned to small boxes. The server box does not offer the range of capabilities possible with a real computer, but it is designed to perform a single task with very little configuration. Because a server box has no monitor, it is often configured through a Web interface. The server box has enough of a built-in Web server to provide Web access to a user working from a browser somewhere on the network. Server boxes currently act as various combinations of the following:

- Print servers
- File servers
- DHCP servers
- Firewalls
- Network address translation devices

The simplicity of a dedicated device makes the server box a useful option for small networks with light network traffic and no professional network administrators on hand.

What Is a Computer Anyway?

Hardware innovations are coming so rapidly that soon it may be difficult to tell what is a computer and what is a bread maker or a light switch. Vendors have recently unveiled plans for an array of new wireless devices. Each device will include a small chip that will make the device accessible over a wireless network. Cell phones, home appliances, televisions, and automobiles will all participate in these wireless device networks. You will be able to communicate with the devices in your house through a palm pilot, cell phone, or wrist watch.

Though some believe this wireless age is a gimmick, others predict these wireless technologies will propel the modern home into an age of science fiction. You have probably heard the scenarios: You will be able to turn on the water in your bathtub while you're heading home on the freeway. Your personal assistant will synchronize its calendar with the coffee maker. Your doorbell will beep your pager when you travel out of state.

Whatever the effect on daily life, it is clear that these wireless technologies will almost certainly have an effect on the local area network (LAN). Although wireless connectivity has been available for several years, the wireless LAN was considered an exception intended for special situations. The new wireless standards will make it easier for vendors to gamble on expanding their wireless product lines. Already wireless network cards are becoming more plentiful and less expensive. In a few years, it is possible that computers, printers, fax machines, and storage devices (at least on small networks) will all communicate without cabling. But a wireless network is still a network, and in this world of talking toasters, you'll still find TCP/IP.

Experts have discussed several concepts for implementing this new wireless technology, but the plan that seems most complete (at least in this writing) is the Bluetooth Protocol Architecture, developed by IBM and a group of other companies. The Bluetooth standard defines the programming environment in which the wireless devices interact. In essence, Bluetooth forms the OSI Data Link and Physical layers (equivalent to the TCP/IP Network Access layer). These layers form the base of the protocol stack and play the role of communicating with network hardware.

The Bluetooth architecture is designed for small personal networks of appliances and devices (as described earlier in this section). Protocols such as the Wireless Application Protocol (WAP) provide wireless networking in more traditional mobile computing scenarios.

The Bluetooth standard does not specify which protocols must operate above the low-level Bluetooth protocols. Vendors are free to implement Bluetooth in a variety of ways.

However, when it comes to connections between Bluetooth devices and computers, there is no reason to believe the popular TCP/IP protocol will be any less popular in a Bluetooth environment. One likely scenario is that the remote device will communicate with the Bluetooth infrastructure through a cell phone–like connection that uses PPP (see Figure 23.7). The TCP/IP protocol stack would reside above PPP, and the Bluetooth protocols could be applied below the PPP layer by some form of Bluetooth-enabled receiver.

FIGURE 23.7

A computer can communicate with the Bluetooth infrastructure using PPP through a cell phone connection.

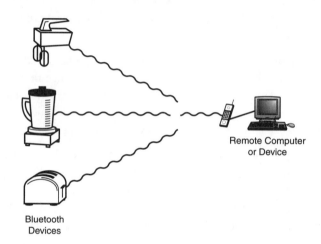

Of course, if a Bluetooth device is to be accessible through the Internet, it must be accessible through TCP/IP. Vendors envision a class of Internet-ready Bluetooth devices accessible through a Bluetooth-enabled Internet bridge (see Figure 23.8). A Bluetooth Data Access Point device acts as a network bridge, receiving incoming TCP/IP transmissions and replacing the incoming Network Access layer with the Bluetooth network access protocols for delivery to a waiting device.

FIGURE 23.8

A Bluetooth-enabled Internet bridge.

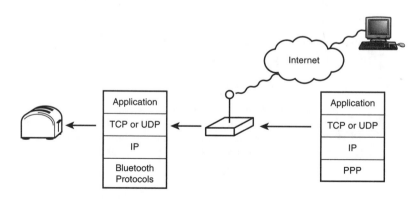

Authors and linguists are delighted that the creators of this technology did not use an acronym for it. But why did they choose the name *Bluetooth*? IBM, of course, always marks its territory with blue, but why the tooth? Because it crunches data? Because it takes bytes? Forget about finding a metaphor. Bluetooth is named for the Viking king Harald Bluetooth, who ruled Denmark and Norway in the eleventh century. King Harald is famous for converting to Christianity after watching a German priest succeed with a miraculous dare.

Bluetooth was loved by many, but his rule was often arbitrary. He seems to be the model for the bad guy in the William Tell legend, having once commanded that one of his subjects shoot an apple off his son's head. The marksman made the shot, but then announced that, if he'd missed, he had three more arrows to shoot into Bluetooth's heart. As we enter the wireless Valhalla, we'll hope the devices ruled by the new Bluetooth do not exhibit this same propensity for spontaneous vengeance.

23

Summary

This hour discussed some recent innovations that will change the character of TCP/IP networking in the next few years. You learned about client technologies such as automated updates, network computers, terminal clients, and the downloadable workspace. You also learned about some server technologies, such as SANs, LDAP, and clustering. This hour also discussed the Bluetooth standard and recent speculation about the future of networkable devices.

Q&A

Q All clerical workers in my office just received new super-charged workstations with over a hundred built-in programs and thousands of configuration options. My TCO consultant is not impressed. Why not?

A The Total Cost of Ownership (TCO) of a workstation is not just the list price of the computer but also the cost of configuring, operating, and maintaining it. A simple system that is easy to configure and doesn't offer superfluous options is often more cost effective than a complicated and advanced system that will be harder to operate and will offer the user more opportunities to get lost.

Q I manage the network for a poor orphanage with a meager endowment. To save money, I'm thinking about deploying a storage area network (SAN) to maintain personal and financial records. When I explain my situation, the vendors won't return my calls. Why not?

A A storage area network is an extremely advanced, high-performing solution that is very expensive. A poor orphanage would not have the money for it. Also, an orphanage probably wouldn't have the need for a storage area network. Storage area networks are designed for mission-critical data centers that hold millions of records.

Q **What are the reasons for deploying a server cluster?**

A Grouping servers into a cluster offers improvements in speed and processing power. A cluster also provides fault tolerance because if one server goes down, the others will continue to provide services.

Key Terms

Review the following list of key terms:

automated update—A service that automatically updates software.

Bluetooth—A protocol architecture for wireless appliances and devices in very close proximity.

cluster—A group of computers configured to operate as a single logical system.

downloadable workspace—A portable, custom work environment available to the user no matter where the user logs in.

Lightweight Directory Access Protocol (LDAP)—A protocol designed for fast lookups of directory-based data structures, such as an online employee directory.

network computer (NC)—A diskless computer that uses Java-based technology.

storage area network—A high-speed and high-performance network of independent storage devices and server nodes.

terminal client—A computer or dedicated terminal device designed to access applications located on another computer.

Total Cost of Ownership (TCO)—The cost of purchasing, operating, and maintaining an electronic devices such as a computer.

Hour 24

Implementing a TCP/IP Network—Seven Days in the Life of Maurice

The preceding hours of this book introduced many of the important components that make up a TCP/IP network. In this hour, you'll witness many of these components in a real, although hypothetical, situation. At the completion of this hour, you'll be able to describe how the components of a TCP/IP network interact.

A Brief History of Hypothetical, Inc.

Hypothetical, Inc., is a large and ponderous company that began with nothing and has magnified it many times. It is one of the largest companies in the world—one of the 1×10^8 largest, to be precise—and is the largest employer in Mordechai, Kansas. Since its birth in 1987, Hypothetical, Inc., has been devoted to the production and distribution of hypotheticals. The mission statement of the company is as follows:

> *To make and sell the best hypotheticals anytime and for any price the buyer will pay.*

In keeping with trends throughout the economy, Hypothetical, Inc., has recently been in transition, and now the strategic focus of the company is to align itself such that a hypothetical is regarded not as a product but rather as a service. This seemingly innocuous change has brought forth severe and extreme measures with regard to implementation, and the tumultuous consequences of those measures have resulted in low employee morale and increased theft of petty business supplies.

A morale committee, consisting of the president, the vice president, the chief of operations, and the president's nephew (who is working in the mail room), analyzed the state of dissatisfaction and agreed the company's longstanding no-computer policy must end. The committee members, some of whom had gained their skills within the public sector, voted immediately to purchase a bulk lot of 1,000 assorted computers at a volume discount, assuming that any disparities of system or hardware would be resolved later.

They placed the 1,000 computers on desktops and countertops and in break rooms and boardrooms throughout the company and wired them together with whatever transmission media they could make fit with the assorted adapter ports. To their astonishment, the network's performance was not within a window of acceptability. In fact, the network did not perform at all, and the search began for someone to blame.

Seven Days in the Life of Maurice

Maurice never doubted that he would find a job, but he didn't think he would find a job so soon after graduating. It didn't occur to him that he would suddenly be presented with an interview at the random corporate office where he had stopped to use the restroom. He was young enough and brash enough to accept the job of network administrator for Hypothetical, Inc., although in hindsight he should have realized that this was not a job for the upwardly mobile. He told the interviewers that he had no experience at all, but that they didn't have to pay him much either. Instead of showing him the door, they immediately placed a W-4 form in front of him and handed him a pen.

Still, he had his library of fine computer books to guide him, including his copy of *Sams Teach Yourself TCP/IP in 24 Hours, Second Edition,* which had provided him with an accessible and well-rounded introduction to TCP/IP.

Day 1: Getting Started

When Maurice arrived at work the first day, he knew his first goal must be to bring all the computers onto the network. A quick inventory of the computers revealed some DOS and Windows machines, some Linux computers, some Macintoshes, several Unix machines, and some other computers that he didn't even recognize. Because this network was supposed to be on the Internet (several of the committee's morale-enhancing measures required visits to certain recreational Web sites), Maurice knew that the network would need to use TCP/IP. He performed a quick check to see if the computers on the network had TCP/IP running. For example, he used the IPConfig utility to output TCP/IP parameters on the Windows computers. On the Unix machines, he used the ifcconfig utility.

In most cases he found that TCP/IP was indeed running, but much to his surprise, he found complete disorganization in assignment of IP addresses. The addresses were seemingly chosen at random. No two addresses had any similar digits that might have served as a network ID. Each computer believed it was on a separate network, and because no default gateway had been assigned to any of the computers, communication within and beyond the network was extremely limited. Maurice asked his supervisor (the nephew who worked in the mailroom) if an Internet network ID had been assigned to the network. Maurice suspected that the network must have some preassigned network ID, because the company had a permanent connection to the Internet. The nephew said he did not know of any network ID.

Maurice asked the nephew whether the value-added retailers who sold them the 1,000 computers had configured any of the computers. The nephew said that they had configured one computer before abruptly leaving the office in a dispute over the contract. The nephew took Maurice to the computer the value-added retailers had configured. It had two computer cables leading from it: one to the corporate network and one to the Internet.

"A multihomed system," Maurice said. The nephew did not seem impressed. "This can serve as a gateway," Maurice told the nephew. "This computer can route messages to the Internet."

The nephew tried to look impatient, hoping for a swift shift to a topic in which he and not Maurice held the greater knowledge. The computer appeared to be a Windows NT system. Maurice considered telling the nephew that he'd never heard of anyone using a multihomed Windows NT box as a corporate gateway and that many experts refer to this type of thing as a "really hokey configuration." It would have been better to purchase a gateway router. But it was his first day, so he didn't offer his advice. A computer, after all, is capable of acting as a router, as long as it is configured for IP forwarding. An ethernet cable led from the gateway computer to the rest of the network. Maurice entered a quick IPConfig for the computer and obtained the IP address of the ethernet adapter.

24

He had a hunch the value-added retailer must have configured the correct network ID into this computer before taking his leave. The IP address was `198.100.145.1`.

Maurice could tell from the first number in the dotted-decimal address (198) that this was a Class C network. On a Class C network, the first three bytes make up the network ID. "The network ID is `198.100.145.0`," he told the nephew. While he was there, he also checked the TCP/IP configuration to ensure that IP forwarding was enabled.

It occurred to Maurice that the network would be capable of supporting only 254 computers with the available host IDs in the Class C address space. But, he concluded, that probably wouldn't matter, because many users did not want their computers anyway. He configured IP addresses for the members of the morale committee:

```
198.100.145.2        (president)

198.100.145.3        (vice-president)

198.100.145.4        (chief of operations)

198.100.145.5        (nephew)
```

and he configured computers for all other possible host IDs. He also entered the address of the gateway computer (`198.100.145.1`) as the default gateway so that messages and requests could be routed beyond the network. For each IP address, he used the standard network mask for a Class C network: `255.255.255.0`.

Maurice used the Ping utility to test the network. For each computer, he typed `ping` and the address of another computer on the network. For instance, from the computer `198.100.145.155`, he entered `ping 198.100.145.5` to ensure that the user of the computer would be able to communicate with the nephew. Also, in keeping with good practice, he always pinged the default gateway:

`ping 198.100.145.1`

For each ping, he received replies from the destination machine, ensuring that the connection was working.

Maurice was thinking that the network had come far for one day, and he was feeling that this would be an easy and rewarding job, but the last computer he configured couldn't ping the other computers on the network. After a careful search, he noticed that the computer appeared to be part of an entirely different type of physical network. Someone had attempted to connect the obscure and obsolete network adapter with the rest of the network by ramming a 10BASE-2 ethernet cable into the ports. When the cable didn't fit, the responsible party had jumped the circuit with a nail and wrapped the whole assembly with so much duct tape that it looked like something they'd used on Apollo 13.

"Tomorrow," Maurice said.

Day 2: Segmenting

When Maurice arrived for work the next day, he brought in something he knew he was going to need: routers. And although he arrived early, many users were already impatient with him. "What's the matter with this network?" they said. "This is really slow!"

Maurice told them that he wasn't finished. The network was working, but the large number of devices competing directly for the transmission medium was slowing things down. Also, some computers that were configured for a different network architecture (such as the computer he'd discovered at the end of the previous day) could not communicate directly with the other computers. Maurice strategically installed some routers so that they would reduce network traffic and integrate the network elements with a differing physical architecture. Of course, he had to find a router that supported the obsolete architecture, but this was not difficult because Maurice had many connections.

Maurice also knew that some subnetting was in order. He decided to divide the final eight bits after the Class C network ID so that he could use three bits for a subnet number and the other five bits for host IDs on the subnetted networks.

To determine a subnet mask, he wrote out an 8-bit binary number (signifying the final octet) with ones for the first three bits (the subnet bits) and zeros for the remaining bits (the host bits):

`11100000`

The last octet of the subnet mask was therefore 32+64+128 or 224, and the full subnet mask was `255.255.255.224`.

Maurice added the new subnet mask for his new subnetted network and assigned IP addresses accordingly. He assigned IP addresses such that the three subnet bits were the same for all computers on a given segment. He also changed default gateway values on many of the computers, because the original gateway was no longer on the subnet. He instead used the IP address of a router port as the default gateway for the computers on the subnet connected to that router port.

Day 3: Dynamic Addresses

The addresnetwork was now functioning splendidly, and Maurice was gaining a reputation for results. Some even suggested him as a possible candidate for the morale committee. The nephew, however, differed with this view. Maurice was not destined for the morale committee or for any committee, the nephew mentioned, because so far he was not meeting the objective of his employment. The committee clearly stated that the network should have 1,000 computers, and so far Maurice had given them a network of only 254. "How can we expect morale to improve if the directives of the morale committee are ignored?" he added.

Actually, the network now had fewer than 254 addresses, because the subnetting implemented in Day 2 left extra unassignable addresses for the all-zeroes host ID and the all-ones broadcast address on each subnet. Maurice did not see a reason for revealing this fact to the nephew.

But how could Maurice bring Internet access to 1,000 computers with fewer than 254 possible host IDs? He knew the answer was that he must configure a DHCP server to lease the IP addresses to users on a temporary basis. "The theory behind DHCP," he explained, "is that all users won't be using their computers all at once." The DHCP server keeps a list of available IP addresses, and when a computer starts and requests an address, the DHCP server issues an address temporarily. As long as users only occasionally access their computers, it is possible to support 1,000 computers with these 254 IP addresses.

Another solution to the address shortage problem would have been to use a network address translation (NAT) device for the Internet connection. If he used a NAT device, Maurice could have assigned any addresses he wanted on the network, regardless of whether the addresses were part of the official address range assigned to the company. However, in a company that economized by using homemade plaster in place of white out, he did not guess that his request for a new device would receive attention. Also, the nephew had grown extremely territorial about the inelegant Windows NT gateway computer and seemed to take a personal stake in its success.

Configuring the DHCP server was easy, at least for Maurice, because he read the documentation carefully and wasn't afraid to look for help on the Web. (He did need to make sure the routers were configured to pass on the DHCP information.) The hard part was manually configuring each of the 1,000 computers to access the DHCP server and receive an IP address dynamically. To configure the 1,000 computers in an eight-hour day, he had to configure 125 computers per hour, or a little more than two per minute. This would have been nearly impossible for anyone but Maurice. He knocked several people down, but he finished in time for the 6:00 p.m. bus.

Day 4: Domain Name Resolution

The next day Maurice realized that his hasty reconfiguration of the network for dynamic address assignment had left some unresolved conflicts. These conflicts would not have occurred at any other company, but at Hypothetical, Inc., they were real and acute.

The president spoke to Maurice privately and informed Maurice that he expected that he, the highest ranking official in the company, would have the computer with the numerically lowest IP address. Maurice had never heard of such a request and could not find reference to it in any of his documentation, but he assured the president that this would not be a problem. He would simply configure the president's computer to use the static IP address 198.100.145.2 and would exclude the president's address from the range of addresses assigned by the DHCP server. Maurice added that he hoped the president understood the importance of not tampering with the configuration of the computer that was acting as an Internet gateway. That computer, which was configured by the value-added retailer, was the only one that would have a lower address: 198.100.145.1. (Actually, Maurice could have changed this address to something higher, but he didn't want to.) The president stated that he did not mind if a computer had a lower IP address as long as that computer didn't belong to another employee. He just didn't want any person to have a lower IP address than his address.

The arrangement between Maurice and the president would have posed no impediment to the further development of the network had not other upper-level managers claimed their own places on this sad ladder of vanity. It was easy enough to give the vice-president and the chief of operations low IP addresses, but a bevy of middle managers, none higher or lower than the others, began to bicker about whose computer would be 198.100.145.33 and whose would be 198.100.145.34. At last, the management team was forced to adjourn to a tennis retreat where they sorted out their differences and tried to begin each match with love.

In the meantime, Maurice implemented a solution he knew they would accept. He set up a DNS server so that each computer could be identified with a name instead of an address. Each manager would have a chance to choose the hostname for his or her own computer. The measure of status, then, would not be who had the numerically lowest computer address but who had the wittiest hostname. Some examples of the middle managers' hostnames included:

- Gregor
- wempy
- righteous_babe
- Raskolnikov

The presence of a DNS server also brought the company closer to the long-term goal of full Internet access. Recently, the users had been able to connect to Internet sites, but only by IP address. The DNS server, through its connection with other DNS servers, gave the company full access to Internet hostnames, such as those used in Internet URLs.

Maurice also took a few minutes to apply for a domain name so that the company would someday be able to sell its hypotheticals through its own Web page on the World Wide Web.

Day 5: NetBIOS Name Resolution

A group of Windows NT workstation users in one of the new subnets told Maurice that some of the other Windows machines they wanted to access were not present in Network Neighborhood. "It all worked fine the first day," they told him. "But on Day 2, the computers in accounting stopped showing up."

Maurice knew that Day 2 was the day he installed the routers and instituted subnetting. He realized suddenly that, after he subdivided the network with routers, NetBIOS names could no longer be resolved through broadcast. Maurice knew he had two choices for implementing network-wide NetBIOS name resolution:

- LMHOSTS
- A Windows Internet Name Service (WINS) server

He chose to implement NetBIOS name resolution using a WINS server. Because the computers received their TCP/IP configurations automatically from the DHCP server, he used the DHCP server to configure the client computers to access WINS.

Day 6: Firewalls

Despite all the recent networking successes, the morale of the company was still very low. Employees were rapidly resigning and departing like moviegoers exiting a bad film. Many of these employees had intimate knowledge of the network, and managers worried that the disgruntled ones might resort to cyber-vandalism as a form of retribution. The managers asked Maurice to implement a plan by which network resources would be protected, but network users would have the fullest possible access to the local network and also the Internet. Maurice asked what the budget was, and they told him he could take some change from the jar by the coffee machine.

Maurice sold approximately 50 of the 1,000 computers and used the money to buy a commercial firewall system that would protect the network from outside attack. (The 50 computers were completely unused and were blocking the hallway to the service entrance. Janitorial personnel had tried to throw them away at least six times.) The firewall provided many security features, but one of the most important was that it allowed Maurice to block off TCP and UDP ports to keep outside users from accessing services on the network. Maurice closed off all non-essential ports. He kept open TCP port 21, which provides access to FTP, because Hypothetical, Inc., information is often dispensed in large paper documents for which FTP is an ideal form of delivery. Maurice carefully configured the firewall so that the port 21 FTP access was authorized only for purposes of connecting to a well-protected FTP server computer.

Day 7: Virtual Private Networking

The chief of operations called Maurice into his office to ask whether federal law prohibited the wagering of large sums of money on sporting events over the Internet. Maurice told the chief that he wasn't a lawyer and didn't know the specifics of gambling law.

The chief asked whether, on an unrelated note, Maurice knew of a way by which all correspondence over the Internet would be strictly private so that no one could find out what he was saying or with whom he was communicating. Maurice told him the best technique he knew about was virtual private networking. A virtual private network (VPN) is a private, encrypted connection over a public line. A VPN provides a connection that is nearly as private as a point-to-point connection.

"I need one of those right away," the chief said, retiring thoughtfully to his inner office.

24

Summary

This hour examined a TCP/IP network in a hypothetical company. You received an inside view of how and why network administrators implement IP addressing, subnet masking, DNS, WINS, DHCP, and other services.

In case you're wondering what happened…

Federal agents arrived at company headquarters sometime after the seven days and arrested the chief of operations. This left an open seat on the morale committee, which the president gratefully offered to Maurice.

Q&A

Q Why did Maurice choose to use three bits for the subnet address?

A The ideal number of subnet bits depends on the number of subnets and the size of the subnets. Committing additional bits to the subnet number leaves fewer bits for the host address. In this case, Maurice made a judgment based on the existing condition of the network. A three-bit mask allows 30 hosts per subnet.

Q Why did Maurice decide to subdivide the network?

A Subdividing the network provided two advantages. First, it reduced traffic. Second, because routers use logical addresses rather than physical addresses, routing offers a means of connecting network segments with dissimilar physical architectures.

Q Why did Maurice use a DNS server instead of configuring hosts files?

A Maurice would have had to configure each hosts file separately, which would have taken a long time. Also, the hosts files would have to be updated whenever a change occurred on the network.

INDEX

I-K

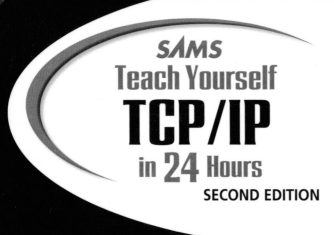

SAMS
Teach Yourself
TCP/IP
in 24 Hours
SECOND EDITION

Learn how to...

- Identify and describe protocols at each layer of the TCP/IP stack
- Use routers and gateways
- Work with IP addresses
- Subnet TCP/IP networks
- Configure TCP/IP name resolution services
- Use TCP/IP utilities such as ping and traceroute
- Use TCP/IP over POTS
- Create your own Web pages
- Use TCP/IP mail protocols such as POP3, IMAP4, and SMTP
- Identify tactics of network attackers
- Implement TCP/IP security
- Use IP Version 6

InformIT
Find IT Solutions at
www.informit.com

Category: Networking
Covers: TCP/IP
User Level: Beginning—Intermediate

www.samspublishing.com

Get Started Now!
24 proven one-hour lessons

In just 24 sessions of one hour or less, you will master the inner workings of TCP/IP. Each lesson builds upon previous lessons for a technical yet refreshingly accessible tour of the elegant protocol suite at the foundation of the Internet.

 Tips point out shortcuts and solutions

 Notes clarify concepts and procedures in a straightforward manner

 Cautions help you avoid common pitfalls

Joe Casad is an engineer who has written widely on PC networking and system administration. He has written or co-written 12 books on computers and networking, includ *MCSE Windows NT Server and Workstation Study Guide MCSE Networking Essentials Training Guide*, *Windows NT Server 4.0 Professional Reference*, and *Windows 98 Professional Reference*. He is the former managing edito of *Network Administrator* magazine and currently is the senior editor of *UNIX Review*.

$24.99 USA / $37.95 CAN / £17.99 Net

ISBN 0-672-32085-1

524